EXPLORATIONS

in

AMERICAN CULTURE

Readings for Critical Thinking, Writing, and Discussion

KATHRINE JASON

Nassau Community College, SUNY

HOLLY POSNER

New York University

Heinle & Heinle Publishers

A division of International Thomson Publishing, Inc.

Boston, Massachusetts 02116 U.S.A.

The ITP logo is a trademark under license.

I(T)P

Pacific Grove • Albany • Bonn • Boston • Cincinnati • Detroit • London • Madrid • Melbourne
Mexico City • New York • Paris • San Francisco • Tokyo • Toronto • Washington

The Publication of *Explorations in American Culture* was directed by the members of the Newbury House Publishing Team at Heinle & Heinle:

Erik Gundersen,   *Editorial Director*
John F. McHugh,   *Market Development Director*
Kristin Thalheimer,   *Production Services Coordinator*
Elizabeth Holthaus,   *Director of Production and Team Leader*

Also participating in the publication of this program were:

Publisher: Stanley J. Galek
Project Manager: Petra Hausberger
Assistant Editor: Karen P. Hazar
Associate Production Editor: Maryellen Eschmann
Manufacturing Coordinator: Mary Beth Hennebury
Interior Designer: Bob Freese
Cover Artist: Jane Mjølness
Photo Researcher: Petra Hausberger

Library of Congress Cataloging-in-Publication Data

Explorations in American Culture: readings for critical thinking,
    writing, and discussion / [compiled by] Holly Posner and Katherine
Jason.
        p.   cm.
    ISBN 0-8384-4069-X
    1. Readers--United States. 2. United States--Civilization-
-Problems, exercises, etc. 3. Critical Thinking--Problems,
exercises, etc. 4. Discussion--Problems, exercises, etc.
5. English Language--Rhetoric. 6. College Readers. I. Posner,
Holly. II. Jason, Katherine.
PE1127.H5E97 1994
808' .042--dc20   94-40613
                                                            CIP

Heinle & Heinle Publishers is a division of International Thomson Publishing, Inc.

Manufactured in the United States of America

ISBN 0-8384-4069-X

10 9 8 7 6 5 4 3

TABLE OF CONTENTS

INTRODUCTORY UNIT   1

EXPLORING AMERICAN CULTURE

This brief introductory unit examines the notion of culture and how it is transmitted both overtly by icons, artifacts, language, and media and covertly by belief systems, stereotypes, attitudes and values.

UNIT ONE   17

AMERICAN DREAMING: THE PURSUIT OF HAPPINESS

Happiness is considered in a broad cultural context by taking into consideration both public—historical and political—and private—spiritual and psychological— aspects of its "pursuit" in America. How has our pursuit of happiness changed over the past two hundred years? To what extent is it equated with material success? Personal fulfillment? Peace of mind?

Preface to the Instructor

What Makes *Explorations* in American Culture Different?

Explorations in American Culture: Readings for Critical Thinking, Writing, and Discussion, as the title suggests, is a content-based reader for advanced English as a Second or Foreign Language (ESL/EFL) students. It is, however, a reader with a difference. Each selection has an apparatus that links reading, oral/listening skills and the writing process through a variety of group tasks. Essentially, *Explorations* is the blueprint of a content-based course, not unlike a college course in which students engage in reading, discussion and writing in a given discipline. All three modalities are integral elements, not only to the mastery of a given intellectual content, but also of language and academic discourse. *Explorations* is also different from many ESL readers in that it has a focused yet broad content area: the American cultural experience, seen from a multicultural perspective and through six foundational categories.

Evolution of the Project

This textbook evolved from a course developed as a bridge-to-college program at the International English Language Institute of Hunter College in New York City. The course was developed in response to research which demonstrated the need for additional preparation for advanced level ESL students who had finished the institute sequence, matriculated and found themselves still unprepared for the rigors of college level reading and writing. For these advanced level students, we designed a course with these four objectives in mind: 1) to give college-bound students an opportunity to read and write intensively in a focused subject area; 2) to familiarize students with fundamental aspects of American culture and history, the knowledge of which is assumed in post-secondary education; 3) to introduce students to a range of authentic texts drawn from journalism, literature and academic writing in various disciplines; (4) and, to give them the opportunity to produce and practice the academic discourse of the American university.

Pedagogical Considerations

Essential to this course and book is the belief that the ESL student must approach the unfamiliar (in this case an aspect of American culture, the discourse of the American college classroom) through what he or she already knows. While the course explores topics in American culture, it necessarily exploits the student's own experience and knowledge, utilizing a cross or multi-cultural perspective. Many ESL students have spent part, if not most, of their lives in their native cultures and have rich reserves of experience of two cultures upon which to draw as readers, writers and thinkers. All of the questions for reading, writing and discussion assume the importance of the student's own cultural experience as a foundation and point of comparison and contrast.

Furthermore, we believe it is important for non-native students to discover that elements of their native culture have been woven into the complex tapestry of American culture and have become part of the public discourse—heard, read and valued.

Both the course and book assume a collaborative, student-based classroom where students grapple with issues and topics together. We see the role of the instructor in a student-centered classroom as threefold: 1) to act as facilitator, directing students in collaborative learning tasks, eliciting group responses and conclusions 2) to act as informant or representative of the culture, providing information and answering questions about American culture 3) to model forms of written and academic discourse.

The Organization of *Explorations*

We begin the book with a brief introductory unit on the topic of culture. Although culture is a word that most foreign students are familiar with, we believe that it bears deeper examination at the outset. A broad consideration of culture also allows students to enter the course by describing and characterizing what they know-their own cultural systems. The reading selection in this unit, "The Values Americans Live By," and its activities should elicit enough discussion and writing to take up the first week of class.

The subsequent units are organized around enduring cornerstones, or foundational concepts, of American society and their corollary issues and controversies. These are 1) *American Dreaming: The Pursuit of Happiness* 2) *The Cult of the Individual: Self Reliance and Self Determination* 3) *Melting Pot or Patchwork Quilt: The Challenge of Multiculturalism* 4) *Defining Gender: Different but Equal* 5) *Right and Wrong in America: Defining Moral Values* 6) *Popular Culture: The Image Shapers*. In each unit, selections were chosen to provide both historical and contemporary perspectives of the unit topic.

Rationale for the Text Selections

We attempt to provide as broad a view as possible of each topic, approaching it through both literary and journalistic readings. We purposely combine poems, stories, and essays with newspaper and popular magazine articles because the culture in which non-native students must function is a continuum that includes both popular, imaginative and academic literature; in college, students must be competent readers of all these forms of writing. However, since actual ESL classes are rarely the homogenous levels we would like them to be, we have included in each chapter readings which range in length and difficulty. After determining the level(s) of their classes, instructors will be able to assign level-appropriate selections.

How to Use the Apparatus

We developed *Explorations* with the assumption that critical thinking and meaningful writing on a given topic can only be produced after topics are adequately presented (i.e., from a variety of perspectives) and contextualized. Thus we have provided not only a balanced selection of readings on controversial issues, but a variety of pre- and post-reading activities designed, we hope, to provoke both spirited debate and thoughtful writing.

The menu of activities and assignments should be approached selectively, as few ESL writing or even reading/writing classes meet for a sufficient number of hours to accommodate the whole menu of tasks in *Explorations*. We envision each chapter taking two weeks to cover. But again, instructors should choose among the six or seven readings in each unit to meet the needs of their different classes.

UNIT OPENERS

Short Takes

Each unit opens with a selection of *Short Takes*, or quotations, to introduce students to the unit topic. These can function as conversation starters or points of departure for freewriting or classroom discussion. Students may agree or disagree with these quotations or compare them to similar ones in their native language. Since the quotes chosen are almost exclusively by Americans, students should be encouraged to look for the underlying cultural generalizations they express.

Introductions

A general *Introduction*, providing a brief historical overview and context for the unit topic opens each unit. Since the units in *Explorations* have more than enough material for the average college or institute term, we did not design exercises to accompany the unit introductions. Instructors are therefore free to assign these readings as homework, in-class readings or even mini-lectures to practice listening and notetaking skills.

BEFORE YOU READ

Every reading selection is preceded by a *Before You Read* activity, which can be done alone for homework, or in groups, using freewriting, questionnaires, charts and graphics to elicit discussion and/or writing. Often this informal writing and discussion can be used as a point of departure for the more complex writing assignments which follow.

AFTER YOU READ

The readings are followed by a *Reading Journal* entry which allows students to react personally to some aspect of the reading. It is our feeling that grammar and correctness should be secondary to content here and that students should view this as an informal writing exercise.

The *Reading For Meaning* questions were designed to test comprehension of the material. There is flexibility in this section as answers may be assigned for homework, done in class in small groups; they may be done orally or submitted as written assignments.

Under the *Exploring Further* section are a variety of activities aimed at broadening the context of the issue under discussion. Many, if not all, of these activities involve group participation.

The Debate

We envision the debates in *Explorations* as informal ones which do not require strict timing and elaborate scoring. We have had success in large classes by dividing the entire class into smaller groups and conducting several mini-debates simultaneously. The secret to a lively debate is preparation, so it is essential that each member take responsibility for his/her team's response.

Another way to organize a debate is to divide the class in half and have each side write its thesis and supporting points on the board. The entire class can then look at such issues as "faulty logic" or "lack of supporting detail" and can make suggestions for improvement.

If the mere idea of debating seems daunting, the topics can be adapted easily for argumentative essay writing assignments.

The Group Presentation

As the name suggests, this activity involves group preparation and oral presentation of a specific topic. The instructor should make sure that all students have a chance to be "presenters" over the course of the semester, by rotating the tasks within the group.

The Research Project

Because of semester time restrictions, we designed our *Research Projects* as informal ones—not subject to the complicated documentation required by the standard college research paper. (We have, for that reason, not included information on MLA or APA guidelines in the *Writer's Guide*.) If, however, instructors choose to include formal research in their course, these assignments can be "formalized" accordingly.

The Interview/Questionnaire

The *Interview/Questionnaire* activities, like the debates and research projects, are loosely structured. Instructors can work with the class as a whole or in small groups, modelling sample questions for the interview and questionnaire on the board and helping students to formulate their questions so that they are readily grasped by their interviewees. Once the interview/questionnaire is designed, a time must be set aside for interviewing and collating the results. (The former must be done outside of class time so interviews and questionnaires must be short and the number of respondents small!) Finally, students should write up and present the findings of their survey and the conclusions they have come to.

Since writing with a time restriction is difficult for most students, we have included a *Timed Writing* section to be used for practice in testing. While we have not dictated a specific time limit for these questions, one hour ought to be sufficient in most cases. Instructors should, however, take this as a suggestion and allow class length and student proficiency level to guide them in deciding their own time limit.

In the *Focused Essay Questions* students are asked to draw on their understanding of the text as they respond. Since students must rely on the texts as support for their arguments, this is an opportunity for them to refer correctly to a text.

UNIT CLOSERS

Extending the Context

At the end of each unit is a section called *Extending the Context* which provides a list of suggested essay topics which ask students to draw upon all the reading, writing and discussion done in the unit. These essays involve more complicated reasoning and more extensive cultural references than do the more narrowly focused essay questions which follow the individual readings.

Video Suggestions

Lastly we have included a list of appropriate *Video Suggestions* to be used as a springboard for debate or additional writing; we encourage instructors to use it as an additional resource. This oral skills component, an integral part of the original bridge course we designed, is an excellent way to broaden the context of a topic. Unfortunately, given the limitations of time, very few ESL reading/writing classrooms have the luxury of utilizing the video component fully. For extensive information on using video material in the classroom, we recommend Susan Stempleski's book on the subject *Video in Action: Recipes for Using Video in Language Teaching*.

How to Use the Writer's Guide

The *Writer's Guide* is to assist students in completing writing assignments and to provide guidelines for various forms of writing and essays. Our objective in including it is to give the students ideas about the forms and functions of paragraphs and essays and to provide writing techniques and strategies. Rhetorical modes are presented as techniques for paragraph, rather than essay, development.

Given its abridged version, instructors should approach the guide as such, and not view it as a writing textbook. Most writing instructors have their own particular approach to writing instruction, and for that reason, the guide is non-directive and open-ended. It is important, however, that instructors set aside some time in the first week of class to familiarize students with the contents of the guide, particularly as it explains in detail the writing assignments they will be asked to undertake.

Finally, grammar instruction is not included in this book, as at this level ESL students should be encouraged to identify their own linguistic weaknesses and to review given trouble spots in a handbook. We believe that if instructors stress editing and revision of all drafts in the writing process and model the importance of student responsibility in all phases of the process, then greater degrees of clarity and correctness will follow.

Using *Explorations* as a Blueprint

Because this text emerged from an actual course designed within the context of a particular institution over a period of four years, we have attempted to recreate in the textbook not the course itself, but a framework and materials for a course in American culture.

Given the differing constraints, policies, and objectives of advanced ESL programs, we have tried to make *Explorations* as open-ended and flexible as possible. Line directions, for example, are purposely not overly prescriptive. We hope that instructors will be able to use *Explorations* to suit their own particular styles and to adapt it to suit the needs and objectives of their classrooms.

Acknowledgments

We would like to thank Pamela McPartland, former Academic Director of the International English Language Institute of Hunter College, CUNY, for her support and encouragement in the development of the original Bridge Course in American Culture. We also thank Debbie Lecesse-Harris, Academic Director of the IELI/Hunter. Holly Posner would like to thank Helen Harper at New York University for her interest in the project. We are particularly grateful to Leslie Taggart for her preparation of the *Writer's Guide*. Thanks go to the reviewers Sheri Handel, Columbia University; Wendy J. Allison, Hunter College; Janis Schiller, University of Texas/Arlington; Meredith Pike-Bakey, University of California/Berkeley and the San Francisco Unified School District; and C. A. Edington, whose comments and constructive criticism helped to shape our final version of *Explorations*. Lastly, we would like to thank our associates at Heinle & Heinle who worked closely with us and cheered us on in moments of difficulty, particularly Erik Gundersen, Lynne Barsky, Karen Hazar and Petra Hausberger.

To Martin, Sarah, Jenna, Peter and Micole

Credits

PHOTOS

p. 159, Bob Daemmrich
32931.002   BAD0138B
©Stock, Boston, Inc. 1986

Michael Grecco
32931.61   MOG0340B
"Grief at the Len Bias Wake"
©Stock, Boston, Inc. 1986

p. 171, Norman Rockwell, "The Golden Rule."
The Norman Rockwell Family Trust,
Thomas Rockwell, Trustee.

p. 203, Andy Warhol
Green Coca-Cola Bottles 1962
oil on canvas
8 1/2 x 57 in. (209.6 x 144.8 cm.)
Collection of Whitney Museum of American Art, New York
Purchase, with funds from the Friends of the Whitney Museum of American Art
68.25

Introductory Unit

EXPLORING AMERICAN CULTURE

JASPER JOHNS, *Three Flags*

INTRODUCTION: WHAT IS CULTURE?

Culture is all around us. We live it daily. In fact, culture is so ubiquitous that we probably take it for granted. Our own culture is second nature to us. But just what do we mean by the term "culture"?

The anthropological definition of culture is "the pattern of activities, beliefs and artifacts characteristic of a group, which is not haphazard or random." American anthropologist E.A. Hobell defines culture as "the integrated system of learned behavior of the members of a society which are characteristic of those members and which are not the results of biological inheritance." In other words, culture is learned, not inherited.

There are four major characteristics of culture. First, it is passed from one generation to the next through the process of *inculturation*. All of us learn to be functioning members of our own culture through inculturation. Second, culture is shared. This is not to say that individual idiosyncracies do not exist, but simply that most members of a given culture share many basic beliefs and attitudes. Third, culture is symbolically expressed and transmitted. For example, the most important symbolic system that all human beings depend upon is language. Through language, each generation passes on its values, information, experiences and history to new generations. Finally, culture is adaptive. This means that human societies are constantly adapting to the environment in order to survive.

In editing *Explorations in American Culture*, we have assumed that students will fall into two groups: foreigners who are visiting the United States to study or work, and Americans of various ethnic backgrounds whose native language is not English. Some of you may be immigrants; some of you may hope to be. But all of you are non-native speakers of English and all of you have your own cultural inheritance.

Precisely because you are straddling two cultures and because "the American experience" is not second nature to you, you are in an ideal position to study American culture. More than the average American, you have the perspective from which to observe, to compare and to evaluate.

Culture shock is an accurate turn of phrase. Part of the thrill of visiting foreign lands is precisely this astonishment of finding oneself in the midst of the spectacle of alien customs, values and beliefs. In fact, most of us are likely to feel "out of step," if not downright perplexed or irritated by a new culture. When these feelings lead us to conclude that our own culture is superior to the culture in question, we are practicing what is called *ethnocentrism*. But as we begin to acclimate ourselves, we are able to view and understand the other culture on its own terms. Anthropologists call this *cultural relativism*. Stepping into other cultural systems reminds us that our own system is by no means universal, or superior, for that matter. It is only familiar. For you to make informed and intelligent observations and conclusions about American culture you must learn to evaluate it from a *relativistic* rather than an *ethnocentric* perspective.

The purpose of this book is not to propagandize American culture, to celebrate it or to criticize it. It is to present some of the fundamental aspects of American life in the hope that you will develop an informed sense of the culture of the United States today and its history.

However, the America we present here is that of a diverse multicultural society. We hope that you will come to see that American culture is a rich and variegated tapestry—woven of many strands of ethnicity, race, class and gender. You will learn of the experiences of African Americans, Asian Americans, Hispanic Americans, and native Americans, as well as those Americans of Eastern and Western European descent.

We hope that you will learn to be good ethnographers—students of culture—and that when you finish the course, you will be better informed and prepared to evaluate and understand American culture.

Exploring Further

1. Of the many symbols used to represent culture, one of the best is that of an iceberg because, like culture, the greater part of it lies hidden beneath the surface. Using the diagram of the iceberg below, fill in as many examples of "visible" and "invisible" culture as you can. (An example of each has been provided for you.) What conclusions can you make from this about understanding a foreign culture?

2. Represent an aspect of American culture graphically—either by drawing a picture or making a collage of words, phrases, and pictures from magazines, newspapers, or other print sources. (You need not be a great artist to do this!) Then write a brief paragraph explaining your concept and present it to the class.

Before You Read

The text you are about to read was written as a brochure to introduce international visitors to life in the United States. "The Values Americans Live By," as the title suggests, describes 13 cultural values which most, if not all, Americans share. Before you begin, answer the following questions:

1. What is a cultural value? Give an example.

2. List two cultural values which you feel are important. Do these values reflect those of your native culture? Why or why not?

3. Before beginning the reading, try to predict at least 5 of the 13 values the article claims are important to Americans. Then turn to Kohl's summary on page 12 and compare your choices with those of the author.

THE VALUES AMERICANS LIVE BY

BY L. ROBERT KOHLS

Dear Visitor:

1   *Most Americans would have a difficult time telling you, specifically, what the values are which Americans live by. They have never given the matter any thought. Even if Americans had considered this question, they would probably, in the end, decide not to answer in terms of a definitive list of values. The reason for this decision is itself one very American value—the belief that every individual is so unique that the same list of values could never be applied to all, or even most, of their fellow citizens.*

2   *Although Americans may think of themselves as being more varied and unpredictable than they actually are, it is significant that they think they are. Americans tend to think they have been only slightly influenced by family, church or schools. In the end, each believes, "I personally chose which values I want to live my own life by."*

3   *Despite this self-evaluation, a foreign anthropologist could observe Americans and produce a list of common values which would fit most Americans. The list of typically American values would stand in sharp contrast to the values commonly held by the people of many other countries.*

4   *We, the staff of the Washington International Center, have been introducing thousands of international visitors to life in the United States for more than a third of a century. This has caused us to try to look at Americans through the eyes of our visitors. We feel confident that the values listed in this booklet describe most (but not all) Americans.*

5   *Furthermore, we can say that if the foreign visitor really understood how deeply ingrained these 13 values are in Americans, he or she would then be able to understand 95% of American actions—actions which might otherwise appear strange, confusing, or unbelievable when evaluated from the perspective of the foreigner's own society and its values.*

6   *The different behaviors of a people or a culture make sense only when seen through the basic beliefs, assumptions and values of that particular group. When you encounter an action, or hear a statement in the United States which surprises you, try to see it as an expression of one or more of the values listed in this booklet. For example, when you ask Americans for directions to get to a particular address in their own city, they may explain, in great detail, how you can get there on your own, but may never even consider walking two city blocks with you to lead you to the place. Some foreign visitors have interpreted this sort of action as showing Americans' "unfriendliness." We would suggest, instead, that the self-help concept (value #6 on our list), is so strong in Americans that they firmly believe that no adult would ever want, even temporarily, to be dependent on another. Also, their future orientation (value #8) makes Americans think it is better to prepare you to find other addresses on your own in the future.*

7   *Before proceeding to the list itself, we should also point out that Americans see all of these values as **very positive ones**. They are not aware, for example, that the people of many Third World countries view change (value #2) as negative or threatening. In fact, all 13 of these American values are judged by many of the world's citizens as negative and undesirable. Therefore, it is not enough simply to familiarize yourself with these values. You must also, as far as possible, consider them without the negative or derogatory connotation which they might have for you, based on your own experience and cultural identity.*

8   *It is important to state emphatically that our purpose in providing you with this list of the most important American values is not to convert you, the foreign visitor, to our values. We couldn't achieve that goal even if we wanted to, and we don't want to. We simply want to help you understand the Americans with whom you will be relating—from their own value system—rather than from yours.*

L. Robert Kohls, Executive Director
The Washington International Center
Washington, D.C.
April 1984

THE VALUES

1. Personal Control Over the Environment

1   Americans no longer believe in the power of Fate, and they have come to look at people who do as being backward, primitive, or hopelessly naive. To be called "fatalistic" is one of the worst criticisms one can receive in the American context; to an American, it means one is superstitious and lazy, unwilling to take any initiative in bringing about improvements.

2   In the United States people consider it normal and right that Man should control Nature, rather than the other way around. More specifically, people believe every single individual should have control over

whatever in the environment might potentially affect him or her. The problems of one's life are not seen as having resulted from bad luck as much as having come from one's laziness in pursuing a better life. Furthermore, it is considered normal that anyone should look out for his or her own self-interests first and foremost.

3   Most Americans find it impossible to accept that there are some things which lie beyond the power of humans to achieve. And Americans have literally gone to the moon because they refused to accept earthly limitations.

4   Americans seem to be challenged, even compelled, to do by one means or another (and often at great cost) what seven-eighths of the world is certain *cannot* be done.

2. Change

5   In the American mind, change is seen as an indisputably good condition. Change is strongly linked to development, improvement, progress, and growth.

6   Many older, more traditional cultures consider change as a disruptive, destructive force, to be avoided if at all possible. Instead of change, such societies value stability, continuity, tradition, and a rich and ancient heritage—none of which are valued very much in the United States.

7   These first two values—the belief that we can do anything and the belief that any change is good—together with an American belief in the virtue of hard work and the belief that each individual has a responsibility to do the best he or she can do, have helped Americans achieve some great accomplishments. So whether these beliefs are "true" is really irrelevant; what is important is that Americans have *considered them to be true* and have acted as if they were, thus, in effect, causing them to happen.

3. Time and Its Control

8   Time is, for the average American, of utmost importance. To the foreign visitor, Americans seem to be more concerned with getting things accomplished on time (according to a predetermined schedule) than they are with developing deep interpersonal relations. Schedules, for the American, are meant to be planned and then followed in the smallest detail.

9   It may seem to you that most Americans are completely controlled by the little machines they wear on their wrists, cutting their discussions off abruptly to make it to their next appointment on time.

10   Americans' language is filled with references to time, giving a clear indication of how much it is valued. Time is something to be "on," to be "kept," "filled," "saved," "used," "spent," "wasted," "lost," "gained," "planned," "given," "made the most of," even "killed."

11   The international visitor soon learns that it is considered very rude to be late—even by 10 minutes—for an appointment in the United States. (Whenever it is absolutely impossible to be on time, you should phone ahead and tell the person you have been unavoidably detained and will be half an hour—or whatever—late.)

12   Time is so valued in America because by considering time to be important one can clearly accomplish more than if one "wastes" time and does not keep busy. This philosophy has proven its worth. It has enabled

Americans to be extremely productive, and productivity itself is highly valued in the United States. Many American proverbs stress the value of guarding our time, using it wisely, setting and working toward specific goals, and even expending our time and energy today so that the fruits of our labor may be enjoyed at a later time. (This latter concept is called "delayed gratification.")

4. Equality/Egalitarianism

13   Equality is, for Americans, one of their most cherished values. This concept is so important for Americans that they have even given it a religious basis. They say all people have been "created equal." Most Americans believe that God views all humans alike without regard to intelligence, physical condition or economic status. In secular terms this belief is translated into the assertion that all people have an equal opportunity to succeed in life. Americans differ in opinion about how to make this ideal into a reality. Yet virtually all agree that equality is an important civic and social goal.

14   The equality concept often makes Americans seem strange to foreign visitors. Seven-eighths of the world feels quite differently. To them, rank and status and authority are seen as much more desirable considerations—even if they personally happen to find themselves near the bottom of the social order. Class and authority seem to give people in those other societies a sense of security and certainty. People outside the United States consider it reassuring to know, from birth, *who* they are and *where* they fit into the complex system called "society."

15   Many highly-placed foreign visitors to the United States are insulted by the way they are treated by service personnel (such as waiters in restaurants, clerks in stores, taxi drivers, etc.). Americans have an aversion to treating people of high position in a deferential manner, and, conversely, often treat lower class people as if they were very important. Newcomers to the United States should realize that no insult or personal indignity is intended by this lack of deference to rank or position in society. A foreigner should be prepared to be considered "just like anybody else" while in the country.

5. Individualism and Privacy

16   The individualism which has been developed in the Western world since the Renaissance, beginning in the late 15th century, has taken its most exaggerated form in 20th century United States. Here, each individual is seen as completely and marvelously unique, that is, totally different from all other individuals and, therefore, particularly precious and wonderful.

17   Americans think they are more individualistic in their thoughts and actions than, in fact, they are. They resist being thought of as representatives of a homogeneous group, whatever the group. They may, and do, join groups—in fact *many* groups—but somehow believe they're just a little different, just a little unique, just a little special, from other members of the same group. And they tend to leave groups as easily as they enter them.

18   Privacy, the ultimate result of individualism, is perhaps even more difficult for the foreigner to comprehend. The word "privacy" does not even

exist in many languages. If it does, it is likely to have a strongly negative connotation, suggesting loneliness or isolation from the group. In the United States, privacy is not only seen as a very *positive* condition, but it is also viewed as a requirement which all humans would find equally necessary, desirable and satisfying. It is not uncommon for Americans to say— and believe—such statements as "If I don't have at least half an hour a day to myself, I will go stark raving mad!"

19   Individualism, as it exists in the United States, does mean that *you will find a much greater variety of opinions (along with the absolute freedom to express them, anywhere and anytime) here.* Yet, in spite of this wide range of personal opinion, almost all Americans will ultimately vote for one of the two major political parties. That is what was meant by the statement made earlier that Americans take pride in crediting themselves with claiming more individualism than, in fact, they really have.

6. Self-Help Concept

20   In the United States, a person can take credit only for what he or she has accomplished by himself or herself. Americans get no credit whatsoever for having been born into a rich family. (In the United States, that would be considered "an accident of birth.") Americans pride themselves in having been born poor and, through their own sacrifice and hard work, having climbed the difficult ladder of success to whatever level they have achieved—all by themselves. The American social system has, of course, made it possible for Americans to move, relatively easily, up the social ladder.

21   Take a look in an English-language dictionary at the composite words that have the word "self" as a prefix. In the average desk dictionary, there will be more than 100 such words, words like self-confidence, self-conscious, self-contained, self-control, self-criticism, self-deception, self-defeating, self-denial, self-discipline, self-esteem, self-expression, self-importance, self-improvement, self-interest, self-reliance, self-respect, self-restraint, self-sacrifice—the list goes on and on. The equivalent of these words cannot be found in many other languages. This list is perhaps the best indication of how seriously Americans take doing things for one's self. The "self-made man or woman" is still very much the ideal in 20th century America.

7. Competition and Free Enterprise

22   Americans believe that competition brings out the best in any individual. They assert that it challenges or forces each person to produce the very best that is humanly possible. Consequently, the foreign visitor will see competition being fostered in the American home and in the American classroom, even on the youngest levels. Very young children, for instance, are encouraged to answer questions for which their classmates do not know the answer.

23   You may find the competitive value disagreeable, especially if you come from a society which promotes *cooperation* rather than competition. But many U.S. Peace Corps volunteers teaching in Third World countries found the *lack* of competitiveness in a classroom situation equally distressing. They soon learned that what they had thought to be one of the universal human characteristics represented only a peculiarly American (or Western) value.

24   Americans, valuing competition, have devised an economic system to go with it—free enterprise. Americans feel very strongly that a highly competitive economy will bring out the best in its people and ultimately, that the society which fosters competition will progress most rapidly. If you look for it, you will see evidence in all areas—even in fields as diverse as medicine, the arts, education, and sports—that free enterprise is the approach most often preferred in America.

8. Future Orientation

25   Valuing the future and the improvements Americans are sure the future will bring means that they *devalue* the past and are, to a large extent, unconscious of the present. Even a happy present goes largely unnoticed because, happy as it may be, Americans have traditionally been hopeful that the future would bring even greater happiness. Almost all energy is directed toward realizing that better future. At best, the present condition is seen as preparatory to a later and greater event, which will eventually culminate in something even more worthwhile.

26   Since Americans have been taught (in value #1) to believe that Man, and not Fate, can and should be the one who controls the environment, this has made them very good at planning and executing short-term projects. This ability, in turn, has caused Americans to be invited to all corners of the earth to plan and achieve the miracles which their goal-setting can produce.

27   If you come from a culture such as those in the traditional Moslem world, where talking about or actively planning the future is felt to be a futile, even sinful activity, you will have not only philosophical problems with this very American characteristic but religious objections as well. Yet it is something you will have to learn to live with, for all around you Americans will be looking toward the future and what it will bring.

9. Action/Work Orientation

28   "Don't just stand there," goes a typical bit of American advice, "do something!" This expression is normally used in a crisis situation, yet, in a sense, it describes most Americans' entire waking life, where action— any action— is seen to be superior to inaction.

29   Americans routinely plan and schedule an extremely active day. Any relaxation must be limited in time, pre-planned, and aimed at "recreating" their ability to work harder and more productively once the recreation is over. Americans believe leisure activities should assume a relatively small portion of one's total life. People think that it is "sinful" to "waste one's time," "to sit around doing nothing," or just to "daydream."

30   Such a "no nonsense" attitude toward life has created many people who have come to be known as "workaholics," or people who are addicted to their work, who think constantly about their jobs and who are frustrated if they are kept away from them, even during their evening hours and weekends.

31   The workaholic syndrome, in turn, causes Americans to identify themselves wholly with their professions. The questions one American will ask another American when meeting for the first time are related to his or her work: "What do you do?" or "Where do you work?" or "What company are you with?"

32   And when such a person finally goes on vacation, even the vacation will be carefully planned, very busy and active.

33   America may be one of the few countries in the world where it seems reasonable to speak about the "dignity of human labor," meaning by that, hard physical labor. In America, even corporation presidents will engage in physical labor from time to time and gain, rather than lose, respect from others for such action.

10. Informality

34   If you come from a more formal society, you will likely find Americans to be extremely informal, and you will probably feel, even disrespectful of those in authority. Americans are one of the most informal and casual peoples in the world, even when compared to their near relatives—the Western Europeans.

35   As one example of this informality, American bosses often urge their employees to call them by their first names and even feel uncomfortable if they are called by the title "Mr." or "Mrs."

36   Dress is another area where American informality will be most noticeable, perhaps even shocking. One can go to a symphony performance, for example, in any large American city nowadays and find some people in the audience dressed in blue jeans and tieless, short-sleeved shirts.

37   Informality is also apparent in Americans greetings. The more formal "How are you?" has largely been replaced with an informal "Hi." This is as likely to be used to one's superior as to one's best friend.

38   If you are a highly placed official in your own country, you will probably, at first, find such informality to be very unsettling. Americans, on the other hand, would consider such informality as a compliment! Certainly it is not intended as an insult and should not be taken as such.

11. Directness, Openness and Honesty

39   Many other countries have developed subtle, sometimes highly ritualistic, ways of informing other people of unpleasant information. Americans, however, have always preferred the direct approach. They are likely to be completely honest in delivering their negative evaluations. If you come from a society which uses the indirect manner of conveying bad news or uncomplimentary evaluations, you will be shocked at Americans' bluntness.

40   If you come from a country where saving face is important, be assured that Americans are not trying to make you lose face with their directness. It is important to realize that an American would not, in such cases, lose face. The burden of adjustment, in all cases while you are in this country, will be on *you*. There is no way to soften the blow of such directness and openness if you are not used to it except to tell you that the rules have changed while you are here. Indeed, Americans are trying to urge their fellow countrymen to become even *more* open and direct. The large number of "assertiveness" training courses which appeared in the United States in the late 1970s reflects such a commitment.

41   Americans consider anything other than the most direct and open approach to be dishonest and insincere and will quickly lose confidence in and distrust anyone who hints at what is *intended* rather than saying it

outright. Anyone who, in the United States, chooses to use an intermediary to deliver the message will also be considered manipulative and untrustworthy.

12. Practicality and Efficiency

42   Americans have a reputation for being an extremely realistic, practical and efficient people. The practical consideration is likely to be given highest priority in making any important decision in the United States. Americans pride themselves in not being very philosophically or theoretically oriented. If Americans would even admit to having a philosophy, it would probably be that of pragmatism.

43   Will it make any money? Will it "pay its own way?" What can I gain from this activity? These are the kinds of questions which Americans are likely to ask in their practical pursuit, not such questions as: Is it aesthetically pleasing? Will it be enjoyable? Will it advance the cause of knowledge?

44   This practical, pragmatic orientation has caused Americans to contribute more inventions to the world than any other country in human history. The love of "practicality" has also caused Americans to view some professions more favorably than others. Management and economics, for example, are much more popular in the United States than philosophy or anthropology; law and medicine are more valued than the arts.

45   Another way in which this favoring of the practical makes itself felt in the United States is a belittling of "emotional" and "subjective" evaluations in favor of "rational" and "objective" assessments. Americans try to avoid being too sentimental in making their decisions. They judge every situation "on its merits." The popular American "trial-and-error" approach to problem-solving also reflects the practical. This approach suggests listing several possible solutions to any given problem, then trying them out, one-by-one, to see which is most effective.

13. Materialism/Acquisitiveness

46   Foreigners generally consider Americans much more materialistic than Americans are likely to consider themselves. Americans would like to think that their material objects are just the natural benefits which always result from hard work and serious intent—a reward, they think, which *all* people could enjoy were they as industrious and hard-working as Americans.

47   But by any standard, Americans *are* materialistic. This means that they value and collect more material objects than most people would ever dream of owning. It also means they give higher priority to obtaining, maintaining and protecting their material objects than they do in developing and enjoying interpersonal relationships.

48   The modern American typically owns:

    one or more color television sets
    an electric hair dryer
    an electric calculator
    a tape recorder and a record player
    a clothes washer and dryer
    a vacuum cleaner

a power lawn mower (for cutting grass)
a refrigerator, a stove and a dishwasher
one or more automobiles
at least one telephone
(Many also own a personal computer.)

Since Americans value newness and innovation, they sell or throw away their possessions frequently and replace them with newer ones. A car may be kept for only two or three years, a house for five or six before trading it in for another one.

Summary

Now that we have discussed each of these 13 values separately, if all too briefly, let us look at them in list form (on the left) and then consider them paired with the counterpart values from a more traditional country (on the right):

U.S. VALUES	SOME OTHER COUNTRYS' VALUES
Personal Control over the Environment	Fate
Change	Tradition
Time and Time Control	Human Interaction
Equality	Hierarchy/Rank/Status
Individualism/Privacy	Group Welfare
Self-Help	Birthright Inheritance
Competition	Cooperation
Future Orientation	Past Orientation
Action/Work Orientation	"Being" Orientation
Informality	Formality
Directness/Openness/Honesty	Indirectness/Ritual/"Face"
Practicality/Efficiency	Idealism
Materialism/Acquisitiveness	Spiritualism/Detachment

Application

Before leaving this discussion of the values Americans live by, consider how knowledge of these values explains many things about Americans.

One can, for example, see America's impressive record of scientific and technological achievement as a natural result of several of these 13 values:

First of all, it was necessary to believe

1. these things *could be* achieved, that Man does not have to simply sit and wait for Fate to bestow them or not bestow them, and that Man does have control over his own environment, if he is willing to take it.

Other values which have contributed to this record of achievement include

2. an expectation of positive results to come from change (and the acceptance of an ever-faster rate of change as "normal");

3. the necessity to schedule and plan one's time;

4. the self-help concept;

5. competition;

6. future orientation;

7. action/work orientation;

8. practicality; and

9. materialism.

By using this approach you will soon begin to understand Americans and their actions. And as you come to understand them, they will seem less "strange" than they did at first.

L. Robert Kohls was the Executive Director of The Washington International Center of Meridian House International in Washington D.C., an organization which, among other things, produces materials to help foreign visitors understand life in the United States.

After You Read

Reading Journal

Have you ever experienced a cross-cultural misunderstanding? Write the details of the incident, the reason for the misunderstanding, and how it was eventually resolved. What did you learn about the differences between the United States and your own native culture as a result?

Reading For Meaning

1. What was the author's purpose in writing this booklet? Who was his intended audience?

2. Kohls writes that each of the thirteen values he lists is seen as positive by Americans. Yet, as he points out, many of the world's cultures interpret these same values negatively. Select two values and interpret them from a non-American viewpoint. What, for example, are their negative consequences?

3. What contradictions does the author find in America's claim to value individualism?

Exploring Further

Group Presentation

> Before you begin, appoint one member of the group as the secretary and another as the presenter of your group's findings to the class.

1. Discuss the sayings below. Assign one of Kohls' values to each.

Example:

Good fences make good neighbors. = *value 5, individualism and privacy*

   a. God helps those who help themselves.
   b. Lost time is never found again.
   c. America, which has the most glorious present still existing in the world today, hardly stops to enjoy it, in her insatiable appetite for the future.
   d. If a man does not keep pace with his companions, perhaps it is because he hears a different drummer. Let him step to the music he hears, however measured or far away.
   e. Happiness is a state of mind in which a man is so busy that he does not know whether he is or is not happy.
   f. America was established not to create wealth but to realize a vision, to realize an ideal—to discover and maintain liberty among men.
   g. Where there's a will, there's a way.

2. Kohls invites his readers to use his list of values to "explain many things about Americans." Using his model, choose four of the above sayings and provide at least one example from your observations to illustrate them.

Example:

Good fences make good neighbors.

An example of this need for privacy would be the frequent use of fences, walls, and dividers such as trees and shrubbery to separate one house from another in the U.S.

Timed Writing Exercise

Americans are often characterized as exceedingly materialistic. From your observations and experience in the United States, do you agree that Americans are more materialistic than people in your native culture? Give concrete examples to support your opinion.

Focused Essay Topics

1. Choose one value from Kohls' list and write an essay in which you either agree or disagree with his assessment of that value. In other words, does what Kohls write ring true for you and your personal experience in the United States? Explain.

2. Kohls wrote "The Values Americans Live By" in 1984 as promotional material for visitors to the United States. Imagine that you are hired as a staff writer to update his brochure. Your assignment is to help visitors understand America's racial problems in light of its stated commitment to equality for all. Write a brief essay in which you attempt to explain this contradiction more fully than Kohls did in the original brochure.

Unit One

AMERICAN DREAMING: THE PURSUIT OF HAPPINESS

JACOB LAWRENCE,
*In a Free Government, the
Security of Civil Rights
Must be the Same*

Short Takes

Unquestionably, it is possible to do without happiness; it is done involuntarily by nineteen-twentieths of mankind.

John Stuart Mill

Remember that happiness is a way of travel—not a destination.

Roy M. Goodman

To be without some of the things you want is an indispensible part of happiness.

Bertrand Russell

We act as though comfort and luxury were the chief requirements of life, when all that we need to make us really happy is something to be enthusiastic about.

Charles Kingsley

The secret of happiness is not in doing what one likes, but in liking what one has to do.

James M. Barrie

The pursuit of happiness, which American citizens are obliged to undertake, tends to involve them in trying to perpetuate the moods, tastes and aptitudes of youth.

Malcolm Muggeridge

When one door of happiness closes, another opens; but often we look so long at the closed door that we do not see the one which has been opened for us.

Helen Keller

Happiness is wanting what you want, getting what you get, and hoping the two will coincide.

Howard Mumford Jones

SUGGESTIONS FOR USING SHORT TAKES:

- Respond in writing to one of the quotations above. Then get together in groups and share what you have written.
- Work with a partner, small group or the entire class to discuss one or more quotations. You may want to agree, disagree, or compare it to similar expressions or sayings in your native language.

INTRODUCTION – AMERICAN DREAMING: THE PURSUIT OF HAPPINESS

This first chapter focuses on that most American of concepts—the pursuit of happiness. What did it mean in 1776, when it was written into the Declaration of Independence? How is it understood today, in an era in which we quantify happiness, like everything else, and then pursue it with a vengeance, often with the help of mental health specialists?

Happiness is a cultural universal. People everywhere aspire to put a measure of happiness in their lives. But the firm conviction that a more or less durable state of happiness is waiting out there for each of us to seize, and then chase after, is perhaps distinctly American. After all, the pursuit of happiness is one of the inalienable rights written into our Declaration of Independence.

But what did Jefferson mean when he drafted the words "We hold these truths to be self-evident, that all men are created equal, that they are endowed by their creator with certain inalienable rights, that among these are Life, Liberty and the pursuit of Happiness"? The men of the Second Continental Congress who adopted this revolutionary document on July 4, 1776, were all propertied white men defending the colonies' right to autonomous rule and freedom from the yoke of Britain. But our interpretation of the "pursuit of happiness" after more than two centuries of cultural and historical evolution is not what the forefathers had in mind.

The promise of a better life—of happiness—is at the heart of the American Dream. For some a better life was basically a political assumption about freedom, equality and justice. Indeed, the first settlers, the Puritans, fleeing religious and political persecution, found in the New World the freedom to practice their religious beliefs and set a precedent for generations of refugees who came to our shores seeking asylum.

For many others, the promise of a better life meant survival from starvation. From the 1840s through the 1920s, great waves of immigration brought penniless Europeans to the United States. For example, in the 1840s and 1850s alone, over 1,700,000 fortunate Irish escaped the infamous Potato Famine. Among them was one Patrick Kennedy, great-grandfather of President John F. Kennedy, the thirty-fifth President of the United States.

In fact, the conviction that the poorest man or woman could put in his or her share of hard work and receive God's reward—wealth—is an essential part of the American mythology. For Americans, the link between success and financial reward goes back to the Puritan conception of hard work and Godly favor. But the American Dream is not solely the acquisition of wealth for its own sake but rather the idea that succeeding generations will move up the social ladder, become more educated and enter professions. The freedom to set one's own goals, the ambition to reach them, and the satisfaction of having achieved, is as much a part of the dream as the corollary financial reward.

However, there are painful contradictions between the myth of the American Dream and the reality. When Jefferson gave the "inalienable rights . . . of Life, Liberty and the pursuit of Happiness to all men, created equal," he didn't literally mean *all men*. Slavery, which Benjamin Franklin called "the sore thumb sticking up through the Constitution" has become, in the late twentieth century, a legacy of inner cities where crime, drugs, and hopelessness reign.

But at the end of the twentieth century, American culture may be at a turning point. Multiculturalism (see Unit 3 for further explanation of the term), the most pervasive ideological trend of the 1990s, is the attempt to open the pursuit to all Americans, regardless of gender, ethnicity, color or creed.

Before You Read

1. On a separate piece of paper make a list of personal requirements for happiness in your native culture. Then make a separate list of what you believe most Americans would require for a happy life. Arrange the two lists in order of importance.

2. Work in small groups to compare lists. Are there any major differences? similarities? Write up a paragraph in which you present your group's findings to the rest of the class.

What is Happiness?   BY CATHERINE HOUCK

Until recently, matters concerning happiness, like those concerning the soul, have been left to philosophers and clergymen. Medicine has been more fascinated with what's wrong with the human psyche than with what's right, and happiness—that most desired, subtle, and elusive of all human moods— has been neglected. But no more—the last decade or two has seen a vigorous proliferation of surveys, studies, and press interviews on the subject. Here's a look at what today's men of science have to say about what the Bible calls that blessed state.

1   Philosophers still debate the definition of happiness, but scientists, who've dubbed it life satisfaction, generally agree on a definition: A state of well-being, filled with positive feelings toward oneself and the world. Philosophers and researchers alike agree on the importance of their subject. "For most people, happiness is the major goal in life," says Jonathan Freedman, who surveyed one hundred thousand people for his book *Happy People*. "Almost every decision we make is based on what we think will bring us the most happiness. Everything important to us—love, faith, success, friendship, sex—is actually a means to the end of achieving happiness."

2   No scientist has been able to produce succinct directions on how to be happy. After thirty years of research and fifty-seven major surveys, however, researchers *have* identified life circumstances that seem most *correlated* with happiness. According to them, happiness is...

3   **Marriage.** Although nearly half of first marriages end in divorce, and 60 percent of second marriages, married people report higher levels of happiness than singles. "Statistically, a happy marriage has been the most important contributor to well-being," says Tom W. Smith, senior study director of the University of Chicago's National Opinion Research Center (NORC). However, a NORC study, published in *Journal of Marriage and the Family*, concludes that marriage in the U.S. is a "weakened and declining institution" because women are dissatisfied. The NORC study and others, including one by Yale psychologist Robert Sternberg, find men happier than women about all aspects of marriage probably because, surmises *Time* magazine, "having a husband means an increased work load rather than the traditional trade-off of homemaking for financial support." Shere Hite's new study, *Women and Love*, finds 98 percent of the forty-five hundred women she interviewed saying they want to make "basic changes" in their love relationships. Single women, conversely, report more life satisfaction than do single men, who have much higher alcoholism and suicide rates.

4   **Meaningful activity.** Some researchers don't agree that marriage is the most reliable predictor of happiness, and would give first place to the amount of time a person spends doing things she finds satisfying and enjoyable—"activity that allows a person to express most fully who she considers herself to be," says Rutgers University research psychologist Daniel Ogilvie. A young mother, for example, might find looking after her child the most meaningful; for others, work may be the most interesting.

5   **Being older.** The University of Michigan's Institute for Social Research, which has surveyed thousands of Americans on personal satisfaction, finds older people happier than the under-thirty group. According to the institute's late Angus Campbell, young adults are more likely to describe their lives as hard, to feel trapped, and to worry about finances, work, marriage, and friendships.

6   In the past, inexperienced young adults, when faced with crucial life decisions, tended to accept the judgment of parents and other authority figures. "Today, young people are more independent—but they pay with increased stress and tension," said Campbell. People over forty-five years old, on the other hand, have the comforting benefit of their own experience to guide them in making important decisions, and they enjoy more self-confidence. They're also likelier to be more realistic in their expectations.

7   **An upbeat attitude.** "Two men looked out through prison bars; one saw mud, the other stars." "Happiness isn't having what you want, it's wanting what you have." "When one door of happiness closes, another opens; but often we look so long at the closed door that we don't see the one that has been opened for us." Such maxims illustrate a quality many researchers now recognize as vital for happiness: the ability to make the most of things and not dwell on worries and setbacks. Psychology researchers, such as Aaron T. Beck, director of the University of Pennsylvania's Center for Cognitive Therapy, have successfully demonstrated that many people are unhappy simply from habitually taking a negative view of reality and becoming enmeshed in patterns of

helpless and hopeless thinking. Happy people, it appears, are always more likely to see the glass as half-full rather than half-empty!

8   **The ability to use time successfully.** Organization is an important component of well-being, says Michael Argyle in *The Psychology of Happiness*. "For happy people, time tends to be organized and planned; they are punctual and efficient. For unhappy people, time is filled with postponements and inefficiency." Equally important for happiness is a sense of being in control of one's life rather than one of being controlled by other people, luck, or fate.

9   **Health.** Researchers have found that illness that causes incapacity or pain destroys well-being. Good health, on the other hand, doesn't automatically *produce* happiness. In his survey, Jonathan Freedman found that most healthy people simply take their health for granted. "They ignore it unless or until it is absent," he says.

The Happiness Chemical

10   The ability to be happy, anthropologists believe, is vital for survival: Without feelings of pleasure and well-being, life wouldn't be worth living and humanity would have no motivation to reproduce. Until recently, no one knew what physical process must take place within the body to produce the sensation called happiness. But now, NIMH neuroscientists have actually located pleasure centers and pathways in the brain region known as the hypothalamus, and have found these centers to be activated largely by endorphins.

11   The common idea that happiness comes from doing one's duty may, it seems, have a biological foundation: The hypothalamus seems to release its pleasure-producing endorphins mostly to reward behavior that's conducive to

survival! To make sure we reproduce, for example, our bodies generously bestow endorphins when we make love; ditto eating, finishing a work project, exercising.

12   **A gift for happiness?** Some people's bodies seem to have a more efficient endorphin-producing mechanism than others—which may explain those fortunate souls apparently born happy. (We've all noticed that with some people no amount of adversity can dim their good cheer; whereas with others, the loveliest good luck is met with complaints and gloom!) "Those who release more endorphins may be happier about any given situation in their lives than those with fewer endorphins," says Yale biochemist Philip B. Applewhite, author of *Molecular Gods*. "Happiness, then, is real and has a molecular basis."

13   **Addictions: The happiness instinct gone awry.** If people with a greater ability to secrete endorphins experience more happiness from the same stimulus—be it love, work, or living well—than do people with fewer endorphins, how do the disadvantaged attempt to make up for this deficiency? "All indications are that some people born with lower levels of endorphins resort to drugs, overeating, drinking, and other addictions as a desperate attempt to compensate for their lack of pleasure," says Michael Hutchison, author of *Megabrain*. Heroin addicts, he points out, have been found to have lower levels of endorphins, as well as fewer receptor sites (places in the brain where the endorphins produce their pleasure-causing effects).

14   In other words, those low in "natural pleasure" eventually learn that they can increase their feelings of happiness and well-being by ingesting a substance—such as alcohol—that artificially stimulates the brain to pour out large quantities of endorphins, or they can engage heavily in behavior

that releases endorphins. Habitual overeaters, for example, need a "fix" every few hours as their body's pleasure chemicals get depleted.

15   The NIMH's biological-psychiatry branch is now investigating the relationship between mental states and brain chemicals. Eventually, scientists hope to learn the most effective ways of dealing with brain-chemical imbalances that lead to addiction and other problems. For the moment, they're experimenting largely with the uses of synthetic drugs, but few researchers believe synthetic chemicals will be the final answer. "Drugs, which assault the whole brain at once, will never be as subtle as our own natural neurochemicals, which can be released just in one spot and not another," says neurochemist Candace Pert, a leading NIMH researcher on endorphins.

Can Money Buy Happiness?

16   A large number of people are convinced that lots of cash would make them happier. This notion isn't far-fetched, researchers have found. "Money matters little to happiness if you have even a moderate amount; but if you don't have enough to live on, it matters a great deal," says Freeman in *Happy People*.

17   Remarking on his poll studying the finances of ten thousand people in seventy countries, statistician George Gallup wrote, "It was hoped that somewhere we'd find a country whose people are poor but happy. We found no such place." Gallup told a Senate committee that "nearly half the world's people are engaged in a struggle for mere survival. Only in the West can inhabitants engage in a pursuit of happiness."

18   Once people have enough money to live with dignity, whether they're rich or poor matters only slightly to happiness. One study of twenty-two big-time lottery winners found no difference between their degree of happiness and that of ordinary people. A British study of 191 pool winners found that 70 percent were lonelier as a result of giving up work and changing neighborhoods.

19   Being rich is no guarantee of happiness, but prospering through one's own efforts *does* bestow a great deal of satisfaction. "Starting out at $12,000 and getting raised to $25,000, or taking a business from red to black is significantly related to happiness," says Tom Smith.

20   Besides making money, how money is *handled* seems to be a factor in happiness. New York psychologist Annette Liebermann, who studied the financial attitudes and behavior of 125 women for her book *Unbalanced Accounts: Why Women Are Still Afraid of Money*, found that the nature of a woman's relationship with her money significantly adds to, or detracts from, her well-being. Effectively using money, the study revealed, bestows a sense of control over life, more self-esteem, freedom, and security. Unfortunately, beyond pleasant thoughts and plans about how to spend it, the majority of women had not learned—or even thought much about—their money. The most common ways of psychologically mishandling funds proved to be the following:

21   **Money blindness.** Thinking about finances makes some so anxious that they can seldom bring themselves to balance checkbooks, plow through financial statements, or even take an interest in discussing money. They don't keep close watch on money they spend. If their money has been invested and they don't understand the investment, they don't consult outside sources to obtain this vital information.

22   **Money denial.** Women often unconsciously regard the need to be

self-supporting as a temporary one and entertain fantasies that a man will come to the rescue. Though 55 percent of the women answered no when asked, "Do you like the idea of being supported by someone else?" a great many of these same women *live* as though they *do* expect someone else to be responsible for them! They spend every penny they earn, give little thought to serious careers, and generally find that the need to make money gets in the way of life.

23   **Money folly.** Women unable to make rational or informed decisions about how to use money blow their paychecks as quickly as possible, attempting to soothe emotional problems by excessive spending. They regard budgets and saving as punishments instead of useful techniques for taking charge of their financial lives; and they blithely sacrifice future security in exchange for immediate gratification.

The Tyranny of Happiness

24   "Happiness is like perfume," goes an old saw. "If you wear it, you share it with everyone around you." A nice thought, but not always true: Too much happiness in the air can make those of us bogged down in everyday humdrum feel bad, because we think that everybody else is happier than we are.

25   Many people believe they should be happier. Friends burble about their delightful lives. Movies, TV (especially commercials), and magazines (such as *People*) not only blitz us with images of the luxuries we're missing but also with the triumphs, romance, and splendid jobs available (to everyone but us). On top of a boring job, financial problems, or whatever, we feel a sense of desperation because life is so short and happiness so near and yet so far.

26   Anyone who is continually miserable, who can't find any reliable source of satisfaction, or who honestly sees no good reason for living, *is* being cheated (or cheating herself) and needs help. The vague sense of deprivation felt by most of us, however, is probably misplaced. To expect to be happy all the time is as foolish as passively accepting constant *unhappiness*. As the English novelist Thomas Hardy wrote, There are no happy lives, only happy moments.

27   According to Michigan's Institute for Social Research, about 30 percent of Americans now say they're very happy (down from 35 percent in the fifties). Even these lucky spirits don't seem to mean that their well-being is constant. After studying the lives of his six hundred men, George Vaillant wrote, "I think I expected to find people who were in no trouble at all. I didn't know people like that, but always assumed that around the corner somewhere were people whose lives were like the quarterbacks in high school whom the girls always wanted. But there was nobody whose life wasn't at times filled with enough pain to send him to a psychiatrist." Life is difficult for everyone.

28   The late Carl R. Rogers, considered the founder of humanistic psychology, has said that such adjectives as *happy, contented,* and *blissful* don't describe the process he would call the good life, even though a person would certainly experience these feelings at times. *Rewarding, challenging, meaningful,* Rogers felt, better described the stretching and growing called for in fully experiencing life.

29   An important component of true well-being, includes recognizing the inevitability of some unhappiness. "I tell my patients there is pain in being single, in being married, and in being alive." says Roberta Temes, assistant professor of psychiatry at New York's

Downstate Medical School. Adds New York psychologist Emery Stein, "Anyone who is *constantly* happy is probably out of touch with reality."

30   One way to deal with everyone else's success, love and privileged life (compared with your dreariness and failures) is to keep in mind that this impression of dazzling happiness is an illusion! If you can't make yourself believe that, go to a meeting of any twelve-step program—AL-ANON, AA, Overeaters Anonymous—and listen to the stories members share. Some of the most attractive and serene-looking members will turn out to have the most heartrending lives, some will be in states of such misery that you'll be shamed by your self-pity. Others will have suffered but triumphed, and will persuade listeners that problems are solvable.

31   Discord and happiness are both part of life. Modern research shows that though the pursuit of happiness is chancy, no one is ever eliminated from the game. Says Freedman, "One of the clearest findings from our study is that no matter how unhappy you are now or were in the past, you can still find happiness in the future."

Catherine Houck's article "What is Happiness?" was excerpted from an article which appeared in *Cosmopolitan Magazine*.

After You Read

Reading Journal

In the opening section, "What is Happiness?" the author refers to people for whom life's glass is "half-full rather than half-empty." Which kind of person are you? Cite several examples which support your argument.

Reading for Meaning

Summarize the major research findings for each of the subsections of the article.

1. "What is Happiness?"

2. "The Happiness Chemical"

3. "Can Money Buy Happiness?"

4. "The Tyranny of Happiness"

Exploring Further

Interview/Questionnaire

Work with a small group. For additional suggestions on questionnaire writing, see the Writer's Guide.

1. Interview at least five Americans to find out what they consider the most important qualities/components of a happy life. You may use the model below or design one of your own.

List in order of importance those things a person needs to be happy.

1.

2.

3.

4.

5.

2. Collate your group's responses. Discuss and write up your findings. For example, how did your findings compare with the lists you prepared in the pre-reading section? Were there any contradictions to the information in the article? If so, how do you account for them?

Timed Writing Exercise

A significant number of Americans consult psychotherapists in order to make their lives happier. In your opinion, is this a useful practice? Why or why not? (You may want to discuss alternatives used in your culture for improving the quality of one's personal life.)

Focused Essay Topics

1. Recent research suggests that some of us are born with more "happiness chemical" than others. Describe your personality and temperament in relation to this substance.

2. Describe a moment or time in your life in which you felt great happiness. Try to analyze this in terms of the article's findings on the subject. Does your personal experience support or contradict any of the author's findings? Explain.

Before You Read

Freewrite on the following: What do you think the author means by his title? Can you imagine getting everything you have ever dreamed of and still not being content? Share your response.

When All You've Ever Wanted Wasn't Enough

BY HAROLD KUSHNER

1   Ask the average person which is more important to him, making money or being devoted to his family, and virtually everyone will answer *family* without hesitation. But watch how the average person actually lives out his life. See where he really invests his time and energy, and what he says he believes. He has let himself be persuaded that if he leaves for work earlier in the morning and comes home more tired at night, he is proving how devoted he is to his family by expending himself to provide them with all the things they have seen advertised.

2   (. . .) Ask the average person what he wants out of life, and he will probably reply, "All I want to be is happy." And I believe him. I believe that he works hard at making himself happy. He buys books, attends classes, changes his lifestyle, in an ongoing effort to find that elusive quality, happiness. But in spite of all that, I suspect that most people most of the time do not feel happy.

3   Why should that sense of happiness be so elusive, eluding both those people who get what they want in life and those who don't? Why should people with so many reasons to be happy feel so acutely that something is missing from their lives? Are we asking too much of life when we say, "All I want is to be happy"? Is happiness, like eternal youth or perpetual motion, a goal that we are not meant to reach, no matter how hard we work for it? Or is it possible for us to be happy, but we are going about it in the wrong way?

4   Oscar Wilde once wrote, "In this world there are only two tragedies. One is not getting what one wants, and the other is getting it." He was trying to warn us that no matter how hard we work at being successful, success won't satisfy us. By the time we get there, having sacrificed so much on the altar of being successful, we will realize that success was not what we wanted. People who have money and power know something that you and I do not know and might not believe even when we are told. Money and power do not satisfy that unnameable hunger in the soul. Even the rich and powerful find themselves yearning for something more. We read about the family problems of the rich and famous, we see their

fictionalized conflicts on television, but we never get the message. We keep thinking that if we had what they have, we would be happy.

5   (. . .) America's Declaration of Independence guarantees every one of us the right to the pursuit of happiness. But because the Declaration is a political document, it does not warn us of the frustration of trying to exercise that right, because the pursuit of happiness is the wrong goal. You don't become happy by pursuing happiness. You become happy by living a life that means something. The happiest people you know are probably not the richest or most famous, probably not the ones who work hardest at being happy by reading the articles and buying the books and latching on to the latest fads. I suspect that the happiest people you know are the ones who work at being kind, helpful, and reliable, and happiness sneaks into their lives while they are busy doing those things. You don't become happy by pursuing happiness. It is always a byproduct, never a primary goal. Happiness is a butterfly—the more you chase it, the more it flies away from you and hides. But stop chasing it, put away your net and busy yourself with other, more productive things than the pursuit of personal happiness, and it will sneak up on you from behind and perch on your shoulder.

> **Harold Kushner**, a Rabbi, lost a young son to a fatal disease, an experience which prompted him to explore in his writing the nature of faith and God in daily life. These themes are reflected in his best-sellers, *When Bad Things Happen To Good People* and *When All You Ever Wanted Wasn't Enough*.

After You Read

Reading Journal

The Declaration of Independence guarantees Americans "life, liberty, and the pursuit of happiness." It has been said that the act of *pursuing happiness* seems to be a uniquely American thing to do. As the author says, we "buy books, attend classes, change lifestyles, in an ongoing effort to find that elusive quality, happiness." Discuss whether you believe that doing these things can make a person happier.

Reading for Meaning

1. In his book *When All You've Ever Wanted Wasn't Enough*, Harold Kushner discusses an apparent contradiction in human nature regarding happiness. What is that contradiction and how does it affect the average person living in America? (In order to answer this question fully you must refer to your impressions of life in the United States. Or, if you prefer, you may refer to impressions you have formed from reading or viewing films about American life.)

2. Make a diagram of Kushner's basic argument (thesis and supporting ideas) regarding the nature of happiness. Compare it with others in your group for accuracy.

Exploring Further

Research Project

Research the kinds of books Kushner refers to in his article. (These will often be found in the "self-help" section of most bookstores.) Choose a book on how to be happy (or a closely related topic) and skim the introduction and table of contents to see what the book promises. Take notes and then later, when you return to class, discuss (a) whether the book seemed to offer useful advice for coping with the problem it addresses, and (b) whether or not you would buy it.

Timed Writing Exercise

In two paragraphs, compare/contrast the elusive happiness that "won't satisfy us" with the kind of happiness that "sneaks into [our] lives." Explain both concepts using examples from your personal experience.

Focused Essay Topics

1. Kushner poses five separate questions in the third paragraph. Choose <u>one</u> question and write an imaginary dialogue in which both you and the author respond. (You may want to use your notes from *Reading for Meaning,* question 2.)

2. Kushner cites Oscar Wilde's contention that "there are only two tragedies. One is not getting what one wants and the other is getting it." What is Wilde suggesting about the human condition? Do you agree or disagree with his view?

Before You Read

1. In 1776, Thomas Jefferson drafted the Declaration of Independence, the document announcing the colonies' intention to free themselves from British rule. In this document he writes:

"We hold these truths to be self-evident, that all men are created equal, that they are endowed by their Creator with certain inalienable Rights, that among these are Life, Liberty and the pursuit of Happiness."

What do you think he meant by the "pursuit of happiness"?

2. The title of the article you are about to read is "In Selfish Pursuit." What do you think the author is trying to say in his title? How might this relate to Jefferson's statement?

IN SELFISH PURSUIT: The road to happiness is often paved with guilt BY ANTHONY BRANDT

1   I want to talk about the pursuit of happiness and the dilemmas it leads us into. But I should explain my own bias, my old habit of contempt for this pursuit, before I begin. Until I looked up the history of the phrase not too long ago, I believed that happiness was an unworthy goal and couldn't understand why Jefferson gave it such weight when he wrote the Declaration of Independence. Life and liberty were inalienable rights clearly enough, but why the pursuit of happiness? Why not something more substantial, like greatness or knowledge?

2   As it turns out, Jefferson did not mean by happiness what we mean by it; we tend to think of happiness as a feeling, an entirely subjective delight, the inner grin that appears when life seems free of problems and disappears when they return. The pursuit of happiness so defined inevitably becomes a matter of managing one's internal state, one's moods. And my moods are characteristically, even genetically, somewhat dour. My father was a Swede by descent and as phlegmatic as that race is supposed to be. My mother was a fierce woman who more often inspired fear in me than delight. One day, I remember, I pulled a muscle so badly she had to take me to the doctor. Walking to the car, I started to groan from the pain; "Keep it to yourself," she snapped. I've hardly allowed myself to groan since. She was a stoic, and her stoicism became the model for my own. Over the years I developed a certain indifference to how I feel. I've lived with minor ailments for years and done nothing about them. I've come to believe that I should ignore my internal emotional state as well.

3   My whole disposition, in short, led me to this contempt for the pursuit of happiness. I am a quiet, occasionally grim, somewhat ascetic man, willing, I've always thought, to leave happiness to those lucky people who are born cheerful. I am of the type that has trouble letting go and having fun. I can't remember jokes when I've heard them. And life has always seemed to me a testing ground; like a fox crossing the ice or a soldier in a minefield, you proceed with great caution, take nothing for granted, and count yourself blessed just to have made it to the other side.

4   But I am a living contradiction; beneath the moods, the stoicism, the seriousness—a happy man. How so? It comes from the conditions of my life. My two children have grown up healthy, bright, and decent; I live in one of the loveliest villages in America. My wife loves and delights me, and I her. Most important of all, I believe to the center of my being that the work I am doing is the work I was meant to do. So this dour man, who can't dance, who worries that he drinks too much, is secretly pleased with himself and is free not to believe in the pursuit of happiness because he has already caught up with it.

5   I don't, however, feel entirely comfortable with this outcome. You will detect the note of self-congratulation in my account of myself. I am aware of it, but I'm not sure what to do about it. Should I deny my feelings? A friend of mine on the West Coast recently wrote me that after two years of trying to adjust to having diabetes and to establish himself in his career at the same time, he had come out whole and modestly successful and he was greatly pleased. Those who love the man can only be pleased for him. He earned it, didn't he? We turn guilty too quickly, I think, when we consider our circumstances and our successes and pronounce them good. I know I react this way; some part of me is sure I'm ripe for tragedy, that whatever success I have and whatever pleasure I take in it will be taken away. I don't really deserve it, I tell myself.

6   It becomes practically a fixed sequence: you arrive at a goal and that makes you happy, but then you notice that the happiness is composed half of relief, half of self-satisfaction; the latter half makes you distinctly nervous, and you fall to chewing on your achievements, discounting them. This then becomes the spur to more achievements, more happiness, more guilt. How much better, I sometimes think, to have no goals, just to live day by day. Would I be happy then? No, my mother's ghost wouldn't allow it. Life is hard, she told me; life is a struggle. So I struggle happily on, running through the sequence again and again, fighting off the impulse to pat myself on the back but remaining, like my friend, fundamentally pleased. That's the American way, isn't it? My contempt for the pursuit of happiness is a joke. I'm playing this game as hard as the next fellow.

7   But I have doubts. There are plenty of ways besides the American way. We Americans identify the pursuit of happiness with the pursuit of success, money, achievement; we think we'll be happy when we make it, although we love to believe that those who do make it are actually quite miserable. But I think of my father, who seemed to have no ambition, perfectly content, as far as I could tell, to work in the same job for the same company for thirty-five years, to come home to his wife and children every single night, read the paper, eat dinner, never go anywhere but to our cottage at the shore for two weeks and weekends during the summer. My father was

intelligent and talented; he had a beautiful singing voice, he could draw with great accuracy, but he made no effort to develop any of his talents. An assistant manager for twenty years, he had no desire to become manager. It used to drive my mother crazy; she was ambitious for him, she wanted him to push. He was immovable. When he retired, he spent the next ten years puttering around in his garden, which he never finished, and doing crossword puzzles. Still driving my mother crazy. I used to think he had wasted his life. Arrogant of me. I remember visiting him in his office and always finding him having a good time with his fellow workers, the very image of a happy man. Was this wasteful? My brother and I are both driven workaholics; my father lived in an entirely different framework. I think of the Greeks in connection with him; their idea of a happy life was a life led outside history, a quiet life like his. Their archetypal illustration was the story Herodotus[1] tells about the lawgiver Solon's conversation with the Lydian king Croesus, who was legendary for his wealth. Solon, who was legendary for his wisdom, was on a ten-year tour of the known world when he met Croesus, who showed him his treasury and then asked him who he thought was the happiest of all men he had met. Croesus believed, of course, that being the richest, he would certainly have to be the happiest. Solon rapidly set him straight. Who is a happy man? He who "is whole of limb" Solon replied, "a stranger to disease, free from misfortune, happy in his children, and comely to look upon." No more is necessary, except that he die well.

8   All of this was true of my father. He had enough money; he was whole of limb; he was almost never sick; he loved his children; he was even relatively good-looking. And he died well. The only time he ever spent in a hospital was the last four days of his life; he had a heart attack, spent four days in intensive care, and then, as quietly as he had lived, died. Here was happiness, not pursued but possessed anyhow.

9   Then there's the price those of us like his two sons pay, and force others to, for our obsession with this will-o'-the-wisp, happiness. A woman I hoped to marry wanted me to give up free-lance writing and get a job in public relations. I was making about six thousand dollars a year at the time and living on my dreams and my MasterCard. We had nothing. It was clear to both of us that we could hardly make a decent life together if my prospects didn't rapidly improve. And I might have made forty thousand dollars a year in PR. I flirted with the idea, saw some people, but nothing came of it. No one will hire me, I told her. You didn't really try, she replied. What do you mean? I said, indignant; of course I did. Of course I didn't. The truth I didn't want to admit to her, or to myself, was that I loved the work I was doing more than I loved her. She left eventually, and I was glad to see her go. I wanted the guilt she represented out of my life.

10   We can be selfish and ruthless in the pursuit of happiness, make choices other people have to live and suffer with, and there's no guarantee that it's going to work out. The odds are, in fact, that we won't make it, whatever "it" is, that the losses will outweigh the gains. The odds are what's keeping my friend Paul, who desperately wants to change his life, from doing it. Paul is thirty-five, married, and has an eleven-year old son.

---

[1] Herodotus: c. 484-425 B.C., Greek historian, known as the father of history.

He works as an advertising copywriter and does well, but what he really wants is to go back to graduate school, get his Ph.D. in English literature, then get a teaching job and write fiction on the side. But to do all this would mean selling his house, asking his wife to go to work and using the savings he has accumulated for his son's education for his own. He tells me that he sometimes spends hours figuring out exactly what he would need, how much the house would bring, how much his wife might make if she got a job, and what his chances are of getting a job in the overcrowded market of Ph.D.s. But no matter how carefully he draws up this budget— the figures, he says, are a simulacrum of his loyalties—there's never enough money.

11   The risks involved in such a choice are enormous, and Paul is at heart not ruthless or selfish enough to take them. If he were alone, he says, sure. And he says his wife is willing to stand behind him whatever he decides. But he can't do it, and this seems in most respects admirable; it was apparently my father's choice, it is the Greek choice, the choice to be content with one's lot and not ask too many sacrifices from other people in the service of something so insubstantial, so vague, as a possibility of happiness beyond what one already has. And yet Paul is not a happy man. He is not ruthless or selfish, no, but he sees this as a lack of courage, a failure to believe in his own talent; he calls himself a coward.

12   I understand Paul and I know what he's going through. I made my choice a long time ago, but it took me a long time to make it. And when I did, it cost me everything I owned, and it cost my ex-wife and my two kids and later my fiancée, not to mention assorted friends and relatives one hell of a lot of pain. And for what? For an old bitch gone in the teeth[2], to reapply Pound's metaphor to my own success, such as it is. I am proud of the work I've done, proud of staying with it when the reward was only six thousand dollars a year and my hair was already starting to turn gray; but I'm not proud of my own ruthlessness and selfishness and I wish I had had it in me to be more like my father.

13   The pursuit of happiness was serious business to Jefferson, but his idea of happiness, as I mentioned at the beginning, was quite different from ours. Happiness at the time of the Declaration was not a state of mind that one pursued in and for oneself, but a version of the common good, an idea of general human felicity that one pursued both for oneself and for all. Jefferson was trying to establish the idea that government has no right to stand in the way of our pursuit of felicity so conceived. The form that felicity took for Jefferson was a society composed very much along the Greek model, with lots of farmers living quiet lives, practicing quiet virtues, making money but not too much, and reading Herodotus by candlelight.

14   It hasn't turned out that way. We have identified happiness with success and we are stuck with it now, so that people like my father seem like washouts to people like my mother and the only happiness we can find is in the struggle to succeed. I suppose it couldn't have happened otherwise. But I am tempted to cry, Enough! To rest easy with what I have, finish reading Herodotus and then move on to Plutarch[3], perhaps take up cross-

---

2 "An old bitch gone in the teeth": literally, an aging, toothless dog. The reference is to a line from a poem by the U.S. poet Ezra Pound (1885-1972).
3 Plutarch: Greek essayist and biographer (c. 46-120 A.D.).

word puzzles, leaving pursuits to others. A gentleman farmer. It was wise of my father not to finish the garden for he would only have had to start another. Now he's gone, I missed the message of his life, I have condemned myself to this pursuit. Oh, I love it, make no mistake, but the pursuit of happiness feels to me sometimes like a dog chasing its tail and half of me thinks that we have made a giant mistake, the American way is little more than the exaltation of greed.

Anthony Brandt, a freelance writer since 1971, is the author of *Reality Police: The Experience of Insanity in America* (1975). Brandt is at work on a book about the myths of American culture.

After You Read

Reading Journal

Now that you have read Brandt's piece, does the pursuit he describes seem particularly American? Why or why not?

Reading for Meaning

1. Read the article again, this time making notes on the contrasting definitions of happiness given by the people below. Then compare your notes with your classmates.

    a. The author

    b. Jefferson

    c. The author's father

    d. The author's friend, Paul

    e. The Greek definition of happiness

2. The author's subtitle is: "The road to happiness is often paved with guilt." What do you think he meant by this?

Exploring Further

Debate

In Brandt's article, two kinds of men are contrasted—one who sacrifices his own ambition for the well-being of his family and one who pursues his personal goals in spite of his family. Debate which alternative seems the better one and for what reasons.

Timed Writing Exercise

As the story of Brandt's friend Paul shows, the pursuit of happiness often requires great sacrifice—both of one's self and others. Do you feel, in certain cases, it is preferable to be content with what you have? Why or why not? Give examples.

Focused Essay Topics

1. Anthony Brandt compares the ways he has pursued happiness with the ways members of his family and friends have pursued it. Summarize these major differences and the attitude of the author in regard to them. In other words, what kind of value judgments does he place on the choices his father, his friends and he himself made? (Use your notes from the *Reading for Meaning* section as a guide, and comment on each.) Which of these attitudes toward the pursuit of happiness most closely resembles your own? Explain and give examples.

2. Describe a member of your family or a close friend in relation to the theme of personal ambition, the realization of life goals, and the pursuit of happiness. Compare his/her attitudes and actions with your own. (Refer back to Brandt for a model.)

Before You Read

1. The title of the short story you are about to read is "The Benefits of American Life." What do you imagine are the "benefits" which attract immigrants to the United States? List them below:

2. Compare your list with that of a partner. Are your lists of benefits similar? If not, discuss where they differ.

3. In small groups or with the entire class, make a master list of benefits. Next, discuss which benefit(s) most influenced you or your family to come to the U.S. and, finally, whether these benefits have been attainable.

The Benefits of American Life

JAMES FARRELL

Ye orphan sons of Greece,
Scattered hither and beyond,
Persecuted and forlorn,
And by all nations beshun.
Guillotine Party

1   Takiss Fillios was a strong shepherd boy whose homeland was located just at the hollow valley of two mountains in Arcadia, Greece, in the central section of the Peloponnesus. He grew up on goats' milk and on pitch black bread whose cinders were not separated so as to produce more bread per pound. His hard-working mother sold a piece of land, which produced enough wheat to pull the family through the whole year, in order to pay his steerage fare to America. For in America the streets were paved with gold; the buildings were taller than mountains; the women all dressed like princesses and the men had their pockets lined with money; every boy had a bicycle; and every man and woman owned an automobile. At the age of thirteen, Takiss, large for his age, arrived in a paradise known as Chicago.

2   He was met at the railroad station, a scared and bewildered boy, by a relative who took him to a home on South Halsted Street. With voluble beneficence, the relative immediately employed Takiss, offering him a salary of fifteen dollars a month and the privilege of sleeping on marble slabs in his candy kitchen. He told Takiss that all successful Greek men started that way, and he showed the boy Greek newspapers with pictures of stern, mustachioed Greek restaurant owners and candy-store proprietors who recounted the story of their rise to fame and offered themselves as favorable candidates for marriage. And as a final word of advice, the relative told Takiss that his mother was getting old now, and that he should send her some of his wages to help her out.

3   Takiss quickly discovered what it meant to live in paradise. It meant working from six in the morning until six in the evening, and until even later on week-ends. It meant sweeping out the store, washing dishes and windows, polishing, arranging, mopping, running errands. It meant attending night school to learn English when he could scarcely keep his eyes open and where he was frequently laughed at for his blundering efforts. It meant walking along, living in the midst of dirty streets where coal dust, soot, smoke, and the poisonous fumes of automobiles choked his nostrils and made him cough. It meant lonesome memories. For a long period, Takiss was a lonely boy remembering his homeland and his Grecian mountains, remembering the long, slow days with the sheep, remembering the games he had played with other boys, remembering the smile and kiss of his old mother, remembering always.

4   And he was afraid of America, and of that tremendous paradise known as Chicago. He worked doggedly day after day, earning his fifteen dollars a month, catching a cough from sleeping on marble slabs. He worked doggedly, and from his wages he saved a pittance which he deposited in an immigrants' savings bank. But he looked ahead to the day when he would be famous, with his picture in the Greek newspapers, a pride and an honor to his native Greece and to the great tradition of the great Socrates about whom his relatives so frequently boasted. He dreamed of the time when he would become like Americans, talk like them, wear their clothes, ride in automobiles just as they did, walk along the streets with pretty American girls.

5   In time, Takiss learned things. He learned American words, but never how to speak them like an American. He learned that he was considered a dirty Greek greenhorn, and that many Americans would have been just as pleased if he and many of his countrymen had never come to their land. And he learned that American girls laughed sardonically at a young Greek greenhorn. Also, he learned of a place owned by a cousin of his, where for a little money he could go and find American girls who did not laugh at a Greek greenhorn, at least for five or ten minutes. He learned how to buy American clothes on installments, to wear a purple silk shirt, purple socks, and an orange tie. And he learned, also, that in the store he could put some of the money received for sales into his pocket instead of into the cash register.

6   Eventually, the cousin employing him discharged him in anger, branding him a crook, a robber, a traitor. In the heated quarrel, Takiss asked him why, if he wanted honesty, he paid only six dollars a week wages,

when he made so much money himself selling bad products and got his picture in the Greek newpapers as a successful pioneer in America.

7   Takiss was employed by other of his countrymen, in fruit stores, soda parlors, at hot-dog stands, and in restaurants. He acquired additional American knowledge, and more American words. And sometimes when he was dressed up, wearing his purple silk shirt with socks to match, and the orange tie, he would walk in the parks or along Halsted Street, seeing American girls, wishing that he had one of his own, a blonde girl with a beautiful pink-white complexion.

8   Time slid from under Takiss, and he was a young man in his early twenties, with his first citizenship papers. He had worked like a dog, and he was still slaving at the same jobs, performing the same tasks and chores as he had always done since he had come to America. He earned eight dollars a week and was busy twelve hours a day in a candy store. He cleaned and he mopped; he scrubbed; he polished; he washed; he waited on trade. And often when he was alone in the store he pocketed money from the cash register. Every week he deposited money in the bank, and almost nightly he looked in his bank book, proud of his savings, thinking of how he was going to achieve fame in America. But he was never able to save money, because he was always quitting or losing jobs and having to use savings to support himself between jobs, as well as to send money to his mother.

9   And he learned another thing . . . he learned how to dance like Americans. A Greek-American friend told him of a dancing school called a taxi-dance hall on West Madison Street, and showed him an advertisement from the Greek-American owner, Professor Christopolos, who stated in the ad that anyone could be as graceful as he if they learned dancing from his beautiful girls at only ten cents a dance. He paid a dollar and was given ten tickets and entered the dimly lighted dancing school of Professor Christopolos on the fourth floor of a dingy and decrepit building. Each ticket was good for one dance which lasted from a minute to a minute and a half. Any girl in the place would dance with him, because she received five cents for each dance. Takiss' tickets were quickly used up, and he bought more. It did not matter if he danced woodenly and clumsily, and the girls acted delighted to teach him. He went to this taxi-dance hall regularly, spending three, four, and five dollars every visit, and once in a while a girl would ask him if he wanted to take her home, and for a few more dollars he could get other favors, too. After he started going to the taxi-dance hall regularly he was able to save less money, and he sent little to his mother.

10   Takiss then spent some of his savings for a suit with bell-bottom trousers. He cultivated a mustache and long side-burns, greased his hair and parted it in the middle with meticulous attention. He began to look like a sheik, and listened to pick up all the words which the American-born sheiks used. He went to public dance halls where there was only an admission fee and longer dances. At these places, there were always swarms of girls, pretty American girls, some of them tall and beautiful blondes with milky skins and red lips like cherries. He would ask them to dance. Often they would dance with him, once. He would talk, and they would catch his accent, and when he asked them for a second dance they would thank him with great regret and exclaim that all their other dances were

taken. So he would quickly be driven to dancing with the homely and ugly girls who were called wallflowers. And then he would go back to Professor Christopolos' dancing school, where all the girls would dance with him for ten cents a dance.

11 One day, Takiss was twenty-five. His native Grecian mountains seemed to have receded in time and he saw them only in painful mists of memory, recalling their details and contours with lessening concreteness. Greece to him was a memory. He had been in America for twelve years, and he was working ten hours a day in a hot-dog stand for ten dollars a week, and able to graft from three to five dollars a week extra. He wanted to make money and to become famous like some of his Americanized countrymen. And when he was a rich man with a hot-dog stand or a restaurant of his own, he would return to Greece with an American wife and act like a millionaire. And he had thirty-five dollars in the bank as a start toward these riches. He wanted to get more money, but not by running a brothel as his fourth cousin George did, and not bootlegging as did George's friend, Mike. He remembered the things his mother, now dead, had told him, and he wanted to make his money and his fame in a way that his mother would have approved of. And then he would have his picture in a Greek-American newspaper.

12 And hard times came to America. Takiss was out of work in the winter, and again his savings melted. He was employed for ten dollars a week in a candy store, still working twelve hours a day, and in four months that job was gone. He worked for seven dollars a week washing dishes in a large restaurant, and then his pay was cut to five dollars, and he went home every night tired, with chafed hands and an aching back. He had less money, also, for taxi dances. And he lost that job.

13 He walked the streets looking for other work, and always he learned the same story . . . hard times. He ate very frugally, lived in a chilly, rat-infested room, and wished that he was back home again in his native Grecian mountains, or else that he was a rich and famous American Greek. Every day he went out looking for a job, and sometimes he found work for a few days or a few weeks and was able to skim along while he tried again to find work.

14 One day he saw an advertisement with large letters at the top . . . DANCE MARATHON. The word Marathon struck him. Greek. He would win it and win another victory for his country as it had been done in ancient times. He would become a famous Greek athlete. He investigated, and learned that it was a contest in which everybody tried to dance longer than the others, and the winner received a five-hundred-dollar prize. And maybe if he won it, he would get a job in the moving pictures and become the idol of American girls, or go on the vaudeville stage, or be hired to dance in a cabaret. And while he was in the contest, he would be cared for, fed, and there would be no room rent to pay. He was strong and husky, even if he had been getting coughs in his chest for years ever since he had slept on those marble slabs. And he could dance. He was used to standing on his feet all day at work. And this was his chance to become rich. He would no longer have to tramp all over town to be told that there were no jobs because it was hard times. This was much better than saving up to own a candy store and grow fat like the American Greeks for whom he had worked. And after he won this contest, and

became famous, he would go back to Greece with a trunk full of clothes and money, and maybe a rich American girl whose skin was like milk.

15   Takiss entered the dance marathon, and when the rules were explained to him, he only understood that he was to stay out on the floor and dance, and if he was able to do that longer than anyone else, he would get five hundred dollars. A number was pinned on his back, and he was assigned a partner named Marie Glenn, a beautiful blonde American girl of the type he had always dreamed of as a possible wife. At first, when she met him, she shuddered, and her face broke into an expression of disgust. But then she saw that he was strong and husky with broad shoulders, and she smiled, offering him a limp hand and sweetly telling him that she knew they were sure going to be the winners.

16   The dance marathon was conducted in a public dance hall on the south side of Chicago. A ring was placed in the center with an orchestra dais at one end. Around the ring there were box seats, and behind them, rising rows of bleacher benches. The opening was described, in advertisements, as gala. An announcer talked through a microphone, and the promoters and judges wearing tuxedoes also addressed a full house. The contestants were introduced and some of them, but not Takiss, spoke to the crowd and the large radio audience all over America. It was all a new and promising, if confusing, world to Takiss, and he walked around the floor, feeling as lost and as out of place as he had on those first days in America. But it was leading at last to paradise.

17   The contest swung into action. They danced for three minutes out of every ten, and walked around and around the floor for the remaining time; and they were given fifteen minutes rest out of every hour. There was glamor in being watched by so many people, in eating sandwiches and drinking coffee before them, in receiving attention from doctors and nurses, and meeting all the others who, like himself, saw at the end of this contest five hundred dollars and fame. As the contestants got to talking to each other, Takiss heard them using one word over and over again . . . celebrity. A celebrity was somebody who was important, like Jack Dempsey and movie stars and Mr. Delphos, the famous American-Greek who was wealthy and owned a large dance hall known as the Bourbon Palace. They all wanted to be celebrities. And Takiss, too, he determined that he was going to be a celebrity.

18   Takiss had not imagined that anyone could dance for more than a week like this, and that maybe after a sleepless and tiring week he would be the winner. In less than twenty-four hours he learned that it was a grind more gruelling than he had calculated, and while he doggedly gritted his teeth, he determined that he would not let himself drop out. Still, he wished that he had not entered it. He wished he were back working in fruit stores and ice cream parlors the way he had been before hard times had come. He wished that he were a shepherd back in the Grecian mountains.

19   When his partner was tired, she put her arms around his neck or hips, laid her head against him, and fell asleep while he dragged her heavily around the floor, and when he fell asleep she did the same with him. Again and again their bodies were jolted, shoved, pushed against each other, and he began wanting her so that her very nearness became excruciating. And he noticed that she, particularly in the early dog hours of the mornings when there were scarcely any spectators in the hall,

began brushing herself against him at every opportunity, looking fever-
ishly into his eyes and telling him smutty jokes. And the other dancers
became the same way, and the fellows used to tell him how much they
wanted one of these girls, any girl.

20   Day after day the marathon grind went on. His eyes grew heavy. His
back ached. His feet became sore and raw, so that each step was pain
and he felt often as if he were walking on fire. The hall was almost continuously stale with cigarette smoke and foul with body odors. He felt
constantly dirty, sweaty, itchy. Dust got into his nostrils and his eyes. He
began to cough again. His muscles knotted. He became like a person
who was always only half awake, and everything took on the semblance
of being a semi-dream. Marie, also, changed. She began to swell around
the buttocks. Deep circles grew under her eyes. She became haggard
and blowsy and looked like a worn-out prostitute. She used more and
more cosmetics, and her face became like a ghastly caricature of the
pretty girl who had entered the contest.

21   In the beginning, particularly because of his accent and Greek heritage, Takiss became the butt of many jokes. Constantly, he would be
asked why he wasn't running a restaurant, and he would be given orders
for a piece zapple pie kid. He was nicknamed Restaurant, Fruit Store,
Socrates and Zapple Pie Kid. In time, this wore down and failed to anger
or disturb him. The grind settled into habitual misery and torture. He, like
the other contestants, would long for fresh air, and during rest periods,
when they were not so tired that they would be dragged like walking som-
nambulists to the rest cots, they would enter the vile and filthy dressing
rooms or the equally unsavory lavatory and jam their heads out of the
windows to breathe fresh air and to look yearningly down at the street
where people walked free to do what they wished, not tired, able to
breathe fresh air, even the fresh air of a city street that was saturated with
carbon monoxide fumes and sootiness.

22   Day after day dragged on. Sometimes Takiss, Marie, or the other contestants would live in stupors of six, twelve hours a day, even longer. As
the time passed, the contestants would switch from affected and over-
stimulated good spirits to nasty, fighting nervousness, and then into that
glaze-eyed stupor. Particularly in those dog hours of the early morning,
they would be raw, if awake, and fight and curse. Sex, too, became a
growing obsession, and in time was almost madness. Living so near to
one another, their bodies touching so frequently, they told smuttier and
smuttier jokes. Perversities and desires or propositions for perversities
sprang up among them. It became a relentless process of both physical
and mental torture. Constipation, diarrhea, sudden inabilities to control
their kidneys so that now and then a contestant would be walking around
the floor, drugged in sleep, with wet lines down his trousers, or if a girl,
down her beach pyjamas which most of them wore regularly. Broken
blood vessels and swollen veins in the legs. Headaches, eye troubles,
sore throats, fevers, colds. Periods of sweatiness, followed by shivers and
chills. And always that returning stupor, caused by sleeplessness and
fatigue, and by the dreams and fantasies which they entertained as relief
from that endless procession around and around the floor. And at the end
of it all, money, the chance to become a celebrity, sex, and clean white
bed sheets and a soft, fresh bed.

23   Ways of making money from day to day quickly developed and were used to the utmost so that all of the contestants started bank accounts. Every one of them developed some trick or act, a song, a dance, a stunt of some kind, and after putting it on, they would be showered with money from the crowd. One of the contestants, a raw country youth of Lithuanian origin with a nasal twang to his voice, chewed razor blades as his stunt. Takiss learned a dance. Stores, theatres, and politicians also paid them fees to wear signs or sweaters and jerseys with advertising printed on the front or back. Money was sent to them, mash notes, written in as ignorant and as bad English as that which Takiss used and wrote in. The various spectators picked favorites, cheered for them, shouted encouragement.

24   And still the days stretched out, past the first month, with contestant after contestant dropping out, and the field narrowing down. One day there would be a birthday party. Another day there was a floor wedding between two of the contestants who had met on the floor, and the wedding provided endless hours of raw jokes and rumor about when they would have their wedding night, until, sex-crazed, both of the newlyweds went temporarily out of their heads and the girl screamed until she was dragged off the floor. Disqualified, they were out of the marathon, and a new note was introduced in the humor. Another day, a girl had an abscessed tooth extracted on the floor, and immediately afterward she rejoined the endless walking procession that tramped around and around in this ever dullening stupor. Another day, an Italian boy, who with his wife had entered the marathon because they were both unemployed and had been evicted, required crutches and ran a high fever. With his eyes intense from the fever, with suffering imprinted on his haggard face, he hobbled around and around. After twelve hours he was forced out by the judges on the advice of a doctor.

25   Again and again Takiss wanted to quit and satisfy himself with the incidental money he had taken in, and as repeatedly he would go patiently on. Like the others, he would fall into that lumbrous sleep, and external means would be necessary to awaken him so that he might continue. The male nurses would slap him in the face with wet towels, put his shoes on the wrong feet, strap him into an electric vibrator machine, poke their fingers down his throat, tickle his calloused soles. During one period, his cough developed into a severe cold in the chest. For another period, he was not out of his stupor for three days. And Marie, his partner, experienced the same tortures. They went on. Days and nights, and days and nights, with the field narrowing to thirteen, ten, eight, five, finally two couples. Then Marie collapsed and was carried off the floor and shipped to a hospital, and Takiss was disqualified. They each collected the two hundred and fifty dollars second place money.

26   After recuperation, Takiss entered other dance marathons, and became a professional. He secured a copy of *Yes, We Have No Bananas* with a Greek translation, and this, with his dance stunt, became very popular. He was able, with both attractions and with a growing audience of fans, to earn from ten to fifteen dollars a day in extra money. Even when he was forced to retire from marathons or was disqualified, he departed with added money. Again the desire to return to his homeland

like a rich American grew upon him, and now his bank account, with foreign exchange rates, would make him very rich in Greece. He was something of a celebrity in this new world of his. His biography and picture appeared in Greek newspapers. A Greek merchant who sold a raisin beverage paid him and Marie each a hundred dollars to be photographed for a newspaper advertisement in which there was their signed testimony that they drank this beverage. He had a run of a week at a small theatre on South Halsted Street where there were many Greeks. Takiss became a famous American Greek.

27   In all, Takiss participated in sixteen dance marathons. In eight of them, he collected money and was the winner of a thousand dollar supermarathon in which only finalists from other marathons were permitted to enter and in which there were no rest periods. He had money now, five thousand dollars. He returned to Greece. But the strain of the marathons had ruined his lungs and he had tuberculosis. Resorts for tuberculosis had been developed in his native mountains, and when he returned it was necessary for him to become a patient in one of them, and the money he had earned was paid out while he lived there with his lungs rotting away on him. Well could he recite his favorite Greek proverb:

> *I ate practically the whole cow,*
> *Why must I forget the tail?*

James Farrell, having grown up in Chicago's South Side slums, was known for his realistic and hard-edged vision of urban life, especially the lives of the disadvantaged. He wrote numerous collections of stories and longer works of fiction, the most famous of which is the novel *Studs Lonigan: A Trilogy* (1935).

After You Read

Reading Journal

What do you think the quality of life was like for new immigrants in the America of the 1930s? Do you think that conditions are the same or different for today's immigrants? Explain.

Reading for Meaning

1. What benefits did Takiss actually find in his life in America? How did they differ from those he imagined he would find?

2. Farrell refers several times to Takiss' acquiring of "American knowledge." What exactly was this knowledge and how did it help Takiss in his search for the American Dream?

3. What is the significance of the proverb in the last paragraph?

Exploring Further

Debate

Some foreigners, in order to secure U.S. citizenship and/or a green card (which enables them to work legally), arrange marriages of convenience in which two people agree to marry and then divorce as soon as the documents come through. Argue whether or not you would do this if you were faced with deportation.

Timed Writing Exercise

By some standards at least, Takiss can be said to have achieved his dream. Yet, along the way he was forced to make compromises—to his morality, his personal happiness and of course, his health. Think of a personal goal and consider how much you would be willing to sacrifice in order to attain it. Be very specific.

Focused Essay Topics

1. Are you more likely to find personal happiness in your native culture or in the U.S.? Explain the reasons behind your choice. (You may want to refer to your *Before You Read* and *Reading Journal* notes.)

2. If you had been Takiss' friend, what "American knowledge" would you have given him about living and adjusting to life in America? How might your advice have changed the course of his story?

Before You Read

1. The following questionnaire examines attitudes concerning success. Answer each statement TRUE or FALSE, first to reflect your personal view and then to reflect what you feel would be the average American view. When you finish, read the "answer key" and share your findings with the group. (Examine, for instance, how many times you disagreed with the "average American." Do you think these differences will effect your chances for success in America?)

SUCCESS QUESTIONNAIRE	Your opinion	Average American opinion
1. Success is best determined by how much money one has.		
2. Success is measured by one's material possessions.		
3. Self-esteem is the secret to success.		
4. Professional success is measured by your salary.		
5. Success is influenced by skin color, religion and ethnic background.		
6. Being successful requires a sacrifice of personal leisure time.		
7. Being successful requires a sacrifice of personal relationships.		
8. In order to succeed, you should only rely on yourself.		
9. Learning how to compete is essential if you want to get ahead.		
10. In order to succeed, sometimes you have to break the rules.		
11. Salary is more important to me than overall job satisfaction.		
12. Success = happiness		
13. The key to success is to take risks.		
14. Anyone can succeed if s/he works at it.		
15. I will probably be more successful than my parents were.		
ANSWER KEY: As you may have guessed, these are all considered to be true by many Americans.		

2. The following article examines the enterprise and material success of Korean immigrants in the United States. As you read, make a check in the left-hand margin of the questionnaire, indicating which of the beliefs about success might play a role in the Korean American success story.

Horatio Alger Kim

BY MATTHEW SCHIFRIN

1   One taste of *kimch'i*, the fiery pickled cabbage with a mindbending aroma that is Korea's national dish, made *Today* show host Jane Pauley lose her composure and drove her off the NBC set after she sampled it for viewers just before the Seoul Olympics. Few other Westerners take to *kimch'i*, either, which helps explain why most Americans have never set foot inside a Korean restaurant in the U.S. Too bad, because if they did, they might get a lesson in economics even more stimulating than a mouthful of *kimch'i*.

2   Korean restaurants are the new home of an ancient Asian practice of savings and capital formation called *kye* (sounds like keh). *Kyes*, prevalent in South Korea, are being used in America to finance thousands of small, Korean-owned businesses.

3   In a typical *kye* a dozen or so friends or alumni meet once a month over a meal of *kimch'i*, rice, barbecued beef and Korean whiskey. Afterward, each person ponies up the same amount, anywhere from $100 to $40,000, in cash, adding to a pot that can sometimes reach $400,000. Every month a different member of the *kye* receives the entire sum raised that month and pays for dinner. There are no credit checks or questions asked. The system is based on trust, and the only requirement is that each member contribute until the last member has had a turn to take home the kitty, and everyone is made whole.

4   *Kye* is just one of the reasons Koreans collectively have emerged as an entrepreneurial powerhouse in the U.S. economy. Surveys indicate that as much as 50% of roughly 1 million Koreans in the U.S. are self-employed, the majority having started their first business within

four years of arriving. Today most Korean shopkeepers earn more than $50,000 a year. Hundreds of them have become millionaires. The thousands of small shops that they operate contribute billions of dollars to the U.S. economy.

5   In New York Koreans own 85% of the $500 million retail greengrocery business, many of the dry cleaners, nail salons, fish markets and a good chunk of the garment industry. Throughout the country they dominate the import and wholesale distribution of South Korean goods like wigs, costume jewelry and leather handbags. In Los Angeles they own most of the liquor and convenience stores and garment factories. In Anchorage the city's 6,000 Korean immigrants are gaining a footing in restaurants, tailoring, gas stations and janitorial services.

6   Koreans in the U.S. are rarely innovators. Rather, they are masters at revitalizing sleepy, small businesses. Take Young Jun Kim, 44, who came to Los Angeles nearly penniless in mid-1983 after ten years as a tuna boat captain based in the South Korean port of Pusan. For four years he and his wife, In Sook, worked long hours, six days a week; he delivered sewing machines to garment factories and his wife worked in one. On Sunday they went to church.

7   In May 1987 Kim bought a run-down liquor/convenience store in East Los Angeles, the city's Mexican barrio. He immediately applied a coat of paint, installed television surveillance and expanded operating hours from 6:30 a.m. until midnight on weekdays, and until 2 a.m. on weekends. Besides a brisk business in José Cuervo Tequila, Kim now also

offers check cashing, lotto tickets, luggage and even tickets for the bus that stops in front of his shop. The Kims—including two sons who work at the shop on weekends—have yet to take a single day off. Kim, who speaks better Spanish than English, hopes to buy a house soon.

8　According to Kim's accountant, Yoon Han Kim, who has over 100 Korean clients, it usually costs around $300,000 to buy a liquor store, and buyers typically put up 50% in cash. So how did Young Jun Kim come up with $150,000 or so, in cash, in just four years? "We saved very much," says Kim, with astonishing understatement. And what about *kye* financing? Kim clearly recognizes the word, but stares blankly and waves his hand as if he doesn't understand.

9　The reason Kim and most other Koreans refuse to talk about *kye* is that they think it is illegal in America. In fact, they're generally wrong. However, in some of the more sophisticated *kyes* members bid for the pool by stating the amount of interest they will pay to get first crack at the money. Those with urgent financial needs might bid 15% interest on a $100,000 pool and take home only $85,000. In such cases, *kye* members are right to fear IRS scrutiny of unreported interest income.

10　Still, *kyes* have become so popular in communities like Los Angeles that Koreatown banks have recently begun offering savings plans structured like *kyes*. At Los Angeles' Hanmi Bank, anyone entering into a 12-month, $10,000 plan is eligible for an advance of the entire amount after four months of saving.

11　But *kyes* are just part of the picture. Ever notice that Korean shops usually are the first ones to crop up in the neighborhoods that have bottomed out and are beginning a rebound? Twenty years ago Los Angeles' Koreatown was a slum; today property values are worth at least 20 times their mid-1960s levels.

12　In Atlanta Koreans dominate the inner city grocery business. In impoverished sections of Washington, D.C. they run many of the small shops. In Philadelphia Koreans set up in distressed Olney; in Chicago, on the South Side. You can find Koreans in the worst sections of Oakland, Calif. and Newark, N.J. In New York there are a disproportionate number of Korean-owned businesses in Harlem, the South Bronx and Manhattan's sleazy area near Herald Square.

13　In this way Koreans suggest nothing so much as a sizable crowd of contrarian investors. They pick businesses in out-of-favor locations because the rents are cheap and growth potential is high.

14　Koreans also show an amazing willingness to adapt to new businesses or lifestyles in order to succeed. Many Koreans who have immigrated here are university educated and have never been self-employed. A disproportionately large number turn out to be the children of North Korean refugees who fled the Communists in the Korean conflict. Lacking roots in South Korea, they began emigrating to the U.S. along with South Koreans in general in the mid-1960s. Emigrants from South Korea are currently arriving in the U.S. at a rate of 35,000 a year. They open labor-intensive small businesses in part because of language problems.

15　"Koreans know that they can only make $30,000 a year with a Ph.D. but can make three times that amount by opening up a laundry," says Michael Lee, executive director of the Korean Chamber of Commerce in Los Angeles. Lee, an M.B.A. and CPA, now owns a Korean restaurant and has also previously owned many different small businesses, including a 7-Eleven franchise. Lee's 55-year-old sister recently sold her house in Seoul for $200,000, moved to Los Angeles and opened up a coin laundry business.

16   By American standards, Koreans seem driven. Consider Cho Hyun Shin, 38, who began his working life in a New York auto body shop, moved up to own a dry cleaner and is now a multimillionaire New York real estate broker. Why real estate? "I went to the library in 1979 and read that 75% of the nation's new millionaires were in real estate," says Shin. "I figured real estate must be the business to go into, because I always wanted to be a millionaire."

17   Adaptability is one reason that a survey by Queens College sociologist Pyong Gap Min, Ph.D., showed that only 9 of the 65 Korean-owned restaurants in Atlanta, Ga. served Oriental food, and only 2 served Korean food.

18   Mr. and Mrs. Chi Jin Ok arrived in the U.S. in the late 1960s and have made a successful career of running American diners formerly owned by Greeks. Chi Jin, 46, a graduate of Cheshin College in Seoul, started as a dishwasher and soon after bought a small coffee shop in a Brooklyn slum for $8,000. The couple now own two Brooklyn diners and are looking to expand into Long Island.

19   "When I first started I didn't know the difference between brisket and corned beef," says Chi Jin, who has never missed work or been outside New York. "Now I can cook every dish on our 200-item menu." The couple recently bought a house in Upper Brookville, on Long Island, where home prices average around $1.1 million and there is a 2-acre minimum lot size. The Oks have 40 employees at their two diners.

20   Such growth suggests that more and more Koreans will soon be facing a familiar business problem, if they are not confronting it already: how to manage the move from small family-run businesses into larger, more structured organizations. "Many Koreans are reaching a plateau and have to go to medium size," says Hanmi Bank President Benjamin Hong. "But they are limited because they don't have management skills."

21   Indeed, most Koreans insist on having total control of the businesses they own. Even diner businessman Ok insists on knowing every facet of his business. "If I don't," he says, "then my cook can throw off his apron and I'm stuck."

22   Andrew Ham, 28, continues to put in ten-hour days even though his $30 million (sales) auto dealership in Los Angeles' Koreatown has made him a millionaire. "You can never totally trust your managers," Ham insists. "You must know the details."

23   As is the case with many immigrant groups that preceded them, the glue that holds the Korean community together in the U.S. is its churches. Besides worship, they are places for socializing, for cultural activities and for making business connections. In Atlanta Koreans first got into the grocery business after a group of Koreans in a local Baptist church got jobs in a regional store chain and began hiring their friends. Today Koreans own 300 grocery stores in Atlanta and dominate the business.

24   According to sociologist Min, only about 25% of South Koreans in the old country are Christian, but no sooner do they arrive in the U.S. than 70% of the immigrants begin attending various Protestant churches, mostly Presbyterian. In the New York City area alone there are over 300 churches with Korean congregations. "Since I came here in 1978, I never missed one week of church," says Suzie Oh, a Bayside, N.Y. nail salon proprietor who rarely went to church in South Korea. Besides the

nail salon, Oh's family owns a car wash in Connecticut, a commercial building in New Jersey and two houses in New York's borough of Queens.

25   Like most Korean churches, the Korean American Presbyterian Church in Flushing, N.Y. sends out a fleet of vans to pick up businessmen and families and bring them to services. Accommodating itself to the frenetic work pace of the faithful, the church offers services as early as 6 a.m. and as late as 8 p.m. The 3,000-strong congregation donates to such organizations as the local police and is about to buy a 500-room resort in the Poconos for religious retreats.

26   Yet for all of their tenacity and success in business, Koreans have still to gain a foothold in U.S. politics. Because of South Korea's persistent political turmoil, most seem to distrust politicians and feel that building an economic base is more important than dabbling in politics anyway.

27   "Our country is small, and for years we have had to survive many bad situations," says Dr. Young Lee, who was cleaning dental laboratories 13 years ago. Today Lee is a dentist with investment holdings that include commercial office buildings and a home in Beverly Hills. He is also chairman of Los Angeles' Korean Chamber of Commerce. Says Lee of the miracle that is his life, "In this country there is freedom, so we know that if we do our best, we can get good results."

Matthew Schifrin's article appeared in *Forbes Magazine* in 1988.

After You Read

Reading Journal

What is your reaction to the profile of the successful Korean? Do you think this kind of success is possible for any ethnic group? If not, what other factors influence success in a new country?

Reading for Meaning

1. Explain the title. (You may have to consult an encyclopedia or large dictionary).

2. What qualities do the successful Koreans presented in the article share?

3. How have successful Koreans adapted their own cultural values and traditions to their pursuit of the "American Dream"?

Exploring Further

Research Project

1. Go to the library and do a newspaper/periodical search on the conflict that emerged between the African American community and the Korean shopkeepers in Brooklyn, New York, in the early part of 1990.

2. Then write an essay that considers both sides of the conflict. First you must describe the situation objectively, from both minorities' point of view, then you must analyze the cultural, social and political motivations for the conflict.

Timed Writing Exercise

Write an overview of your personal goals and objectives. What qualities, training and skills will you need to accomplish them? And finally, do you think it will be harder for you, as a non-native speaker of English, to succeed in realizing your ambitions?

Focused Essay Topics

1. Do a profile of a figure or personality commonly considered successful in your native culture (e.g., an entertainer, an entrepreneur, etc.). Do research, if necessary. Tell the story of this person's rise to success, describing the qualities s/he has that are valued in your culture. How do they compare with the Korean success formula as described in the article?

2. Cohesiveness and a strong sense of group identity have obviously helped some Korean immigrants succeed in their new lives. However, Koreans have also been involved in confrontations with other ethnic/racial minorities in the United States. Discuss the possible drawbacks to maintaining a strong identification with one's own group. For example, how might it interfere with a fuller integration into American society at large? Use your own experience and observation to respond.

Before You Read

The poem you are about to read was written by the African American writer Langston Hughes in the late 1930s. Speculate on what he might have meant by his title.

Let America Be
America Again   BY LANGSTON HUGHES

1   Let America be America again.
    Let it be the dream it used to be.
    Let it be the pioneer on the plain
    Seeking a home where he himself is free.

5   (America never was America to me.)

    Let America be the dream the dreamers dreamed—
    Let it be that great strong land of love
    Where never kings connive nor tyrants scheme
    That any man be crushed by one above.

10 (It never was America to me.)

    O, let my land be a land where Liberty
    Is crowned with no false patriotic wreath,
    But opportunity is real, and life is free,
    Equality is in the air we breathe.

15 (There's never been equality for me,
    Nor freedom in this "homeland of the free.")

    Say who are you that mumbles in the dark?
    And who are you that draws your veil across the stars?

    I am the poor white, fooled and pushed apart,
20 I am the red man driven from the land.
    I am the refugee clutching the hope I seek—
    But finding only the same old stupid plan
    Of dog eat dog, of mighty crush the weak.
    I am the Negro, "problem" to you all.
25 I am the people, humble, hungry, mean—
    Hungry yet today despite the dream.
    Beaten yet today—O, pioneers!
    I am the man who never got ahead,
    The poorest worker bartered through the years.

30 Yet I'm the one who dreamt our basic dream
In that Old World while still a serf of kings,
Who dreamt a dream so strong, so brave, so true,
That even yet its mighty daring sings
In every brick and stone, in every furrow turned
35 That's made America the land it has become.
O, I'm the man who sailed those early seas
In search of what I meant to be my home—
For I'm the one who left dark Ireland's shore,
And Poland's plain, and England's grassy lea,
40 And torn from Black Africa's strand I came
To build a "homeland of the free."

The free?
Who said the free? Not me?
Surely not me? The millions on relief today?
45 The millions who have nothing for our pay
For all the dreams we've dreamed
And all the songs we've sung
And all the hopes we've held
And all the flags we've hung,
50 The millions who have nothing for our pay—
Except the dream we keep alive today.

O, let America be America again—
The land that never has been yet—
And yet must be—the land where *every* man is free.
55 The land that's mine—the poor man's, Indian's, Negro's, ME—
Who made America,
Whose sweat and blood, whose faith and pain,
Whose hand at the foundry, whose plow in the rain,
Must bring back our mighty dream again.

60 O, yes,
I say it plain,
America never was America to me,
And yet I swear this oath—
America will be!

(James) Langston Hughes was a major voice in the Harlem Renaissance, an
African American movement that emerged in the 1930s and embraced all the
arts. Hughes wrote both poetry and fiction, most notably the collection of
stories *The Ways of White Folks*.

After You Read

Reading Journal

Explore your own feelings about "letting America be America again."
It might help to focus on one line or passage. Do you think we have
reason to be optimistic about a return to a more ideal state today?

Reading for Meaning

1. Who are the "dreamers" Hughes refers to in line 6?

2. What is the effect of the parenthetical lines 5, 10, 15-16?

3. Who is speaking in lines 17-18? To whom is s/he speaking?

4. What evidence is there in the poem which contradicts the ideal of the "American Dream"?

5. Who does the poet feel should be responsible for resurrecting the "dream"?

Exploring Further

Group Presentation

> Before you begin, appoint one member of the group as the secretary and choose your "actors" from among the remaining members.

Give a dramatic reading of Hughes's poem for the class. Before you can do this, you must decide how many speakers there are in the poem, and how to divide up the lines in order to best present each dramatic "voice."

Timed Writing Exercise

"Translate" the eighth stanza (lines 19-41) into a prose paragraph. You do not have to work line-by-line, but rather idea-by-idea. First, decide what overall impression of America's past Hughes was trying to create. Try for a strong opening sentence that will convey both the poet's tone and main idea.

Focused Essay Topics

1. Discuss the irony in Hughes's belief that "America will be." What do you think the poet means by this optimistic future tense? What do you think will have to change in order for America "to be" again? Consider the question in light of past and current racial struggles in the U.S. (You may want to use your *Reading Journal* entry as a point of departure.)

2. Go to the library and get a copy of Martin Luther King's "I have a dream" speech. Re-read Hughes's poem. In the first part of your essay compare/contrast these two documents of hope. What do they share? How do they differ? In the second half, discuss how close you feel we are today to these "dreams."

EXTENDING THE CONTEXT

> These questions are designed for further discussion or essay writing. Your responses should reflect the thinking, reading and writing you have done on the unit topic thus far.

1. Review all of your reading/writing/class discussion on happiness. Then write an extended personal definition of the term. Be sure to indicate how your definition compares/contrasts with that of the authors you have chosen by referring to your own life experiences.

2. Argue for or against the "rags to riches" myth which claims that hard work and determination will lead to a piece of the American Dream. Use at least two of the readings to support your argument. (Suggested: "Horatio Alger Kim" and "Benefits of American Life.")

3. Do you think happiness is determined/influenced by gender? In your native country are there different criteria or opportunities for happiness for men than for women? Explain.

4. To what extent can one separate happiness from material success? Use the readings to support your thesis.

5. If you have not done so before, turn to the *Short Takes* section at the beginning of the chapter and select one of the quotes to respond to in an essay. How have the readings changed or reinforced your opinion about American happiness? (Be sure to refer directly to the texts in your argument.)

6. Alistair Cooke claimed in his book on America that "Every other country scorns American materialism while striving in every big and little way to match it." Do you agree or disagree? Explain this contradiction in your essay and use your knowledge of the United States and your own culture as support.

7. Look back at Anthony Brandt's "In Selfish Pursuit" and the way in which he compares three basic kinds of ambition and success. Compare this American model of success, which emphasizes individual desire and action, with that of the Korean immigrants' success model, which stresses group or communal effort. Which model do you feel more affinity for? Explain.

8. Go to the library and find the results of opinion polls conducted to measure the happiness and satisfaction of the American people. (The American Enterprise Institute for Public Policy conducts one such poll; ask the reference librarian for others.) What does this tell you about Americans and the American Dream? Alternatively, you may research one particular ethnic group's share of the American Dream. In either case, try to come to some conclusions which either support or contradict the position taken by one of the authors in this unit.

VIDEO SUGGESTIONS

The video selections are offered as suggestions for viewing in or out of class to enrich the unit topic.

Moscow on the Hudson　　　*It's a Wonderful Life*
Citizen Kane　　　　　　　*West Side Story*
The Great Gatsby　　　　　*Kramer vs. Kramer*
Christmas in July

The Cult of the Individual: Self-Reliance and Self-Determination

Jonathan Borofsky,
*I Dreamed the Letters
ME were Written on My
Forehead at 2,218,321*

Short Takes

It is always through those who are unafraid to be different that advance comes to human society.

Raymond B. Fosdick

Democracy is a small hard core of common agreement, surrounded by a rich variety of individual differences.

James Bryant Conant

If individuality has no play, society does not advance; if individuality breaks out of all bounds, society perishes.

Thomas Henry Huxley

To be nobody but myself in a world which is doing its best, night and day, to make you everybody else means to fight the hardest battle which any human being can fight, and never stop fighting.

e.e. cummings

We can't reach old age by another man's road.

Mark Twain

We must be our own before we can be another's.

Ralph Waldo Emerson

The individual is not accountable to society for his actions, insofar as these concern the interests of no person but himself.

John Stuart Mill

Selfness is an essential fact of life. The thought of non-selfness, precise sameness, is terrifying.

Lewis Thomas

SUGGESTIONS FOR USING SHORT TAKES:

- Respond in writing to one of the quotations above. Then get together in groups and share what you have written.
- Work with a partner, small group or the entire class to discuss one or more quotations. You may want to agree, disagree, or compare it to similar expressions or sayings in your native language.

INTRODUCTION – THE CULT OF THE INDIVIDUAL: INDIVIDUALISM AND SELF-RELIANCE

In American ideology, the individual reigns supreme. Historically, our culture has championed no single group, but it has championed the idea of the individual man or woman. The historian Frederick Jackson Turner proposed that the westward expansion and frontier experience of the nineteenth century was a major force in shaping this aspect of our national character. He wrote, "That restless, nervous energy; that dominant individualism, working for good and for evil, and withal that buoyancy and exuberance which comes with freedom—these are traits of the frontier."

In fact, we train our children to define and distinguish themselves from their peers, to be self-reliant and autonomous. Indeed, from a very early age, selfhood and independence are stressed. Children learn they must stand on their own two feet in a competitive world where self-reliance and self-realization are the name of the game. The expression "self-made" man or woman expresses that American ideal perfectly.

It is not surprising then that in comparison to many other cultures, we are more tolerant of individual differences, idiosyncracies and non-conformity. Perhaps it must be so in a culture as diverse as ours, a culture made up of so many subcultures. Although attitudes towards conformity have not been fixed historically and have changed over time, in general, Americans seem to dread the idea of being, acting and looking just like their neighbors.

Indeed, Americans have ambivalent feelings about neighbors. This ambivalence reflects the tension we feel over our loyalties to group and to self and which of the two takes precedence. In other cultures, the group clearly takes precedence. However, in the United States, whether in city or country, we draw boundaries around individuals and circumscribe their "space." We conceptualize this space as privacy which protects the individual from the outside and from others. It is a concept that many foreigners find odd, even offensive. But again, it is the individual that is valued over the group, whether that group is a family, corporation, or community.

Although American individualism grows out of eighteenth and nineteenth century experience, it has been further bolstered in this century by the civil rights, anti-war and feminist movements of the 1960s and early 1970s. African Americans, women and other traditionally disadvantaged groups began to demand the equal opportunities which had historically been denied them. The U.S. Supreme Court, as well as courts on the state and local level throughout the nation, passed legislation that made discriminatory practices illegal and set new precedents for equal opportunities. These ideologies profoundly altered the way we think about the rights of both individuals and groups. Also during the progressive climate of the 1960s, the individual was encouraged to "do his own thing." And many did! Mores, beliefs, and traditions regarding codes of behavior, both public and private, that had changed little for generations, were suddenly questioned and cast aside.

In a society as pluralistic as our own, where there is little consensus on what constitutes "the greater good" and where diverse traditions, world views and moral systems compete, it is inevitable that conflicts arise. More and more, these conflicts over individual rights, from abortion and surrogate motherhood to euthanasia and custody disputes, are debated and decided by the courts, thus taking on political and legislative significance. Given an increasingly complex social fabric and a constant introduction of new technologies, it is likely that such social and ethical dilemmas will continue to emerge, creating debate and conflict among individuals and groups of different cultural backgrounds.

Before You Read

Imagine this situation: You have been offered a one-time-only scholarship to study at a prestigious university in the United States. The week before you are planning to leave, your father has a heart attack. His recovery requires that he remain at home for at least six months. Without his income to pay the rising medical expenses, your family will experience severe economic hardship. As the oldest child, you are asked to make a choice between your needs and those of your family. What do you do? Explain your decision and how you arrived at it.

The Group and the Self: New Focus on a Cultural Rift   DANIEL GOLEMAN

1   While Americans say the squeaky wheel gets the grease, in Japan the maxim is "the nail that stands out gets pounded down." And while American children who won't finish their food are given stern warnings not to waste it, Japanese children are told, "Think how bad the farmer who raised this food for you will feel if you don't eat it."

2   Such contrasts have emerged from a rapidly growing body of scientific studies that show how deeply individualism runs in most Western cultures, and how shallow that vein is in most others.

3   The new cross-cultural studies are confirming what many observers have long noticed: that the cardinal American virtues of self-reliance and individualism are at odds with those of most non-Western cultures. They also suggest that the nature of American individualism has been changing toward a greater emphasis on raw self-interest, and that the rise of individualism in a society goes hand in hand with economic growth.

4   The work contrasts individualism with "collectivism," in which a person's loyalty to a group like a family or tribe overrides personal goals. Recent studies say this outlook predominates in most cultures of Asia, Africa, the Middle East and Latin America.

5   The late Raoul Narrol, a professor of anthropology at the State University of New York at Buffalo, found in a 1983 study that such societies have among the lowest rates of homicide, suicide, juvenile delinquency, divorce, child abuse and alcoholism. They also tend to have lower economic productivity, though as countries like Japan become more affluent, they also tend to become more individualistic.

6   The collectivist cultures comprise about 70 percent of the world's population, according to the studies. But virtually all the data of modern psychology

and most other social sciences come from the most individualistic cultures, like the United States. As a result, some social scientists say, many Western assumptions about the universals of human behavior actually apply to a minority of people, albeit those in the most advanced economies.

7   "There are many kinds of individualism," said Robert N. Bellah, a sociologist at the University of California at Berkeley who wrote "Habits of the Heart: Individualism and Commitment in American Culture" (University of California Press, 1985). "The individualism that's on the rise recently in the U.S. is one of 'What's in it for me?' with immediate gratification of one's own needs coming before all other loyalties. Commitments like marriage only hold while they pay off."

8   Leading the study of individualism or its absence, and the argument for its importance in understanding people around the world, is Harry C. Triandis, a psychologist at the University of Illinois who came to America as a college student from his native Greece.

9   Writing in the current issue of *The Nebraska Symposium on Motivation*, an influential journal, and reviewing over 100 scientific studies, Dr. Triandis argues that the distinction between individualism and collectivism holds the key to understanding a range of telling contrasts from culture to culture.

10   Though many seem minor, they bespeak vast differences in how people see the world and themselves:

11   □ A lecturer in the West will be introduced as "distinguished," while speakers in Asia will always begin by saying how little they know about the topic at hand.

12   □ A telephone operator in Greece will be rude and unhelpful until the caller establishes his identity, while American operators tend to be uniformly friendly to everyone.

13   □ In countries like Pakistan, Peru and Singapore, people take it for granted that those at the top of the social hierarchy are very different from those at the bottom and that they should keep their distance. In countries like the United States, Australia and the Netherlands, such an attitude is seen as offensively anti-egalitarian.

14   Perhaps most critical for understanding contemporary events is the role of the collectivist outlook in generating friction between ethnic groups. "While collectivists are very nice to those who are members of their own groups, they can be very nasty, competitive and uncooperative toward those who belong to other groups," said Dr. Triandis. "There is an unquestioned obedience to one's own group and even a willingness to fight and die for it, and a distrust of those in other groups."

15   This attitude, he said, encourages the kind of ethnic fighting common in many parts of the world, including sub-Saharan Africa, India and the Middle East.

16   In an individualist culture, people's personal goals take priority over their allegiance to groups like the family or the employer. The loyalty of individualists to a given group is very weak; they feel they belong to many groups and are apt to change their membership as it suits them, switching churches, for example, or leaving one employer for another.

17   In such cultures, people subscribe to values like "winning is everything" and "to be superior, a man must stand alone," Dr. Triandis wrote in the November issue of *The Journal of Personality and Social Psychology*. The article includes findings from studies of people in Illinois, Hawaii, Hong Kong, Peking, the Philippines, Japan and Europe.

Different Commandments

18   Collectivist societies put high value on self-discipline, accepting one's position in life, honoring parents and elders, and preserving one's public image for the sake of the group, Dr. Triandis reported. Individualists stress equality, freedom, having an exciting and varied life, and personal enjoyment.

19   Child rearing in collectivist cultures is intrusive; children have virtually no privacy or autonomy. "A child's dependence on parents is considered good, as is breaking the will of the child to obtain complete obedience," Dr. Triandis said. When there is conflict between personal and group goals, the group takes precedence. People feel comfortable in hierarchies, and place a premium on harmony within their group.

20   People with a collective focus tend to think in terms of long-term goals, which benefit the whole group, Dr. Triandis said; their time frame is likely to include "a chain of generations." Individualists, by contrast, "look for immediate rewards for their efforts."

21   In collectivist cultures, Dr. Triandis found, family integrity is of the utmost importance. People strongly believe, for instance, that children should live at home with their parents until they get married, and that aging parents should live at home with their children.

22   "In short, the values that are most important in the West are least important worldwide," said Dr. Triandis.

Most Individualistic: The U.S.

23   The difference can be seen readily in literature, according to a 1983 analysis by Francis Hsu, an anthropologist recently retired from Northwestern University. Dr. Hsu found that novels in the West typically focus on a lone fig-ure seeking private goals, while those of the East commonly celebrate duty to kin or other authorities, despite personal temptations. A Western prototype is Huckleberry Finn, striking out on his own; an Eastern one is Krishna in the Bhagavad-Gita, being persuaded to do his duty and plunge into battle.

24   In a worldwide study of 116,000 employees of I.B.M. in 1980, Geert Hofstede, a Dutch psychologist, was able to rank 40 cultures according to the strength of individualism or collectivism.

25   The five most strongly individualist cultures were the United States, Australia, Great Britain, Canada and the Netherlands, in that order. The other countries of Northern Europe also ranked high.

26   The five where collectivism was strongest were Venezuela, Colombia, Pakistan, Peru and Taiwan. It was also strong in Thailand, Singapore, Hong Kong, Turkey and some countries of Southern Europe, including Greece and Portugal.

27   Growing affluence and geographic mobility contribute to the spread of individualism in a culture, Dr. Triandis finds. Likewise, within a given society, "individualism is higher among the affluent, socially and geographically mobile, more modern segments," he said. But as countries like Japan become more prosperous, people start to show more signs of individualism, especially the young and urban.

28   The most individualistic people in a collectivist society tend to be "rebels ready to migrate from the oppression of the culture," said Dr. Triandis. That may partly explain why societies like Canada, the United States and Australia, all settled by immigrants, are among the most individualistic.

29   "People in different cultures have very different premises about what defines a person, with different consequences

for how they think, feel and act," said Shinobu Kitiyama, a psychologist at the University of Oregon, who, with Hazel Markus, a psychologist at the University of Michigan, will publish research on the subject next year in the journal Psychological Review.

30   "In white middle-class America people think of themselves as a bundle of traits, preferences and desires," Dr. Kitiyama said. "But in Asian culture people conceive themselves in terms of a dense web of social relations."

Traps for Social Scientists

31   One telling difference between American and Asian cultures, Dr. Kitiyama found, emerged when people described their contribution to a collaboration. "When you ask Americans to give a percent figure that estimates how much each member of a team contributes to the overall effort, the total is almost always greater than 100 percent. People overestimate how much weight they pull."

32   But in Asia, the reverse was true. People underestimated their contribution, so the total for the group was usually less than 100 percent. Such self-effacement, Dr. Kitiyama said, is part of the way people in a collectivist culture preserve harmony within their group. Studies in China, for example, show that people who are modest about their successes are better-liked than those who take pride in them.

33   The difference in life goals between such cultures was evident in a 1978 survey of Pacific and Asian nations by Yasumata Tanaka, a psychologist

at Gakushin University in Tokyo. He found that 64 percent of New Zealanders and 50 percent of Australians subscribed to the goal of "doing whatever I think worth doing," while only 32 percent of Japanese and 12 percent of Indians agreed with that strongly individualistic goal.

34   Some social scientists say the American focus on individualism has gone overboard. Barry Schwartz, a psychologist at Swathmore College, has written that failure to realize the limited appeal of individualism around the world leads to basic errors in social sciences like economics. The pitfall is in overgeneralizing how essential a part of human nature individualism is; a "greedy self-interest" cannot be assumed as "an eternal law of human nature," Dr. Schwartz wrote in "The Battle for Human Nature" (Norton, 1986).

35   Dr. Bellah, the Berkeley sociologist, sees a broader danger. "In earlier days," he said, "the individualism in America was one that also honored community values. Today we have an ideology of individualism that simply encourages people to maximize personal advantage. This leads to a consumer politics in which 'What's in it for me?' is all that matters, while considerations of the common good are increasingly irrelevant.

36   "There's perhaps a better model in the democracies of Europe," he went on. "There you find a strong sense of the dignity of the individual with an equally strong social responsibility."

 Daniel Goleman was senior editor of the popular magazine *Psychology Today* and is the author of numerous books, including some basic reference works. He currently writes on psychology, psychotherapy and related matters for *The New York Times*.

After You Read

Reading Journal

Explain, in your own words, the American saying "It's the squeaky wheel that gets the grease," and the Japanese saying "The nail that stands out gets pounded down." Then give an example from everyday life to illustrate each maxim. Which cultural value defines you better?

Reading For Meaning

1. In paragraph 22, one researcher says, "the values that are most important in the West are least important worldwide." Go through the article and make two lists of the contrasting values mentioned in the research.

2. Research shows that individualism is strongest among "the affluent, socially and geographically mobile, more modern segments" of society. Why do you think this is so?

3. In your own words explain what Dr. Kitiyama meant in paragraph 30, when he said, "In white, middle-class America people think of themselves as a bundle of traits, preferences and desires, but in Asian culture people conceive [of] themselves in terms of a dense web of social relations." Give examples from your own experience of these two different ways of viewing the self.

4. What dangers do Goleman (and the researchers he cites) see in American individualism? How does it differ from European individualism?

Exploring Further

Research Project

In paragraph 23, Goleman talks about literary prototypes, like Huckleberry Finn and Krishna in the *Bhagavad-Gita*, which embody cultural attitudes toward individualism. Reflect back to your elementary and high school years. What famous literary figure in your native language represents your culture's stand on individualism or collectivism? Go to the library and find a copy of this work (in translation if possible). Write up a brief report to share with the class, using quotes from the work to support your point.

Timed Writing Exercise

In a well-developed essay, argue for or against the following: Parents should encourage their children to be leaders first and followers second.

Focused Essay Topics

1. Using the response you made to question 4 in *Reading for Meaning* as a guide, discuss how Americans might encourage others to incorporate *one* of the more positive aspects of collectivism: increased community involvement, stronger family ties, or greater interest in the global environment.

2. Much American advertising promotes products which speak to individual needs and desires. Accordingly, the right running shoes or the right toothpaste assure you a first place in life's "race." Analyze the "hidden message" which glorifies individualism in a print or TV advertisement of your choosing.

Before You Read

1. How is entrance to the university system in your native country regulated, if at all? For example, is access based on school performance, or solely on entrance exams? (If you have been educated in the U.S., discuss what you know about getting into an American college.) How accurate do you think the current system is in predicting an individual's potential to succeed in college?

2. The story you are about to read, "Open Admissions and the Inward I," was written while the author was a student at a public college in New York City. What do you think his title might mean?

Open Admissions and the Inward I

PETER J. RONDINONE

1   The fact is, I didn't learn much in high school. I spent my time on the front steps of the building smoking grass with the dudes from the dean's squad. For kicks we'd grab a freshman, tell him we were undercover cops, handcuff him to a banister, and take his money. Then we'd go to the back of the building, cop some downs[1], and nod away the day behind the steps in the lobby. The classrooms were overcrowded anyhow, and the teachers knew it. They also knew where to find me when they wanted to make weird deals: If I agreed to read a book and do an oral report, they'd pass me. So I did it and graduated with a "general" diploma. I was a New York City public school kid.

2   I hung out on a Bronx streetcorner with a group of guys who called themselves "The Davidson Boys" and sang songs like "Daddy-lo-lo." Everything we did could be summed up with the word "snap." That's a "snap." She's a "snap." We had a "snap." Friday nights we'd paint ourselves green and run through the streets swinging baseball bats. . . . Even though I'd seen a friend stabbed for wearing the wrong colors and another blown away with a shotgun for "messin'" with some dude's woman, I was too young to realize that my life too might be headed toward a violent end.

3   Then one night I swallowed a dozen Tuminols and downed two quarts of beer at a bar in Manhattan. I passed out in the gutter. I puked and rolled under a parked car. Two girlfriends found me and carried me home. My over-protective brother answered the door. When he saw me—eyes rolling toward the back of my skull like rubber—he pushed me down a flight of stairs. My skull hit the edge of a marble step with a thud. The girls

---

[1] Cop some downs: to take drugs (barbituates)

screamed. My parents came to the door and there I was: a high school graduate, a failure, curled in a ball in a pool of blood.

4   The next day I woke up with dried blood on my face. I had no idea what had happened. My sister told me. I couldn't believe it. Crying, my mother confirmed the story. I had almost died! That scared the hell out of me. I knew I had to do something. I didn't know what. But pills and violence didn't promise much of a future.

5   I went back to a high school counselor for advice. He suggested I go to college.

6   I wasn't aware of it, but it seems that in May 1969 a group of dissident students from the black and Puerto Rican communities took over the south campus of the City College of New York (CCNY). They demanded that the Board of Higher Education and the City of New York adopt an open-admission policy that would make it possible for anybody to go to CCNY without the existing requirements: SATs and a high school average of 85. This demand was justified on the premise that college had always been for the privileged few and excluded minorities. As it turned out, in the fall of 1970 the City University's 18 campuses admitted massive numbers of students—15,000—with high school averages below 85. By 1972, I was one of them.

7   On the day I received my letter of acceptance, I waited until dinner to tell my folks. I was proud.

8   "Check out where I'm going," I said. I passed the letter to my father. He looked at it.

9   "You jerk!" He said. "You wanna sell ties?" My mother grabbed the letter.

10   "God," she said. "Why don't you go to work already? Like other people."

11   "Screw that," I said. "You should be proud."

12   At the time, of course, I didn't understand where my parents were coming from. They were immigrants. They believed college was for rich kids, not the ones who dropped downs and sang songs on streetcorners.

13   My mother had emigrated from Russia after World War II. She came to the United States with a bundle of clothes, her mother and father, a few dollars, and a baby from a failed marriage. Her first job was on an assembly line in a pen factory where she met my father, the production manager.

14   My father, a second-generation Italian, was brought up on the Lower East Side of Manhattan. He never completed high school. And when he wasn't working in a factory, he peddled Christmas lights door to door or sold frankfurters in Times Square.

15   My family grew up in the South Bronx. There were six children, and we slept in one room on cots. We ate spaghetti three times a week and were on welfare because for a number of years my father was sick, in and out of the hospital.

16   Anyhow, I wasn't about to listen to my parents and go to work; for a dude like me, this was a big deal. So I left the dinner table and went to tell my friends about my decision.

17   The Davidson Boys hung out in a rented storefront. They were sitting around the pool table on milk boxes and broken pinball machines, spare tires and dead batteries. I made my announcement. They stood up and circled me like I was the star of a cockfight. Sucio stepped to the table with a can of beer in one hand and a pool stick in the other.

18   "Wha' you think you gonna get out of college?" he said.

19   "I don't know, but I bet it beats this," I said. I shoved one of the pool balls across the table. That was a mistake. The others banged their sticks on the wood floor and chanted. "Oooh-ooh—snap, snap." Sucio put his beer on the table.

20   "Bullshit!" he yelled. "I wash dishes with college dudes. You're like us— nuttin', man." He pointed the stick at my nose.

21   Silence.

22   I couldn't respond. If I let the crowd know I thought their gig was uncool[2], that I wanted out of the club, they would have taken it personally. And they would have taken me outside and kicked my ass. So I lowered my head. "Aw, hell, gimme a hit of beer," I said, as if it were all a joke. But I left the corner and didn't go back.

23   I spent that summer alone, reading books like *How to Succeed in College* and *30 Days to a More Powerful Vocabulary*. My vocabulary was limited to a few choice phrases like, "Move over, Rover, and let Petey take over." When my friends did call for me I hid behind the curtains. I knew that if I was going to make it, I'd have to push these guys out of my consciousness as if I were doing the breaststroke in a sea of logs. I had work to do, and people were time consuming. As it happened, all my heavy preparations didn't amount to much.

24   On the day of the placement exams I went paranoid. Somehow I got the idea that my admission to college was some ugly practical joke that I wasn't prepared for. So I copped some downs and took the test nodding. The words floated on the page like flies on a crock of cream.

25   That made freshman year difficult. The administration had placed me in all three remedial programs: basic writing, college skills, and math. I was shocked. I had always thought of myself as smart. I was the only one in the neighborhood who read books. So I gave up the pills and pushed aside another log.

26   The night before the first day of school, my brother walked into my room and threw a briefcase on my desk. "Good luck, Joe College," he said. He smacked me in the back of the head. Surprised, I went to bed early.

27   I arrived on campus ahead of time with a map in my pocket. I wanted enough time, in case I got lost, to get to my first class. But after wandering around the corridors of one building for what seemed like a long time and hearing the sounds of classes in session, the scrape of chalk and muted discussions, I suddenly wondered if I was in the right place. So I stopped a student and pointed to a dot on my map.

28   "Look." He pointed to the dot. "Now look." He pointed to an inscription on the front of the building. I was in the right place. "Can't you read?" he said. Then he joined some friends. As he walked off I heard someone say, "What do you expect from open admissions?"

29   I had no idea that there were a lot of students who resented people like me, who felt I was jeopardizing standards, destroying their institution. I had no idea. I just wanted to go to class.

30   In Basic Writing I the instructor, Regina Sackmary, chalked her name in bold letters on the blackboard. I sat in the front row and reviewed my *How to Succeed* lessons: Sit in front/don't let eyes wander to cracks on

---

2 Their gig was uncool: their behavior was unacceptable

ceilings/take notes on a legal pad/make note of all unfamiliar words and books/listen for key phrases like "remember this," they are a professor's signals. The other students held pens over pads in anticipation. Like me, they didn't know what to expect. We were public school kids from lousy neighborhoods and we knew that some of us didn't have a chance; but we were ready to work hard.

31   Before class we had rapped about[3] our reasons for going to college. Some said they wanted to be the first in the history of their families to have a college education—they said their parents never went to college because they couldn't afford it, or because their parents' parents were too poor—and they said open admissions and free tuition ($65 per semester) was a chance to change that history. Others said they wanted to be educated so they could return to their neighborhoods to help "the people"; they were the idealists. Some foreigners said they wanted to return to their own countries and start schools. And I said I wanted to escape the boredom and the pain I had known as a kid on the streets. But none of them said they expected a job. Or if they did they were reminded that there were no jobs.

32   Ms. Sackmary told us that . . . we weren't in basic writing because there was something wrong with us—we just needed to learn the basics, she said. Somehow I didn't believe her. After class I went to her office. She gave me a quick test. I couldn't write a coherent sentence or construct a paragraph. So we made an agreement: I'd write an essay a day in addition to my regular classwork. Also, I'd do a few term papers. She had this idea that learning to write was like learning to play a musical instrument—it takes practice, everyday practice.

33   In math I was in this remedial program for algebra, geometry, and trigonometry. But unlike high school math, which I thought was devised to boggle the mind for the sake of boggling, in this course I found I could make a connection between different mathematical principles and my life. For instance, there were certain basics I had to learn—call them 1, 2, and 3—and unless they added up to 6 I'd probably be a failure. I also got a sense of how math related to the world at large: unless the sum of the parts of a society equaled the whole there would be chaos. And these insights jammed my head and made me feel like a kid on a Ferris wheel looking at the world for the first time. Everything amazed me!

34   Like biology. In high school I associated this science with stabbing pins in the hearts of frogs for fun. Or getting high snorting small doses of the chloroform used for experiments on fruit flies. But in college biology I began to learn and appreciate not only how my own life processes functioned but how there were thousands of other life processes I'd never known existed. And this gave me a sense of power, because I could deal with questions like, Why do plants grow? not as I had before, with a simple spill of words: " 'Cause of the sun, man." I could actually explain that there was a plant cycle and cycles within the plant cycle . . . .

35   To deal with the heavy workload from all my classes, I needed a study schedule, so I referred to my *How to Succeed* book. I gave myself an hour for lunch and reserved the rest of the time between classes and evenings

---

3 Rapped about: talked about

for homework and research. All this left me very little time for friendships. But I stuck to my schedule and by the middle of that first year I was getting straight A's. Nothing else mattered . . . .

36   God, those early days were painful. Professors would tear up my papers the day they were due and tell me to start over again, with a piece of advice— "Try to say what you really mean." Papers I had spent weeks writing. And I knew I lacked the basic college skills; I was a man reporting to work without his tools . . . .

37   And there were nights I was alone with piles of notebooks and textbooks. I wanted to throw the whole mess out the window; I wanted to give up. Nights the sounds of my friends singing on the corner drifted into my room like a fog over a graveyard and I was afraid I would be swept away. And nights I was filled with questions but the answers were like moon shadows on my curtains: I could see them but I could not grasp them.

38   Yet I had learned a vital lesson from these countless hours of work in isolation: My whole experience from the day I received my letter of acceptance enabled me to understand how in high school my sense of self-importance came from being one of the boys, a member of the pack, while in college the opposite was true. In order to survive, I had to curb my herd instinct.

39   Nobody, nobody could give me what I needed to overcome my sense of inadequacy. That was a struggle I had to work at on my own. It could never be a group project. In the end, though people could point out what I had to learn and where to learn it, I was always the one who did the work; and what I learned I earned. And that made me feel as good as being one of the boys. In short, college taught me to appreciate the importance of being alone. I found it was the only way I could get any serious work done.

40   But those days of trial and uncertainty are over, and the open-admission policy has been eliminated. Anybody who enters the City University's senior colleges must now have an 80 percent high school average. And I am one of those fortunate individuals who in a unique period of American education was given a chance to attend college. But I wonder what will happen to those people who can learn but whose potential doesn't show in their high school average; who might get into street crime if not given a chance to do something constructive? I wonder, because if it weren't for open admissions, the likelihood is I would still be swinging baseball bats on the streets on Friday nights.

Peter Rondinone is a professor of English and Director of Journalism at LaGuardia Community College, CUNY.

After You Read

Reading Journal

Explore your feelings about Rondinone's story. For example, was his experience similar to or different from your own? How do you feel about the choices he made?

Reading For Meaning

1. How did Rondinone's family affect his developing sense of self?

2. How does the author explain his parents' disapproval of his going to college? Is this attitude common in your own culture? Explain.

Exploring Further

Debate

Argue for or against the following: America owes everyone who is motivated, regardless of ability, the right to pursue a higher education.

Timed Writing Exercise

If your college waived the English language requirement (ESL classes) for those students who showed they could perform well in their other college courses, would you choose to drop this basic requirement? Why or why not? What might be the long-term effect of this policy on the college community as a whole?

Focused Essay Topics

1. When the open admissions policy was instituted its critics said it lowered standards for the entire public university system in New York, to the detriment of the better students and faculty. How would you address this argument? (Use your *Debate* notes, if applicable.)

2. Rondinone's decision to pursue a college education went against his family's and community's expectation that he "get a job" and earn a living. In this sense, he put his individual needs and values before those of his family. How would you have behaved in his situation? (Look back at your *Reading Journal* entry before you begin.)

Before You Read

In the reading that follows, a Native American father attempts to instruct his son's teacher in the value of diversity in the classroom. Reflect back on your early school experience. Which seemed to you to be valued more by your school—conformity to a homogenous standard, or development of individual skills, background and temperament? Give examples from the daily routine or curriculum to support your answer.

An Indian Father's Plea

By Robert Lake (Medicine Grizzlybear)

Dear Teacher,

1   I would like to introduce you to my son, Wind-Wolf. He is probably what you would consider a typical Indian kid. He was born and raised on the reservation. He has black hair, dark brown eyes, and an olive complexion. And, like so many Indian children his age, he is shy and quiet in the classroom. He is five years old, in kindergarten, and I can't understand why you have already labeled him a "slow learner."

2   He has already been through quite an education compared with his peers in Western society. He was bonded to his mother and to the Mother Earth in a traditional native childbirth ceremony. And he has been continuously cared for by his mother, father, sisters, cousins, aunts, uncles, grandparents, and extended tribal family since this ceremony.

3   The traditional Indian baby basket became his "turtle's shell" and served as the first seat for his classroom. It is the same kind of basket our people have used for thousands of years. It is specially designed to provide the child with the kind of knowledge and experience he will need to survive in his culture and environment.

4   Wind-Wolf was strapped in snugly with a deliberate restriction on his arms and legs. Although Western society may argue this hinders motorskill development and abstract reasoning, we believe it forces the child to first develop his intuitive faculties, rational intellect, symbolic thinking, and five senses. Wind-Wolf was with his mother constantly, closely bonded physically, as she carried him on her back or held him while breast-feeding. She carried him everywhere she went, and every night he slept with both parents. Because of this, Wind-Wolf's educational setting was not only a "secure" environment, but it was also very colorful, complicated, sensitive, and diverse.

5   As he grew older, Wind-Wolf began to crawl out of the baby basket, develop his motor skills, and explore the world around him. When frightened or sleepy, he could always return to the basket, as a turtle withdraws

into its shell. Such an inward journey allows one to reflect in privacy on what he has learned and to carry the new knowledge deeply into the unconscious and the soul. Shapes, sizes, colors, texture, sound, smell, feeling, taste, and the learning process are therefore functionally integrated— the physical and spiritual, matter and energy, and conscious and unconscious, individual and social.

6   It takes a long time to absorb and reflect on these kinds of experiences, so maybe that is why you think my Indian child is a slow learner. His aunts and grandmothers taught him to count and know his numbers while they sorted materials for making abstract designs in native baskets. And he was taught to learn mathematics by counting the sticks we use in our traditional native hand game. So he may be slow in grasping the methods and tools you use in your classroom, ones quite familiar to his white peers, but I hope you will be patient with him. It takes time to adjust to a new cultural system and learn new things.

7   He is not culturally "disadvantaged," but he is culturally "different." If you ask him how many months there are in a year, he will probably tell you 13—not because he doesn't know how to count properly, but because he has been taught there are 13 full moons in a year and really 13 planets in our solar system and 13 tail feathers on a perfectly balanced eagle, the most powerful kind of bird to use in ceremony and healing.

8   But he also knows that some eagles may have only 12 tail feathers, or seven, that they do not all have the same number. He knows that the flicker has exactly 10 tail feathers; that they are red and black, representing the directions of east and west, life and death; and that this

bird is considered a "fire" bird, a power used in native doctoring and healing. He can probably count more than 40 kinds of birds, and tell you and his peers what kind of bird each is, where it lives, the seasons in which it appears, and how it is used in a sacred ceremony.

9   He may have trouble writing his name on a piece of paper, but he knows how to say it and many other things in several different Indian languages. He is not fluent yet because he is only five and required by law to attend your educational system and learn your language, your values, your ways of thinking, and your methods of teaching and learning.

10   So you see, all of these influences together make him somewhat shy and quiet—and perhaps "slow" according to your standards. But if Wind-Wolf was not prepared for your world, neither were you appreciative of his. On the first day of class, you wanted to call him Wind, insisting that Wolf somehow must be his middle name. The students in class laughed at him.

11   As you try to teach him your new methods, helping him learn new tools for self-discovery and adapt to his new learning environment, he may be looking out the window as if daydreaming. Why? Because he has been taught to watch and study the changes in nature. It is hard for him to make the appropriate psychic switch from the right to the left hemisphere of the brain when he sees the leaves turning bright colors, the geese heading south, and the squirrels scurrying around for nuts to get ready for a harsh winter. In his heart, in his young mind, and almost by instinct, he knows that this is the time of year he is supposed to be with his people gathering and preparing fish, deer meat, and native plants

and herbs, and learning his assigned tasks in this role. He is caught between two worlds, torn by two distinct cultural systems.

12   Yesterday, for the third time in two weeks, he came home crying and said he wanted his hair cut. He said he doesn't have any friends at school because they make fun of his long hair. I tried to explain that in our culture, long hair is a sign of masculinity and balance and is a source of power. But he remained adamant.

13   To make matters worse, he recently encountered his first harsh case of racism. Wind-Wolf had managed to adopt at least one good school friend and asked his new pal if he wanted to come home to play with him until supper. That was OK with Wind-Wolf's mother, who was walking with them. But the other boy's mother lashed out, "It is OK if you have to play with him at school, but we don't allow those kind of people in our house!" When my wife asked why not, she answered, "Because you are Indians, and we are white, and I don't want my kids growing up with your kind of people."

14   So now my young Indian child does not want to go to school anymore (even though we cut his hair). He feels he does not belong. He is the only Indian child in your class, and he is well aware of it. Instead of being proud of his race, heritage, and culture, he feels ashamed.

15   When he watches television, he asks why the white people hate us and always kill us in movies and take everything from us. He asks why the other kids in school are not taught about the power, beauty, and essence of nature or provided with an opportunity to experience the world around them firsthand. He says he hates living in the city and that he misses his Indian cousins and

friends. He asks why one young white girl at school who is his friend always tells him, "I like you, Wind-Wolf, because you are a good Indian."

16   Now he refuses to sing his native songs, play with his Indian artifacts, learn his language, or participate in his sacred ceremonies. When I ask him to help me with a sacred ritual, he says no because "that's weird" and he doesn't want his friends at school to think he doesn't believe in God.

17   So, dear teacher, I want to introduce you to my son, Wind-Wolf, who is not really a "typical" little Indian kid after all. He stems from a long line of hereditary chiefs, medicine men and women, and ceremonial leaders whose accomplishments and unique forms of knowledge are still being studied and recorded in contemporary books. He has seven different tribal systems flowing through his blood; he is even part white.

18   I want my child to succeed in school and in life. I don't want him to be a dropout or juvenile delinquent or to end up on drugs and alcohol because he is made to feel inferior or because of discrimination. I want him to be proud of his rich heritage and culture, and I would like him to develop the necessary capabilities to adapt to, and succeed in, both cultures. But I need your help.

19   What you say and do in the classroom, what you teach and how you teach it, and what you don't say and don't teach will have significant effect on the potential success or failure of my child. Please remember that this is the primary year of his education and development.

20   All I ask is that you work with me, not against me, to help educate my child in the best way. If you don't have the knowledge, preparation, experience, or training to effectively

deal with culturally different children, I am willing to help you with the few resources I have available or direct you to such resources.

21   Millions of dollars have been appropriated by Congress and are being spent each year for "Indian Education." All you have to do is take advantage of it and encourage your school to make an effort to use it in the name of "equal education." My Indian child has a constitutional right to learn, retain, and maintain his heritage and culture. By the same token, I strongly believe that non-Indian children also have a constitutional right to learn about our Native American heritage and culture, because Indians play a significant part in the history of Western society. Until this reality is equally understood and applied in education as a whole, there will be a lot more school children in grades K-2 identified as "slow learners."

22   My son Wind-Wolf, is not an empty glass coming into your class to be filled. He is a full basket coming into a different environment and society with something special to share. Please let him share his knowledge, heritage, and culture with you and his peers.

Robert Lake (Medicine Grizzlybear) is Associate Professor of Education at Gonzaga University in Spokane, Washington, where he specializes in Native American education.

After You Read

Reading Journal

If it is true that Wind-Wolf must function and compete in an American classroom of "Western society," should his father's plea be heeded? What do you think his teacher could or should do with the knowledge he has gained from this letter?

Reading For Meaning

1. Robert Lake suggests that the cultural values and socialization of Native Americans and mainstream American children are opposed in some ways. List the values that are at variance with one another.

2. Which examples of Wind-Wolf's knowledge appear to be "useless" in the mainstream classroom and culture at large?

3. How does the author distinguish between "culturally disadvantaged" and "culturally different"? What are the long-term implications of this distinction for his child?

4. When Lake writes that his child is required by law to attend the American educational system, perhaps he is suggesting that this is unjust. Could you imagine a situation which would better serve native American children?

Exploring Further

Debate

Argue for or against the following: A child is like an empty vessel, waiting to be filled by the greater experience, knowledge and training of his teachers.

Timed Writing Exercise

Using your notes from either the pre-reading or the reading journal entry, write an essay either defending or criticizing the need for children of different cultures to conform to one homogeneous standard.

Focused Essay Topics

1. Imagine that you are Wind-Wolf's father or mother. How would you deal with your young son's increasing rejection of his native heritage? (See paragraphs 13-16 for details of the problems he is encountering.)

2. Imagine that you are the principal of an American elementary school and that you have received letters from Lake and several other parents of minority students, each asking that the school and teachers find ways to value and include their children's native culture. Write a speech which you will deliver to the PTA (Parent-Teacher Association) detailing how your administration hopes to address this issue in the coming school year.

Before You Read

1. As we saw in the first unit, Americans value privacy and, as a result, often isolate themselves from others by building fences or walls. Robert Frost's poem, "Mending Wall," which you are about to read, contains a line familiar to most Americans: "Good fences make good neighbors." What do you think Frost meant by this?

2. As a class, brainstorm as many different kinds of "walls," both visible and invisible, as you can. Make two lists, one for real walls (e.g., fences, gates, trees, office cubicles) and the other for symbolic ones (e.g., use of personal space, body language). Make a master list on the board to use as a checklist.

Mending Wall   ROBERT FROST

1   Something there is that doesn't love a wall,
    That sends the frozen-ground-swell under it,
    And spills the upper boulders in the sun;
    And makes gaps even two can pass abreast.
5   The work of hunters is another thing:
    I have come after them and made repair
    Where they have left not one stone on a stone,
    But they would have the rabbit out of hiding,
    To please the yelping dogs. The gaps I mean,
10 No one has seen them made or heard them made,
    But at spring mending-time we find them there.
    I let my neighbor know beyond the hill;
    And on a day we meet to walk the line
    And set the wall between us once again.
15 We keep the wall between us as we go.
    To each the boulders that have fallen to each.
    And some are loaves and some so nearly balls
    We have to use a spell to make them balance:
    "Stay where you are until our backs are turned!"
20 We wear our fingers rough with handling them.
    Oh, just another kind of outdoor game,
    One on a side. It comes to little more:
    There where it is we do not need the wall:
    He is all pine and I am apple orchard.
25 My apple trees will never get across
    And eat the cones under his pines, I tell him.
    He only says, "Good fences make good neighbors."

Spring is the mischief in me, and I wonder
If I could put a notion in his head:
30   "*Why* do they make good neighbors? Isn't it
Where there are cows? But here there are no cows.
Before I built a wall I'd ask to know
What I was walling in or walling out,
And to whom I was like to give offense.
35   Something there is that doesn't love a wall,
That wants it down." I could say "Elves" to him,
But it's not elves exactly, and I'd rather
He said it for himself. I see him there,
Bringing a stone grasped firmly by the top
40   In each hand, like an old-stone savage armed.
He moves in darkness as it seems to me,
Not of woods only and the shade of trees.
He will not go behind his father's saying,
And he likes having thought of it so well
45   He says again, "Good fences make good neighbors."

Robert Frost 1874-1963, is known for having brought both nineteenth and twentieth century impulses to his work. Frost won numerous major awards, including a gold medal from the United States Senate in 1960. Many remember Frost as the poet who read at the Presidential inauguration of John F. Kennedy.

After You Read

Reading Journal

Have you ever built a symbolic wall? Describe it and the purpose it served for you.

Reading For Meaning

1. Who is the "we" Frost refers to in line 15? What activity are the two men engaged in and why do they do it?

2. Frost repeats his first line: "Something there is that doesn't love a wall" in line 35. What exactly is this "something"?

3. In your own words, describe the essential area of disagreement between the two neighbors. Which lines could be used to sum up the two opposing sides of the argument?

4. Read the following lines: ". . . I see him there,/Bringing a stone grasped firmly by the top/In each hand, like an old-stone savage armed./He moves in darkness as it seems to me,/Not of woods only and the shade of trees." How do they contribute to our picture of the neighbor?

5. Paraphrase line 43: "He will not go behind his father's saying." What does this suggest about the neighbor's way of thinking?

6. There have been several symbolic interpretations of Frost's poem by literary critics over the years. What universal contradiction in human nature does the poem suggest to you?

Exploring Further

Group Presentation

1. Plan a short excursion, either by car or by public transportation, to an area near your school. (If possible plan to visit city, suburbs and rural areas.) As you travel, make note of the presence or absence of American "walls." In other words, look for ways in which people have created private space for themselves.

2. Use the data you collect as support for your group's short report on the nature, frequency and/or purpose of American wall-building.

Debate

Argue for or against the following: "Good fences make good neighbors," particularly in the United States today where so many cultural groups must co-exist.

Timed Writing Exercise

In thinking about Frost's two neighbors, which one are you—the one who would tear down life's walls or the one who believes that they are necessary for survival and harmony? Why?

Focused Essay Topics

1. What are the consequences of building walls in one's life? As you think about this, consider, as Frost says, who you are "walling in or walling out, and to whom (you) are giving offense."

2. Is there a sense of community where you live? How is this expressed or not expressed? (Refer to Frost's poem as a point of departure.)

Before You Read

Imagine for a moment that you are projected far into the future and that all people, thanks to the perfection of cloning[1], are equal in both intelligence and physical attractiveness. Speculate in writing what the consequences of this kind of sameness might be. Would you like to live in this society? Why or why not? Keep your responses in mind as you read Vonnegut's short story.

Harrison Bergeron KURT VONNEGUT

1   The year was 2081, and everybody was finally equal. They weren't only equal before God and the law. They were equal every which way. Nobody was smarter than anybody else. Nobody was better-looking than anybody else. Nobody was stronger or quicker than anybody else. All this equality was due to the 211th, 212th, and 213th Amendments to the Constitution, and to the unceasing vigilance of agents of the United States Handicapper General.

2   Some things about living still weren't quite right, though. April, for instance, still drove people crazy by not being springtime. And it was in that clammy month that the H-G men took George and Hazel Bergeron's fourteen-year-old son, Harrison, away.

3   It was tragic, all right, but George and Hazel couldn't think about it very hard. Hazel had a perfectly average intelligence, which meant she couldn't think about anything except in short bursts. And George, while his intelligence was way above normal, had a little mental handicap radio in his ear. He was required by law to wear it at all times. It was tuned to a government transmitter. Every twenty seconds or so, the transmitter would send out some sharp noise to keep people like George from taking unfair advantage of their brains.

4   George and Hazel were watching television. There were tears on Hazel's cheeks, but she'd forgotten for the moment what they were about.

5   On the television screen were ballerinas.

6   A buzzer sounded in George's head. His thoughts fled in panic, like bandits from a burglar alarm.

7   "That was a real pretty dance, that dance they just did," said Hazel.

8   "Huh?" said George.

9   "That dance—it was nice," said Hazel.

10   "Yup," said George. He tried to think a little about the ballerinas. They weren't really very good—no better than anybody else would have been,

---

[1] Cloning is a genetic engineering process by which scientists can reproduce in the laboratory genetically identical organisms from a single ancestor.

anyway. They were burdened with sashweights and bags of birdshot, and their faces were masked, so that no one, seeing a free and graceful gesture or a pretty face, would feel like something the cat drug in. George was toying with the vague notion that maybe dancers shouldn't be handicapped. But he didn't get very far with it before another noise in his ear radio scattered his thoughts.

11   George winced. So did two out of the eight ballerinas.

12   Hazel saw him wince. Having no mental handicap herself, she had to ask George what the latest sound had been.

13   "Sounded like somebody hitting a milk bottle with a ballpeen hammer," said George.

14   "I'd think it would be real interesting, hearing all the different sounds," said Hazel, a little envious. "All the things they think up."

15   "Um," said George.

16   "Only, if I was Handicapper General, you know what I would do?" said Hazel. Hazel, as a matter of fact, bore a strong resemblance to the Handicapper General, a woman named Diana Moon Glampers. "If I was Diana Moon Glampers," said Hazel, "I'd have chimes on Sunday—just chimes. Kind of in honor of religion."

17   "I could think, if it was just chimes," said George.

18   "Well—maybe make 'em real loud," said Hazel. "I think I'd make a good Handicapper General."

19   "Good as anybody else," said George.

20   "Who knows better'n I do what normal is?" said Hazel.

21   "Right," said George. He began to think glimmeringly about his abnormal son who was now in jail, about Harrison, but a twenty-one-gun salute in his head stopped that.

22   "Boy!" said Hazel, "that was a doozy, wasn't it?"

23   It was such a doozy that George was white and trembling, and tears stood on the rims of his red eyes. Two of the eight ballerinas had collapsed to the studio floor, were holding their temples.

24   "All of a sudden you look so tired," said Hazel. "Why don't you stretch out on the sofa, so's you can rest your handicap bag on the pillows, honeybunch." She was referring to the forty-seven pounds of birdshot in a canvas bag which was padlocked around George's neck. "Go on and rest the bag for a little while," she said. "I don't care if you're not equal to me for a while."

25   George weighed the bag with his hands. "I don't mind it," he said. "I don't notice it any more. It's just a part of me."

26   "You been so tired lately—kind of wore out," said Hazel. "If there was just some way we could make a little hole in the bottom of the bag, and just take out a few of them lead balls. Just a few."

27   "Two years in prison and two thousand dollars fine for every ball I took out," said George. "I don't call that a bargain."

28   "If you could just take a few out when you come home from work," said Hazel. "I mean—you don't compete with anybody around here. You just set around."

29   "If I tried to get away with it, " said George, "then other people'd get away with it—and pretty soon we'd be right back to the dark ages again, with everybody competing against everybody else. You wouldn't like that would you?"

30   "I'd hate it," said Hazel.

31   "There you are," said George. "The minute people start cheating on laws, what do you think happens to society?"

32   If Hazel hadn't been able to come up with an answer to this question, George couldn't have supplied one. A siren was going off in his head.

33   "Reckon it'd fall all apart," said Hazel.

34   "What would?" said George blankly.

35   "Society," said Hazel uncertainly. "Wasn't that what you just said?"

36   "Who knows?" said George.

37   The television program was suddenly interrupted for a news bulletin. It wasn't clear at first as to what the bulletin was about, since the announcer, like all announcers, had a serious speech impediment. For about half a minute, and in a state of high excitement, the announcer tried to say, "Ladies and gentlemen—"

38   He finally gave up, handed the bulletin to a ballerina to read.

39   "That's all right—" Hazel said of the announcer, "he tried. That's the big thing. He tried to do the best he could with what God gave him. He should get a nice raise for trying so hard."

40   "Ladies and gentlemen—" said the ballerina, reading the bulletin. She must have been extraordinarily beautiful, because the mask she wore was hideous. And it was easy to see that she was the strongest and most graceful of all the dancers, for her handicap bags were as big as those worn by two-hundred-pound men.

41   And she had to apologize at once for her voice, which was a very unfair voice for a woman to use. Her voice was a warm, luminous, time-less melody. "Excuse me—" she said, and began again, making her voice absolutely uncompetitive.

42   "Harrison Bergeron, age fourteen," she said in a grackle squawk, "has just escaped from jail, where he was held on suspicion of plotting to over-throw the government. He is a genius and an athlete, is under-handicapped, and should be regarded as extremely dangerous."

43   A police photograph of Harrison Bergeron was flashed on the screen— upside down, then sideways, upside down again, then right side up. The picture showed the full length of Harrison against a background cali-brated in feet and inches. He was exactly seven feet tall.

44   The rest of Harrison's appearance was Halloween and hardware. Nobody had ever borne heavier handicaps. He had outgrown hindrances faster than the H-G men could think them up. Instead of a little ear radio for a mental handicap, he wore a tremendous pair of earphones, and spectacles with thick wavy lenses. The spectacles were intended to make him not only half blind, but to give him whanging headaches besides.

45   Scrap metal was hung all over him. Ordinarily, there was a certain symmetry, a military neatness to the handicaps issued to strong people, but Harrison looked like a walking junkyard. In the race of life, Harrison carried three hundred pounds.

46   And to offset his good looks, the H-G men required that he wear at all times a red rubber ball for a nose, keep his eyebrows shaved off, and cover his even white teeth with black caps at snaggle-tooth random.

47   "If you see this boy," said the ballerina, "do not—I repeat, do not—try to reason with him."

48   There was the shriek of a door being torn from its hinges.

49   Screams and barking cries of consternation came from the television set. The photograph of Harrison Bergeron on the screen jumped again and again, as though dancing to the tune of an earthquake.

50   George Bergeron correctly identified the earthquake, and well he might have—for many was the time his own home had danced to the same crashing tune. "My God—" said George, "that must be Harrison!"

51   The realization was blasted from his mind instantly by the sound of an automobile collision in his head.

52   When George could open his eyes again, the photograph of Harrison was gone. A living, breathing Harrison filled the screen.

53   Clanking, clownish, and huge, Harrison stood in the center of the studio. The knob of the uprooted studio door was still in his hand. Ballerinas, technicians, musicians, and announcers cowered on their knees before him, expecting to die.

54   "I am the Emperor!" cried Harrison. "Do you hear? I am the Emperor! Everybody must do what I say at once!" He stamped his foot and the studio shook.

55   "Even as I stand here—" he bellowed, "crippled, hobbled, sickened—I am a greater ruler than any man who ever lived! Now watch me become what I *can* become!"

56   Harrison tore the straps of his handicap harness like wet tissue paper, tore straps guaranteed to support five thousand pounds.

57   Harrison's scrap-iron handicaps crashed to the floor.

58   Harrison thrust his thumbs under the bar of the padlock that secured his head harness. The bar snapped like celery. Harrison smashed his headphones and spectacles against the wall.

59   He flung away his rubber-ball nose, revealed a man that would have awed Thor, the god of thunder.

60   "I shall now select my Empress!" he said, looking down on the cowering people. "Let the first woman who dares rise to her feet claim her mate and her throne!"

61   A moment passed, and then a ballerina arose, swaying like a willow.

62   Harrison plucked the mental handicap from her ear, snapped off her physical handicaps with marvelous delicacy. Last of all, he removed her mask.

63   She was blindingly beautiful.

64   "Now—" said Harrison, taking her hand, "shall we show the people the meaning of the word *dance*? Music!" he commanded.

65   The musicians scrambled back into their chairs, and Harrison stripped them of their handicaps, too. "Play your best," he told them, "and I'll make you barons and dukes and earls."

66   The music began. It was normal at first—cheap, silly, false. But Harrison snatched two musicians from their chairs, waved them like batons as he sang the music as he wanted it played. He slammed them back into their chairs.

67   The music began again and was much improved.

68   Harrison and his Empress merely listened to the music for a while—listened gravely, as though synchronizing their heartbeats with it.

69   They shifted their weights to their toes.

70   Harrison placed his big hands on the girl's tiny waist, letting her sense the weightlessness that would soon be hers.

71   And then, in an explosion of joy and grace, into the air they sprang!

72   Not only were the laws of the land abandoned, but the law of gravity and the laws of motion as well.

73   They reeled, whirled, swiveled, flounced, capered, gamboled, and spun.

74   They leaped like deer on the moon.

75   The studio ceiling was thirty feet high, but each leap brought the dancers nearer to it.

76   It became their obvious intention to kiss the ceiling.

77   They kissed it.

78   And then, neutralizing gravity with love and pure will, they remained suspended in air inches below the ceiling, and they kissed each other for a long, long time.

79   It was then that Diana Moon Glampers, the Handicapper General, came into the studio with a double-barreled ten-gauge shotgun. She fired twice, and the Emperor and the Empress were dead before they hit the floor.

80   Diana Moon Glampers loaded the gun again. She aimed it at the musicians and told them they had ten seconds to get their handicaps back on.

81   It was then that the Bergerons' television tube burned out.

82   Hazel turned to comment about the blackout to George. But George had gone out into the kitchen for a can of beer.

83   George came back in with the beer, paused while a handicap signal shook him up. And then he sat down again. "You been crying?" he said to Hazel.

84   "Yup," she said.

85   "What about?" he said.

86   "I forget," she said. "Something real sad on television."

87   "What was it?" he said.

88   "It's all kind of mixed-up in my mind," said Hazel.

89   "Forget sad things," said George.

90   "I always do," said Hazel.

91   "That's my girl," said George. He winced. There was the sound of a riveting gun in his head.

92   "Gee—I could tell that one was a doozy," said Hazel.

93   "You can say that again," said George.

94   "Gee—" said Hazel, "I could tell that one was a doozy."

Kurt Vonnegut, Jr. a prolific writer, has written 12 novels, two collections of stories, plays, screenplays, essays and children's books. His interest in science has caused him to be labeled as a science fiction writer; however, the fundamental concerns of Vonnegut's fiction are human and social issues.

After You Read

Reading Journal

Now that you have finished Vonnegut's story, have you modified the position you took in the pre-reading exercise? Explain.

Reading For Meaning

1. What methods were used to insure equality in Vonnegut's society? Who was in charge of enforcing "equality" ? Give specific examples from the story.

2. What is the reason for the government's aggressive policy on equality? What, according to George and Hazel, would happen if society permitted individual difference?

3. What kind of society is Vonnegut ridiculing in his satire? Who does the figure of Harrison Bergeron symbolize? What are the consequences of his action?

Exploring Further

Interview/Questionnaire

Design a short interview sheet in which you ask six respondents (three from your native culture and three native born Americans) their views on total equality.

1. Begin your interview by asking how your respondents feel about genetic engineering and whether they would like to live in a totally "equal" society.

2. Write a short summary of the Vonnegut story in your group. Give the summary to each respondent to read.

3. Then, design questions which ask respondents to list pros and cons of "total equality" in Vonnegut's sense of the term. (For example, you might ask: "Do you think total equality in business would be good or bad? Why?")

4. Collate your findings, come to some conclusions about the feelings people have about total equality, and share them with the class.

Timed Writing Exercise

Imagine that you are a reporter chosen to write an opinion piece for your paper on the earth as it will be in 2100. Thanks to a time machine, you discover a radically different universe inhabited by a genetically cloned race of superior (rather than average) men and women. Describe this hypothetical universe to your readers and be sure to conclude with an opinion on the desirability of living in such a place.

Focused Essay Topics

1. Write an extended definition of the word *equality*. Make sure to distinguish between equality of rights under the law and equality in "every which way" in Vonnegut's sense.

2. Discuss the effects of removing all competition from a society. You may want to concentrate on one area such as education, sports, business or technology. Use examples from the short story to illustrate your ideas.

EXTENDING THE CONTEXT

These questions are designed for further discussion or essay writing. Your responses should reflect the thinking, reading and writing you have done on the unit topic thus far.

1. In American films, the cowboy and the detective are two figures which can be said to typify the rugged individualist—someone who repeatedly defends the laws and values of the society he remains outside of. Rent several western or detective movies from the video store to watch and write an essay in which you describe in what ways these film heros represent American individualism.

2. Write an essay in which you discuss one incident in recent U.S. current events in which the American notion of individualism helped form U.S. policy.

3. Write a personal definition of individualism.

4. What evidence is there in the daily life of Americans that either confirms or refutes the notion that American individualism is simply "What's in it for me?" Draw your examples from the readings and from current newspapers or periodicals.

5. In 1993 a young Japanese exchange student was gunned down by a homeowner who suspected him of trespassing. The fatal misunderstanding occured when the young Japanese, not understanding the meaning of "freeze," lurched forward, alarming the homeowner and causing him to shoot. The case was brought to trial and the homeowner was acquitted on the grounds that he had the right to own and operate a gun for self-protection. This case, among others, fuels the debate in America between those who feel easy access to firearms has led to increased violence and gun-related deaths and those who (like the National Rifle Association) feel that an individual's right to bear arms should take precedence. Go to the library and research the above incident. Write a defense of or argument against gun control.

6. Choose another controversial issue in which individual rights pose a conflict for Americans. Some suggested topics include: smoking in public, freedom of the press versus the right of individual privacy, reproductive rights, divorce. Present both sides of the argument and take a position.

7. In his article, Daniel Goleman writes "as countries like Japan become more affluent, they also tend to become more individualistic." Has the emphasis on personal goals or satisfaction increased in recent years in your native culture? Is this the result of economic change or some other cultural influence? Explain, giving examples to support your argument.

8. Americans, especially the younger generation, express their individuality in terms of the objects and accessories they buy. Women, in particular, express a sense of personal style through fashion and decor. Describe yourself or a person you know well in terms of individual style. Analyze the message s/he is trying to convey behind the facade.

VIDEO SUGGESTIONS

The video selections are offered as suggestions for viewing in or out of class to enrich the unit topic.

Five Easy Pieces   *Dead Poets' Society*
Marty   *The Fountainhead*
Stand and Deliver   *Malcolm X*

MELTING POT OR PATCHWORK QUILT: THE CHALLENGE OF MULTICULTURALISM

JACOB LAWRENCE,
*Men Exist for the Sake
of One Another*

Short Takes

Everyone is a prisoner of his own experiences. No one can eliminate prejudices—just recognize them.

Edward R. Murrow

We hate some persons because we do not know them; and will not know them because we hate them.

Charles Caleb Colton

We are now at the point where we must decide whether we are to honor the concept of a plural society which gains strength through diversity, or whether we are to have bitter fragmentation that will result in perpetual tension and strife.

Earl Warren

When asked by an anthropologist what the Indians called America before the white man came, an Indian said simply, "Ours."

Vine Deloria, Jr.

There is a tendency to judge a race, a nation or any distinct group by its least worthy members.

Eric Hoffer

I have a dream that my four little children will one day live in a nation where they will not be judged by the color of their skin but by the content of their character.

Martin Luther King, Jr.

The highest result of education is tolerance.

Helen Keller

SUGGESTIONS FOR USING SHORT TAKES:

- Respond in writing to one of the quotations above. Then get together in groups and share what you have written.
- Work with a partner, small group or the entire class to discuss one or more quotations. You may want to agree, disagree, or compare it to similar expressions or sayings in your native language.

INTRODUCTION – MELTING POT OR PATCHWORK QUILT: THE CHALLENGE OF MULTICULTURALISM

On every U.S. coin you find the familiar slogan *E pluribus unum*, Latin for "one formed by many." These words are not only a description of American society but also a political ideal, even if a battered one. On the threshold of the twenty-first century, the American ideal of equality and unity is far from being realized.

For decades, the term *melting pot* was used to describe American society. In this imaginary cauldron, the immigrant's original national, racial and ethnic characteristics were boiled down, purified, and transformed into a novel identity—that of the American. The melting pot metaphor thus stressed the immigrant American's new hybrid form.

However, as we know, American society has historically given greater priority and value to the Anglo-Saxon elements of culture. Those who were farthest from the Anglo-Saxon ideal—African Americans, Asian Americans, native Americans, and European Jews, among others—all suffered prejudice and discrimination. It took 100 years, from the end of the Civil War in 1865 to the beginnings of the civil rights movement in the early 1960s for the African American to gain those basic civic, educational and professional opportunities afforded his fellow white Americans.

Although lack of equal opportunity for all Americans is still one of our most troubling national issues, there has been progress. Gradually over the past decades, the political climate has been changing. Today we are more aware of the wealth of our national diversity, and of the need to preserve and value the numerous threads that make up the American fabric. The melting pot metaphor—in which the immigrant's traditions and heritage were obliterated—has been replaced by new terms like *patchwork quilt, rainbow coalition* and *cultural pluralism*. These terms value the *pluribus*—the myriad of distinct cultural and national traditions that form the American experience—rather than the ideal of a homogeneous *unum* which erases these distinctions in favor of Anglo-conformity.

It may be that this cultural, political and moral evolution is being forced by our new demographics. Some telling statistics were brought out in a recent *Time* magazine article. For example, already one out of every four Americans is Hispanic or non-white. And, by 2056, the average American will be non-European in origin.

In some cities, the demographic balance has already shifted. In New York City, over 40% of the student population belongs to an ethnic minority; within a decade this group will account for half. In California, white students are already in the minority. In fact, whites of all ages make up only 58% of California's population. In San Jose, California, for example, the Vietnamese surname Nguyen covers 14 columns in the white pages of the telephone book as compared to only 8 columns of Joneses. More than 200,000 people of Middle Eastern descent have settled in the greater Detroit area, while 12,000 Hmong refugees from Laos have settled in St. Paul, Minnesota. According to Molefi Asante, chairman of the African-American studies department at Temple University, "Once America was a microcosm of Europe. Today America is a microcosm of the world."

American history suggests that political and social accommodation of our new demographics is likely to be explosive. Already we have seen fresh battle lines drawn between the newest immigrants and older ethnic groups with a history of disadvantage. For example, in some African American neighborhoods, conflicts have arisen between blacks and Korean shopkeepers. As Asians, and in some areas, Hispanics, become the largest minorities, some African Americans fear that they will once again be neglected. In fact, affirmative action[1] now includes other minorities such as women, Hispanics, native Americans, and in some cities, Italian Americans.

---

[1] Affirmative action: any plan or program that promotes the employment of women and members of minority groups.

Not only is the battle being fought in political and economic arenas; the classroom has also become a battleground of multiculturalism. The battle cry "Whose classroom is this and whose history, whose culture will be taught here?" has brought sweeping changes to curricula, from public elementary and secondary schools to universities across the nation.

A case in point is the radical overhaul of the New York State curriculum recently by a State Task Force which concluded that "African Americans, Asian Americans, Puerto Ricans and Native Americans have all been victims of an intellectual and educational oppression . . . . Negative characterizations, or the absence of positive references, have had a terribly damaging effect on the psyche of young people." Their suggested changes included not only a "politically correct"[2] syllabus but changes in language as well. For example, the once neutral word "mankind," they suggested, should be replaced in textbooks by the less gender specific "humankind." And in colleges around the nation, the European humanistic tradition (Greek, Latin, European and male) is under pressure from various factions to be more inclusive. This means the inclusion of required courses that reflect the historical contributions of Africa, Asia, the Caribbean and the study of women and their experience.

Some scholars are outraged by these reforms, claiming that not all cultures and civilizations are equal in stature and deserving of study, especially on the eve of the twenty-first century when students must master so much information within a limited time frame. Other scholars claim that the revisions of academic traditions and canons[3] may be "politically" but not necessarily historically correct or intellectually valuable. Andrew Hacker, Professor of Political Science at Queens College, CUNY, for example, takes exception to the New York State Task Force recommendation "that children be taught how native Americans were here to welcome new settlers from Holland, Senegal, England, Indonesia, France, the Congo, Italy, China and Iberia." Hacker responds: "Did the Indians really welcome all those groups? Were they at Ellis Island when the Italians started to arrive? This is not history but a myth intended to bolster the self-esteem of certain children, and just possibly, a platform for advocates of various ethnic interests."

Just as possibly, however, the traditional canon of American history was a platform for advocates of one cultural, if not ethnic, interest—that of the white, male intellectual, if not himself of European origin, at least of European tradition in his training and outlook.

As we move into the next century, the once-revered symbol of the melting pot no longer serves our vision of America. In fact, Maya Angelou's rousing poem, read at President Clinton's 1993 inauguration, made the politics of inclusion explicit:

> *Humankind—the Asian, the Hispanic, the Jew*
> *The African, the Native American, the Sioux,*
> *The Catholic, the Muslim, the French, the Greek,*
> *The Irish, the Rabbi, the Priest, the Sheik,*
> *The Gay, the Straight, the Preacher,*
> *The privileged, the homeless, the Teacher . . .*

Undoubtedly we will coin new metaphors and slogans that better represent the ever-increasing diversity of our *E pluribus unum*. And, with a president in office committed to representing our national diversity in his own cabinet and government, we may witness in this last decade of the century some movement toward this democratic ideal.

---

[2] Politically correct: a term used to describe efforts made to encourage a more inclusive society in which racism, sexism and prejudice of all sorts are eliminated, particularly as they are reflected in language.

[3] Canon: the accepted complete works of an author or authors.

Before You Read

Freewrite on the following topic and share your response: Several metaphors have been used over the years to express the process of immigration and assimilation, most notably "melting pot" and "patchwork quilt." Which of these two terms do you think is a better description of our vision of American society today? Explain.

Assimilation in America: Theory and Reality

MILTON M. GORDON

1   Three ideologies or conceptual models have competed for attention on the American scene as explanations of the way in which a nation, in the beginning largely white, Anglo-Saxon, and Protestant, has absorbed over 41 million immigrants and their descendants from variegated sources and welded them into the contemporary American people. These ideologies are Anglo-conformity, the melting pot, and cultural pluralism. They have served at various times, and often simultaneously, as explanations of what has happened—descriptive models—and of what should happen—goal models. Not infrequently they have been used in such a fashion that it is difficult to tell which of these two usages the writer has had in mind. In fact, one of the more remarkable omissions in the history of American intellectual thought is the relative lack of close analytical attention given to the theory of immigrant adjustment in the United States by its social scientists.

2   The story of America's immigration can be quickly told for our present purposes. The white American population at the time of the Revolution was largely English and Protestant in origin, but had already absorbed substantial groups of Germans and Scotch-Irish and smaller contingents of Frenchmen, Dutchmen, Swedes, Swiss, South Irish, Poles, and a handful of migrants from other European nations. Catholics were represented in modest numbers, particularly in the middle colonies, and a small number of Jews were residents of the incipient nation. With the exception of the Quakers and a few missionaries, the colonists had generally treated the Indians and their cultures with contempt and hostility, driving them from the coastal plains and making the western frontier a bloody battleground where eternal vigilance was the price of survival.

3   Although the Negro at that time made up nearly one-fifth of the total population, his predominantly slave status, together with racial and cultural prejudice, barred him from serious consideration as an assimilable element of the society. And while many groups of European origin started out as determined ethnic enclaves, eventually, most historians believe,

considerable ethnic intermixture within the white population took place. "People of different blood" [sic]-write two American historians about the colonial period, "English, Irish, German, Huguenot, Dutch, Swedish— mingled and intermarried with a little though of any difference."[1] In such a society, its people, predominantly English, its white immigrants of other ethnic origins either English-speaking or derived largely from countries of northern and western Europe whose cultural divergences from the English were not great, and its dominant white population excluding by fiat the claims and considerations of welfare of the non-Caucasian minorities, the problem of assimilation understandably did not loom unduly large or complex.

4   The unfolding events of the next century and a half with increasing momentum dispelled the complacency which rested upon the relative simplicity of colonial and immediate post-Revolutionary conditions. The large-scale immigration to America of the famine-fleeing Irish, the Germans, and later the Scandinavians (along with additional Englishmen and other peoples of northern and western Europe) in the middle of the nineteenth century (the so-called "old immigration"), the emancipation of the Negro slaves and the problems created by post-Civil War recon- struction, the placing of the conquered Indian with his broken culture on government reservations, the arrival of the Oriental, first attracted by the discovery of gold and other opportunities in the West, and finally, begin- ning in the last quarter of the nineteenth century and continuing to the early 1920's, the swelling to proportions hitherto unimagined of the tide of immigration from the peasantries and "pales" of southern and eastern Europe—the Italians, Jews, and Slavs of the so-called "new immigra- tion," fleeing the persecutions and industrial dislocations of the day—all these events constitute the background against which we may consider the rise of the theories of assimilation mentioned above. After a neces- sarily foreshortened description of each of these theories and their his- torical emergence, we shall suggest analytical distinctions designed to aid in clarifying the nature of the assimilation process, and then conclude by focusing on the American scene.

Anglo-Conformity

5   "Anglo-conformity"[2] is a broad term used to cover a variety of viewpoints about assimilation and immigration; they all assume the desirability of maintaining English institutions (as modified by the American Revolution), the English language, and English-oriented cultural patterns as dominant and standard in American life. However, bound up with this assumption are related attitudes. These may range from discredited notions about race and "Nordic" and "Aryan" racial superiority, together with the nativist political programs and exclusionist immigration policies which such notions entail, through an intermediate position of favoring immigration from northern and western Europe on amorphous, unreflective grounds ("They are more like us"), to a lack of opposition to any source of immigration, as long as these

[1] Allan Nevins and Henry Steele Commager, *America: The Story of a Free People* (Boston, Little, Brown, 1942), p. 58.
[2] The phrase is the Coles's. See Stewart G. Cole and Mildred Wiese Cole, *Minorities and the American Promise* (New York, Harper & Brothers, 1954), ch. 6.

immigrants and their descendants duly adopt the standard Anglo-Saxon cultural patterns. There is by no means any necessary equation between Anglo-conformity and racist attitudes.

6   It is quite likely that "Anglo-conformity" in its more moderate aspects, however explicit its formulation, has been the most prevalent ideology of assimilation goals in America throughout the nation's history. As far back as colonial times, Benjamin Franklin recorded concern about the clannishness of the Germans in Pennsylvania, their slowness in learning English, and the establishment of their own native-language press.[3] Others of the founding fathers had similar reservations about large-scale immigration from Europe. In the context of their times they were unable to foresee the role such immigration was to play in creating the later greatness of the nation. They were not at all men of unthinking prejudices. The disestablishment of religion and the separation of church and state (so that no religious group—whether New England Congregationalists, Virginian Anglicans, or even all Protestants combined—could call upon the federal government for special favors or support, and so that man's religious conscience should be free) were cardinal points of the new national policy they fostered. "The Government of the United States," George Washington had written to the Jewish congregation of Newport during his first term as president, "gives to bigotry no sanction, to persecution no assistance."

7   Political differences with ancestral England had just been written in blood; but there was no reason to suppose that these men looked upon their fledgling country as an impartial melting pot for the merging of the various cultures of Europe, or as a new "nation of nations," or as anything but a society in which, with important political modifications, Anglo-Saxon speech and institutional forms would be standard. Indeed, their newly won victory for democracy and republicanism made them especially anxious that these still precarious fruits of revolution should not be threatened by a large influx of European peoples whose life experiences had accustomed them to the bonds of despotic monarchy. Thus, although they explicitly conceived of the new United States of America as a haven for those unfortunates of Europe who were persecuted and oppressed, they had characteristic reservations about the effects of too free a policy. "My opinion, with respect to immigration," Washington wrote to John Adams in 1794, "is that except of useful mechanics and some particular descriptions of men or professions, there is no need of encouragement, while the policy or advantage of its taking place in a body (I mean the settling of them in a body) may be much questioned; for, by so doing, they retain the language, habits and principles (good or bad) which they bring with them." Thomas Jefferson, whose views on race and attitudes towards slavery were notably liberal and advanced for his time, had similar doubts concerning the effects of mass immigration on American institutions, while conceding that immigrants, "if they come of themselves . . . are entitled to all the rights of citizenship."

8   Anglo-conformity received its fullest expression in the so-called Americanization movement which gripped the nation during World War I.

---

[3] Maurice R. Davie, *World Immigration* (New York, Macmillan, 1936), p. 36, and (cited therein) "Letter of Benjamin Franklin to Peter Collinson," 9th May.

While "Americanization" in its various stages had more than one emphasis, it was essentially a consciously articulated movement to strip the
immigrant of his native culture and attachments and make him over into
an American along Anglo-Saxon lines—all this to be accomplished with
great rapidity. To use an image of a later day, it was an attempt at
"pressure-cooking assimilation." It had prewar antecedents, but it was
during the height of the world conflict that federal agencies, state gov-
ernments, municipalities, and a host of private organizations joined in the
effort to persuade the immigrant to learn English, take out naturalization
papers, buy war bonds, forget his former origins and culture, and give
himself over to patriotic hysteria.

The Melting Pot

9   While Anglo-conformity in various guises has probably been the most
prevalent ideology of assimilation in the American historical experience,
a competing viewpoint with more generous and idealistic overtones has
had its adherents and exponents from the eighteenth century onward.
Conditions in the virgin continent, it was clear, were modifying the institutions which the English colonists brought with them from the mother
country. Arrivals from non-English homelands such as Germany,
Sweden, and France were similarly exposed to this fresh environment.
Was it not possible, then, to think of the evolving American society not
as a slightly modified England but rather as a totally new blend, culturally and biologically, in which the stocks and folkways of Europe, figura-
tively speaking, were indiscriminately mixed in the political pot of the
emerging nation and fused by the fires of American influence and inter-
action into a distinctly new type?

10   Such, at any rate, was the conception of the new society which motivated that eighteenth-century French-born writer and agriculturalist,
J. Hector St. John Crèvecoeur, who, after many years of American residence, published his reflections and observations in *Letters from an
American Farmer*. Who, he asks, is the American?

11   He is either an European, or the descendant of an European,
        hence that strange mixture of blood, which you will find in no
        other country. I could point out to you a family whose grandfather
        was an Englishman, whose wife was Dutch, whose son married a
        French woman, and whose present four sons have now four wives
        of different nations. *He* is an American, who leaving behind him
        all his ancient prejudices and manners, receives new ones from
        the new mode of life he has embraced, the new government he
        obeys, and the new rank he holds. He becomes an American by
        being received in the broad lap of our great *Alma Mater*. Here
        individuals of all nations are melted into a new race of men,
        whose labours and posterity will one day cause great changes in
        the world.

12   Some observers have interpreted the open-door policy on immigration
of the first three-quarters of the nineteenth century as reflecting an underlying faith in the effectiveness of the American melting pot, in the belief
"that all could be absorbed and that all could contribute to an emerging
national character." No doubt many who observed with dismay the nativist

agitation of the times felt as did Ralph Waldo Emerson that such conformity-demanding and immigrant-hating forces represented a perversion of the best American ideals. In 1845, Emerson wrote in his Journal:

13   I hate the narrowness of the Native American Party. It is the dog in the manger.[4] It is precisely opposite to all the dictates of love and magnanimity; and therefore, of course, opposite to true wisdom . . . . Man is the most composite of all creatures . . . .Well, as in the old burning of the Temple at Corinth, by the melting and intermixture of silver and gold and other metals a new compound more precious than any, called Corinthian brass, was formed; so in this continent,—asylum of all nations,—the energy of Irish, Germans, Swedes, Poles, and Cossacks, and all the European tribes,—of the Africans, and of the Polynesians,—will construct a new race, a new religion, a new state, a new literature, which will be as vigorous as the new Europe which came out of the smelting-pot of the Dark Ages, or that which earlier emerged from the Pelasgic and Etruscan barbarism.

14   Eventually, the melting-pot hypothesis found its way into historical scholarship and interpretation. While many American historians of the late nineteenth century, some fresh from graduate study at German universities, tended to adopt the view that American institutions derived in essence from Anglo-Saxon (and ultimately Teutonic) sources, others were not so sure. One of these was Frederick Jackson Turner, a young historian from Wisconsin, not long emerged from his graduate training at Johns Hopkins. Turner presented a paper to the American Historical Association, meeting in Chicago in 1893. Called "The Significance of the Frontier in American History," this paper proved to be one of the most influential essays in the history of American scholarship, and its point of view, supported by Turner's subsequent writings and his teaching, pervaded the field of American historical interpretation for at least a generation. Turner's thesis was that the dominant influence in the shaping of American institutions and American democracy was not this nation's European heritage in any of its forms, nor the forces emanating from the eastern seaboard cities, but rather the experiences created by a moving and variegated western frontier. Among the many effects attributed to the frontier environment and the challenges it presented was that it acted as a solvent for the national heritages and the separatist tendencies of the many nationality groups which had joined the trek westward, including the Germans and Scotch-Irish of the eighteenth century and the Scandinavians and Germans of the nineteenth. "The frontier," asserted Turner, "promoted the formation of a composite nationality for the American people . . . . In the crucible of the frontier the immigrants were Americanized, liberated, and fused into a mixed race, English in neither nationality nor characteristics. The process has gone on from the early days to our own." And later, in an essay on the role of the Mississippi Valley, he refers to "the tide of foreign immigration which has risen so steadily that it has made a composite American people whose amalgamation is destined to produce a new national stock."

---

[4] Dog in the manger: one who will neither enjoy the use of something himself, nor allow anyone else to enjoy it.

Cultural Pluralism

15   Probably all the non-English immigrants who came to American shores in any significant numbers from colonial times onward—settling either in the forbidding wilderness, the lonely prairie, or in some accessible urban slum—created ethnic enclaves and looked forward to the preservation of at least some of their native cultural patterns. Such a development, natural as breathing, was supported by the later accretion of friends, relatives, and countrymen seeking out oases of familiarity in a strange land, by the desire of the settlers to rebuild (necessarily in miniature) a society in which they could communicate in the familiar tongue and maintain familiar institutions, and, finally, by the necessity to band together for mutual aid and mutual protection against the uncertainties of a strange and frequently hostile environment. This was as true of the "old" immigrants as of the "new." In fact, some of the liberal intellectuals who fled to America from an inhospitable political climate in Germany in the 1830's, 1840's, and 1850's looked forward to the creation of an all-German state within the union, or, even more hopefully, to the eventual formation of a separate German nation, as soon as the expected dissolution of the union under the impact of the slavery controversy should have taken place. Oscar Handlin, writing of the sons of Erin in mid-nineteenth-century Boston, recent refugees from famine and economic degradation in their homeland, points out: "Unable to participate in the normal associational affairs of the community, the Irish felt obliged to erect a society within a society, to act together in their own way. In every contact therefore the group, acting apart from other sections of the community, became intensely aware of its peculiar and exclusive identity." Thus cultural pluralism was a fact in American society before it became a theory—a theory with explicit relevance for the nation as a whole, and articulated and discussed in the English-speaking circles of American intellectual life.

16   Early in 1915 there appeared in the pages of *The Nation* two articles under the title "Democracy *versus* the Melting-Pot." Their author was Horace Kallen, a Harvard-educated philosopher with a concern for the application of philosophy to societal affairs, and, as an American Jew, himself derivative of an ethnic background which was subject to the contemporary pressures for dissolution implicit in the "Americanization," or Anglo-conformity, and the melting-pot theories. In these articles Kallen vigorously rejected the usefulness of these theories as models of what was actually transpiring in American life or as ideals for the future. Rather he was impressed by the way in which the various ethnic groups in America were coincident with particular areas and regions, and with the tendency for each group to preserve its own language, religion, communal institutions, and ancestral culture. All the while, he pointed out, the immigrant has been learning to speak English as the language of general communication, and has participated in the over-all economic and political life of the nation. These developments in which "the United States are in the process of becoming a federal state not merely as a union of geographical and administrative unities, but also as a cooperation of cultural diversities, as a federation or commonwealth of national cultures," the author argued, far from constituting a violation of historic American political

principles, as the "Americanizers" claimed, actually represented the inevitable consequences of democratic ideals, since individuals are implicated in groups, and since democracy for the individual must by extension also mean democracy for his group.

17   The processes just described, however, as Kallen develops his argument, are far from having been thoroughly realized. They are menaced by "Americanization" programs, assumptions of Anglo-Saxon superiority, and misguided attempts to promote "racial" amalgamation. Thus America stands at a kind of cultural crossroads. It can attempt to impose by force an artificial, Anglo-Saxon oriented uniformity on its peoples, or it can consciously allow and encourage its ethnic groups to develop democratically, each emphasizing its particular cultural heritage. If the latter course is followed, as Kallen puts it at the close of his essay, then,

18   the outlines of a possible great and truly democratic commonwealth become discernible. Its form would be that of the federal republic; its substance a democracy of nationalities, cooperating voluntarily and autonomously through common institutions in the enterprise of self-realization through the perfection of men according to their kind. The common language of the commonwealth, the language of its great tradition, would be English, but each nationality would have for its emotional and involuntary life its own peculiar dialect or speech, its own individual and inevitable esthetic and intellectual forms. The political and economic life of the commonwealth is a single unit and serves as the foundation and background for the realization of the distinctive individuality of each *natio* that composes it and of the pooling of these in a harmony above them all. Thus "American civilization" may come to mean the perfection of the cooperative harmonies of "European civilization"—the waste, the squalor and the distress of Europe being eliminated— a multiplicity in a unity, an orchestration of mankind.

Milton M. Gordon's *Assimilation in American Life* (1964) is a classic of sociological analysis. He is professor emeritus of Sociology at the University of Massachusetts, Amherst, and author of *The Scope of Sociology* (1988).

After You Read

Reading Journal

Some critics of multiculturalism say that the danger of stressing diversity is the loss of an agreed-upon "American" culture. Do you agree or disagree? Explain.

Reading for Meaning

1. What is the difference between a description model and a goal model as Gordon explains it? Which of his models best describes American culture/society as it stands today, and which do you believe would best serve as a goal model?

2. What evidence does Gordon give that the founding fathers had reservations about "too free" an immigration policy? Explain why the author feels Anglo-conformity has been the most prevalent position toward immigration until quite recently.

3. In your own words, explain the idea of the "frontier crucible." In what ways would the frontier experience be different from the urban experience of immigrants?

Exploring Further

Research Project

With a partner or group, plan to visit and observe an ethnic neighborhood. Before you go, check to see what information is available on this neighborhood in the library or chamber of commerce. Remember, you will be looking for evidence of cultural diversity—customs, language, dress, food, etc. Look also for signs of assimilation to American culture (such as bilingual signs). What generalizations can you make based on your observation of this neighborhood? Write your findings up in a short paper and share them with the class.

Timed Writing Exercise

If you become or are a permanent resident/citizen of the U.S., what cultural and social links would you wish to maintain with your native cultural identity and heritage, if any? Be specific and explain the reasons for your choices.

Focused Essay Topics

1. Do you think Kallen's description of the American society he envisions is too utopian or idealistic, or is it a realizable goal? Is it still realizable given the identity of the new immigrant groups, many of whom are not European and come from radically different cultural backgrounds than that of the U.S.? (Make sure you summarize Kallen's view in your essay.)

2. Interview an immigrant (preferably of your own ethnic group) who has lived in the United States for at least 15 or 20 years to find out how important his or her native ethnic identity has been. Which of Kallen's models best describes his/her experience?

Before You Read

Freewrite on the following and share your response: In all likelihood, as an entering college freshman, you attended an orientation session.[1] Increasingly, these sessions have focused on ethnic, gender and racial diversity in order to dispel negative stereotypes, preconceptions and misconceptions. Does this kind of orientation program seem useful or necessary on the college campus? Explain how it might make you feel more or less comfortable about your identity.

Welcome, Freshman!
Oppressor or Oppressed?   BY HEATHER MACDONALD

1   It is never too soon to learn to identify yourself as a victim. Such, at least, is the philosophy of today's college freshman orientation, which has become a crash course in the strange new world of university politics. Within days of arrival on campus, "new students" (the euphemism of choice for "freshmen") learn the paramount role of gender, race, ethnicity, class and sexual orientation in determining their own and others' identity. Most important, they are provided with the most critical tool of their college career: the ability to recognize their own victimization.

2   An informal survey shows that two themes predominate at freshman orientation programs — oppression and difference — foreshadowing the leitmotifs of the coming four years. Orientations present a picture of college life in which bias lurks around every corner. This year, for example, the University of California at Berkeley changed the focus of its freshman orientation from "stereotyping" to "racism, homophobia, status-ism, sexism, and age-ism."

3   According to Michele Frasier, assistant director of the new student program at Berkeley, the program organizers "wanted to talk more specifically about specific issues the students will face." The objective of the emphasis on discrimination is "to make students aware [of the] issues they need to think about, so they're not surprised when they face them."

Various Forms of "Isms"

4   Dartmouth's assistant dean of freshmen, Tony Tillman, offered no less bleak a vision of the academic community. A mandatory program for freshmen, "Social Issues," presented skits on "the issues first year students face," which he defined as "the various forms of 'isms': sexism, racism, classism, etc." If the content of the skits overlapped, such overlap was, according to Mr. Tillman, unavoidable.

[1] If you have not experienced this directly, respond hypothetically to the questions posed.

The experience of discrimination cannot be compartmentalized: "It's not as if today, I have a racist experience, tomorrow, a sexist [one]. In any one day, one may be up against several issues. Some issues of sexism have a racist foundation, and vice versa."

5   The point of the program (and, indeed, of much of the subsequent education at Dartmouth and other schools) is to "try to weave a common thread" through these various instances of oppression.

6   If one can't fit oneself into the victim role, however, today's freshmen orientation offers an alternative: One can acknowledge oneself as the oppressor. Columbia University brought in a historian from the National Museum of American History in Washington to perform, in effect, an ideological delousing of the students. Her mission, as she said in her speech, was to help students recognize their own beliefs that foster inequality. By describing the stereotypes in American society that support racism and prejudice, she hoped to give students a chance to "re-evaluate [and] learn new things."

7   Learning to see yourself as a victim is closely tied to seeing yourself as different. At Columbia, freshmen heard three of their classmates read essays on what being different — gay, black, and Asian-American — had meant in their lives. According to assistant dean Michael Fenlon, "the goal is to initiate an awareness of difference and the implications of difference for the Columbia community. And this is not a one-shot program. We expect it will continue through their four years here, not just in the classrooms, but in the residence halls, on the playing fields, and in every aspect of student life."

8   "Faces of Community," a program organized by Stanford's "multicultural educator," presented freshmen with a panel of students and staff who each embodied some officially recognized difference. James Wu, orientation coordinator of Stanford's Residential Education program, says that the "Faces" program "gives students a sense that everyone's different." At Bowdoin, the assistant to the president for multicultural programs hosted a brown-bag lunch for freshmen entitled "Defining Diversity: Your Role in Racial-Consciousness Raising, Cultural Differences, and Cross-Cultural Social Enhancers." Oberlin shows its new students a performance piece on "differences in race, ethnicity, sexuality, gender, and culture," and follows up with separate orientation programs for Asian-Americans, blacks, Latinos, and gay, lesbian and bisexual students.

9   The presupposition behind the contemporary freshman initiation is the need for political re-education. Columbia's assistant dean for freshmen, Kathryn Balmer, explained that "you can't bring all these people together and say, 'Now be one big happy community,' without some sort of training. . . . It isn't an ideal world, so we need to do some education." That students have somehow managed for years to form a college community in the absence of such "education" has apparently escaped administrative attention.

10   Stanford's outgoing multicultural educator, Greg Ricks, revealed the dimensions of the task: "White students need help to understand what it means to be white in a multicultural community. We have spent a lot of money and a lot of time trying to help students of color, and women students, and gay and disabled students to figure out what it means for them. But for the white heterosexual male who feels disconnected and marginalized by multiculturalism, we've got to do a lot of work here."

11   Anticipating the amount of "work" that faces the multicultural re-educator,

Duke University got a head start on its mission. Over the summer, it sent each freshman a glossy booklet entitled "A Vision for Duke," which included full-page photos of scrupulously diverse groups of students. A letter from Duke's president, H. Keith H. Brodie, M.D., accompanied the book.

12 President Brodie's letter leaves no doubt that multiculturalism is not an optional occupation at Duke. It crisply informs each student that, after listening to a speech by Maya Angelou, "you and your classmates *will* engage in a discussion of questions raised by Ms. Angelou and by the enclosed booklet" (emphasis added).

13 "A Vision for Duke" begins less sternly with a bit of New Age wisdom, typeset as if it were poetry: "To have a vision is to see with imagination; / it is to perceive that which does not exist. / Reality is that which is not imaginary; / it is that which is actually true." But the book immediately reveals that its role is not to soothe but to judge: "By refusing to face reality, a community lies about its past and present. / . . . A healthy community acknowledges its reality honestly, / [and] admits its gap [between vision and reality] sorrowfully."

Obsessive Emphasis on Difference

14 If all this sounds more appropriate for a war-crimes trial than for the first year of college, the incoming student can at least look forward to one unexpected area of freedom at Duke. According to President Brodie, "gender" is a "preference" that should be respected. Anyone who feels oppressed by their chromosomes can apparently simply "prefer" to be of the opposite sex.

15 Today's freshman orientations, prelude to the education to come, raise one of the great unexplained mysteries of our time; how the obsessive emphasis on "difference" and victimization will lead to a more unified, harmonious culture. Students who have been taught from day one to identify themselves and their peers with one or another oppressed or oppressing group are already replicating those group divisions in their intellectual and social lives.

16 In a time of budget cuts and rising tuitions, alumni should demand that their schools stop devoting their resources to the inculcation of separatism. The bureaucratic machinery behind multiculturalism is enormous and growing yearly. It would be inaccurate to say that college administrators have jumped on the lucrative bandwagon of multiculturalism and political correctness. Properly speaking, they have hijacked the wagon and are heading for territories all but inaccessible without their assistance. It is long past time that schools start directing the minds, rather than the souls, of their students.

Heather MacDonald's piece appeared on the opinion page of *The Washington Post.* She is an attorney and lives in New York City.

After You Read

Reading Journal

Do you agree or disagree with MacDonald that "it is long past time that schools start directing the minds, rather than the souls, of their students"?

Reading for Meaning

1. What does the freshman orientation, with its emphasis on difference, suggest about American culture at large?

2. What do you think the colleges mentioned in the article wish to accomplish through these programs? Do you think acceptance of difference is possible?

3. Why would the "white male" student now feel "on the outs"? Do you agree that this is so?

4. What is the author's attitude towards these orientation programs? Do you agree or disagree with her?

Exploring Further

Interview/Questionnaire

MacDonald writes that "students have managed for years to form a college community. . ." without specifically being "educated" as to how to go about it. Working alone and using the notes you have from the *Before You Read* section, interview three students (of different ethnic backgrounds, if possible) on campus as to their feelings about the need for educating the student body on diversity and tolerance. Write up your findings and share them with the class.

Timed Writing Exercise

One of the most important outcomes of a multicultural agenda is a change in curricula and textbooks to include coverage of all the component cultures in the United States. This means that every student will be required to study some aspect of non-white, non-European culture. Do you feel such a requirement is justified or not?

Focused Essay Topics

1. Write a personal essay in which you describe your experience or that of someone you know as being either "oppressor" or "oppressed." (Be sure to refer directly to the article when you use these terms.)

2. MacDonald argues that the "obsessive emphasis on 'difference' and victimization" in freshman orientations works against the goal of a "more unified, harmonious culture." Do you agree or disagree? Use examples from your personal experience to support your argument.

Before You Read

Barbara Ehrenreich explores the effects of what she calls her "cultural baggage" on her identity as an American. What do you think the author is referring to when she uses this term?

Cultural Baggage   BARBARA EHRENREICH

1   An acquaintance was telling me about the joys of rediscovering her ethnic and religious heritage. "I know exactly what my ancestors were doing 2,000 years ago," she said, eyes gleaming with enthusiasm, "and I can do the same things now." Then she leaned forward and inquired politely, "And what is your ethnic background, if I may ask?"

2   "None," I said, that being the first word in line to get out of my mouth. Well, not "none," I backtracked. Scottish, English, Irish — that was something, I supposed. Too much Irish to qualify as a WASP; too much of the hated English to warrant a "Kiss Me, I'm Irish" button; plus there are a number of dead ends in the family tree due to adoptions, missing records, failing memories and the like. I was blushing by this time. Did "none" mean I was rejecting my heritage out of Anglo-Celtic self-hate? Or was I revealing a hidden ethnic chauvinism in which the Britannically derived serve as a kind of neutral standard compared with the ethnic "others"?

3   Throughout the 1960's and 70's I watched one group after another — African-Americans, Latinos, Native Americans — stand up and proudly reclaim their roots while I just sank back ever deeper into my seat. All this excitement over ethnicity stemmed, I uneasily sensed, from a past in which their ancestors had been trampled upon by my ancestors, or at least by people who looked very much like them. In addition, it had begun to seem almost un-American not to have some sort of hyphen at hand, linking one to more venerable times and locales.

4   But the truth is I was raised with none. We'd eaten ethnic foods in my childhood home, but these were all borrowed, like the pasties, or Cornish meat pies, my father had picked up from his fellow miners in Butte, Montana. If my mother had one rule, it was militant ecumenism in all matters of food and experience. "Try new things," she would say, meaning anything from sweetbreads to clams, with an emphasis on the "new."

5   As a child, I briefly nourished a craving for tradition and roots. I immersed myself in the works of Sir Walter Scott. I pretended to believe that the bagpipe was a musical instrument. I was fascinated to learn from my grandmother that we were descended from certain Highland clans and longed for a pleated skirt in one of their distinctive tartans.

6   But in Ivanhoe, it was the dark-eyed "Jewess" Rebecca I identified with, not the flaxen-haired bimbo Rowena. As for clans: Why not call them "tribes," those bands of half-clad peasants and warriors whose idea of cuisine was stuffed sheep gut washed down with whisky? And then in my early teens I was stung by Disraeli's remark to the effect that his ancestors had been leading orderly, literate lives when my ancestors were still rampaging through the highlands daubing themselves with blue paint.

7   Motherhood put the screws on me, ethnicity-wise. I had hoped that by marrying a man of Eastern European-Jewish ancestry I would acquire for my descendants the ethnic genes that my own forebears so sadly lacked. At one point, I even subjected the children to a Passover seder of my own design, which included a little talk about the flight from Egypt and its relevance to modern social issues. But the kids insisted on buttering their matzohs and snickering through my talk. "Give me a break, Mom," the older one said. "You don't even believe in God."

8   After the tiny pagans had been put to bed, I sat down to brood over Elijah's wine. What had I been thinking? The kids knew that their Jewish grandparents were secular folks who didn't hold seders themselves. And if ethnicity eluded me, how could I expect it to take root in my children, who are not only Scottish-English-Irish, but Hungarian-Polish-Russian to boot?

9   But, then, on the fumes of Manischewitz, a great insight took form in my mind. It was true, as the kids said, that I didn't "believe in God." But this could be taken as something very different from an accusation — a reminder of a genuine heritage. My parents had not believed

in God either, nor had my grandparents or any other progenitors going back to the great-great level. They had become disillusioned with Christianity generations ago — just as, on the in-law side, my children's other ancestors had shaken off their Orthodox Judaism. This insight did not exactly furnish me with an "identity," but it was at least something to work with: we are the kind of people, I realized — whatever our distant ancestors' religions — who do not believe, who do not carry on traditions, who do not do things just because someone has done them before.

10   The epiphany went on: I recalled that my mother never introduced a procedure for cooking or cleaning by telling me, "Grandma did it this way." What did Grandma know, living in the days before vacuum cleaners and disposable toilet mops? In my parents' general view, new things were better than old, and the very fact that some ritual had been performed in the past was a good reason for abandoning it now. Because what was the past, as our forebears knew it? Nothing but poverty, superstition and grief. "Think for yourself," Dad used to say. "Always ask why."

11   In fact, this may have been the ideal cultural heritage for my particular ethnic strain — bounced as it was from the Highlands of Scotland across the sea, out to the Rockies, down into the mines and finally spewed out into high-tech, suburban America. What better philosophy, for a race of migrants, than "think for yourself"? What better maxim, for a people whose whole world was rudely inverted every 30 years or so, than "try new things"?

12   The more tradition-minded, the newly enthusiastic celebrants of Purim and Kwanzaa and Solstice, may see little point to survival if the

survivors carry no cultural freight — religion, for example, or ethnic tradition. To which I would say that skepticism, curiosity and wide-eyed ecumenical tolerance are also worthy elements of the human tradition and are at least as old as such notions as "Serbian" or "Croation," "Scottish" or "Jewish." I make no claims for my personal line of progenitors except that they remained loyal to the values that may have induced all of our ancestors, long, long ago, to climb down from the trees and make their way into the open plains.

13   A few weeks ago, I cleared my throat and asked the children, now mostly grown and fearsomely smart, whether they felt any stirrings of ethnic or religious identity, etc., which might have been, ahem, insufficiently nourished at home. "None," they said, adding firmly, "and the world would be a better place if nobody else did, either." My chest swelled with pride, as would my mother's, to know that the race of "none" marches on.

Barbara Ehrenreich was trained as a biologist and worked in the health sciences before she turned to writing. She is best known for her ambitious feminist studies and social critiques, among them *The Hearts of Men* (1983) and *Fear of Falling: The Inner Life of The Middle Class* (1989). She has won numerous awards for her work.

After You Read

Reading Journal

What "cultural baggage" do you bring with you to the United States? Has it helped or hindered your adjustment to American life? Explain.

Reading for Meaning

1. Why did Ehrenreich first answer "none" in response to the questions about her roots?

2. Paraphrase the following: "Or was I revealing a hidden ethnic chauvinism in which the Britannically derived serve as a kind of neutral standard compared with the ethnic 'others'?"

3. What did Ehrenreich hope to gain for her children by adopting the Passover tradition of her husband's Jewish family?

4. Explain the author's revelation about her own genuine tradition or identity.

Exploring Further

Debate

Argue for or against the following: The world would be a better place if parents did not nourish strong ethnic, cultural or religious identity in their children.

Timed Writing Exercise

Ehrenreich claims the sayings "think for yourself," "always ask why," and "try new things," expressed her family's values of "skepticism, curiosity and wide-eyed ecumenical tolerance." Think of an expression used in your family and the value it has for you. Describe how this value was taught and whether or not you consider it important today.

Focused Essay Topics

1. Do you agree with the author that a lack of "cultural freight" (as Ehrenreich refers to ancestral tradition and identity) is beneficial to new immigrants whose lives must be "rudely inverted," or do you think that native traditions are an asset in a new culture? Support your opinion with concrete examples. (You may want to refer to your *Reading Journal* entry when doing this essay.)

2. In Ehrenreich's formulation, the motto "think for yourself" seems to be at odds with the body of traditional values handed down from one's forbears. Must these be mutually exclusive? Use your own experience in a new culture to explore this question.

Before You Read

There is a tendency for non-Asians to define all the peoples from across the Pacific Basin as either "Japanese" or "Chinese." The article you are about to read discusses the successes and failures of assimilation of the many distinct cultures which make up the second largest immigrant group in America.

Take the following quiz. Then work in small groups to compare your answers. Read the article to see whether or not you were correct.

True or False   T   F

1. The majority of Asian Americans have settled in New York. ☐   ☐

2. Japanese Americans and Asian Indians possess the largest family incomes among all ethnic groups, including whites. ☐   ☐

3. Koreans constitute the largest Asian American ethnic group. ☐   ☐

4. Asia has replaced Europe as the leading foreign source of U.S. engineers, doctors and technical workers. ☐   ☐

5. Asian Americans are rarely victims of racial discrimination. ☐   ☐

6. Asian cultural values are seldom in conflict with American cultural values. ☐   ☐

7. Being seen as a "model minority" has helped all Asian Americans. ☐   ☐

8. Asian Americans vote more frequently than either whites or blacks. ☐   ☐

9. There are virtually no Asian Americans who suffer from devastating poverty, joblessness, and lack of hope. ☐   ☐

10. Most Asian Americans cut their ties both culturally and financially with their homelands as soon as they arrive in the U.S. ☐   ☐

Strangers in Paradise   BY HOWARD G. CHUA-EOAN

*Even as they stake claims to the American West, Asians experience
the ambivalence of assimilation and the perils of prosperity.*

1   At the western edge of America, where the continent falls into the Pacific as it follows the sun, the coast has always seemed an image of Eden, a garden of earthly delights. "There is an island called California, on the right hand of the Indies, very near the Earthly Paradise," wrote a 16th century Spanish fantasist in a novel that gave the Golden State its name. California and other stretches of the Pacific shore would become the fated and fateful destinations of adventurous journeys westward by European settlers, cowboys, miners, Forty-Niners and dreamers. There the travelers would pass, or so they hoped, from their old lives—and the Old World—into a heaven on earth. As Robert Louis Stevenson wrote in 1879 at the end of a long trip West, "At every turn we could see farther into the land and our own happy futures . . . For this was indeed our destination; this was the 'good country' we had been going to so long."

2   In spite of the seemingly inexorable European settlement of the Pacific Coast, there are strangers in the Western paradise. Other peoples too have sought the "good country," though instead of crossing the continent, they have crossed an ocean; instead of looking back to Europe, they trace their bloodlines to Asia. The profound impact they have made on the West is a case study of the changes that will sweep the nation as it gradually moves beyond the melting pot. As Asians bring vitality and a renewed sense of purpose to the region, is history repeating itself with a twist? Just as Europeans took the region from Native Americans, is the West being won all over again by Korean entrepreneurs, Japanese financiers, Indian doctors, Filipino nurses, Vietnamese restaurateurs and Chinese engineers?

3   What often passes for Asian ghettos bustle with the pride and promise of middle-class America with an exotic cast. Churches hold services in English—and Korean, Chinese and Tagalog. The curved eaves of Buddhist temples share suburbia with the flat roofs of ranch-style homes. Asian shopping malls are stocked with everything from disposable diapers to dried sea cucumbers that sell for up to $1,000 per lb. Signs in English and Spanish compete with those in the Korean Hankul alphabet and in Chinese ideograms. When Roman letters appear, they are often tricked out in the rococo accents of the Vietnamese.

4   The ties that bind the West Coast to Asia are not merely cultural but also financial. At the news of the earthquake that ravaged the San Francisco Bay area last October, Wall Street barely blinked. But in Tokyo, Manila and Hong Kong, stock markets dipped nervously. The Pacific coastland is a 20th century Asia Minor, a continent in miniature, with a diversity of mores and languages not matched anywhere else. Among those who have sunk roots are Cambodians, Thais, Filipinos, Koreans, Japanese, Indians, Vietnamese, Indochinese hill people, and Chinese from the People's Republic, Taiwan and Southeast Asia. Most hold on to vibrant links across the Pacific Basin. East may be East and West West, but in this case

the West seems more and more East as well.

5 Even as they stake their claims to the American West, Asians are encountering problems: racism, the ambivalence of assimilation, the perils of prosperity, ethnic jealousies and the sometimes dire inequities of a laissez-faire society. Asians in general are still strangers in the Western paradise, and they are keenly aware of their status.

6 Many have found success and prosperity in their new home. A decade ago, a 1½-mile strip of Bolsa Avenue between Garden Grove and Westminster in Orange County, Calif., was a ragged quilt of vacant lots and small stores, bean fields and discount emporiums. Today the stretch is as alive as payday in a port city—specifically, Saigon. Between 20,000 and 50,000 Vietnamese flock each weekend to 800 shops and restaurants, buying herbal medicine and dining out on snail-tomato-rice-noodle soup. In the mornings people may attend Buddhist ceremonies in makeshift temples; in the evenings they can applaud Elvis Phuong, who complete with skintight pants and sneer, does Presley Vietnamese-style.

7 More than 80,000 refugees have made the area, known locally as Little Saigon, the center of one of the largest Vietnamese enclaves outside Indochina. Says Frank Jao, the Vietnamese-American developer of Bolsa Avenue: "The Chinese, the Japanese, the Italians and the Jews grouped together when they came to the U.S. There seemed to be no reason why the Vietnamese wouldn't follow the same tradition."

8 Southern California is full of Asian immigrants who are doing just that. Across the intersection of Crenshaw and Olympic boulevards in Los Angeles is Koreatown, with its thousands of Korean businesses: mom-and-pop curio stores, multinational banks, tiny storefronts, gleaming glass buildings. Upwards of 300,000 Korean Americans live in or near Koreatown.

9 Some 15 miles away, near the intersection of Coldwater Canyon and Roscoe boulevards, in the San Fernando Valley working-class section of North Hollywood, Buddhist monks pray in a Thai temple pungent with incense and dominated by a 10-ft. statue of Buddha. On weekends Thai families turn the temple's parking lot into a festival straight out of Bangkok.

10 To the east of Los Angeles is Monterey Park, a city of 60,000 people, approximately half of whom are of Chinese descent. The rest of the population is 32% white and 16% Hispanic. After a Chinese-American developer placed an ad in Hong Kong and Taiwan newspapers, an explosion of real estate sales occurred in Monterey Park. Dozens of shopping centers sprouted to cater to new Chinese residents.

11 Asians fill the professions and the universities. Already Asia has replaced Europe as the leading foreign source of U.S. engineers, doctors and technical workers. The 400 Silicon Valley electronics firms owned by Asian Americans last year earned revenues of $2.5 billion. From 1975 to 1985, the number of full-time Asian faculty members in colleges throughout the U.S. nearly doubled, to 19,000. Asians make up 10% of California's population but 12.2% of the state's university enrollment. At the University of California's Berkeley campus, the proportion is 20.8%. In February the University of California named Chang-lin Tien, a Chinese American, as head of the prestigious campus. Still, Asian parents complain of quotas that limit the access of their children to the top schools.

12 With the influx from across the Pacific have come Asian trade and Asian money. New immigrants do

business with friends and relatives in their home countries, tapping into Tokyo and the expanding capital markets of Hong Kong, Taipei, Singapore and Bangkok. Healthy stakes in real estate, banking, medicine, engineering, commerce and finance give Asians in America the appearance of a gilded community. According to the latest U.S. Census, Japanese Americans and Asian Indians possessed the largest average family incomes among all ethnic groups, including whites.

13   Yet there is no pan-Asian prosperity, just as there is no such thing as an "Asian American." There are comfortably middle-class, fourth-generation Japanese Americans, and there are prospering new immigrants from Taiwan and South Korea, all driven by an admirable work ethic. There are also fragmented Filipino families headed by women, and Hmong tribesmen who know little of technology and are dependent upon public assistance.

14   "There *are* people without hope in the Asian-American community," says Michael Woo, the lone Asian member of the Los Angeles city council. It is a strange notion to those whose only awareness of Asian Americans is of whiz-kid scholars and hardworking greengrocers.

15   The record of the largest Asian ethnic group in the U.S. is ambivalent, with success stories alternating with tales of the underclass. Numbering nearly 1 million in California alone, Filipinos have found their situation complicated by the practice of pressing the Philippine immigration level—currently close to 50,000 a year—to the fullest in order to bring along as many relatives as possible, including those who have little education and work experience.

16   Furthermore, prosperous Asian-American families are not immune to fragmentation, even among the Koreans, who are perhaps the most entrepreneurial of the new immigrants. Long hours at the store and the office have taken their toll. The all-consuming work ethic has robbed some Korean youths of parental supervision and, by extension, a sense of identity. Says Youngbin Kim, program coordinator for the Korean Youth Center in Los Angeles: "We see a lot of problems with identity and self-esteem. These kids look Korean, but they don't want to be Korean. They only sense that they are Asian, and then they join Asian gangs." In fact, gangs of Korean teenagers from affluent homes have replaced an earlier generation of Korean gangs that dealt mainly with turf protection and peaked in the mid-80's. The new gangs focus on criminal activity and are made up of Filipinos and Vietnamese as well.

17   The most troubled Asian Americans are the ones from Indochina. The 40,000 Cambodians in Southern California have settled primarily in one area, Long Beach, 20 miles south of downtown Los Angeles. They have few marketable skills and thus enter the work force at the lowest levels. Often they have only the most basic of business instincts—including imitation. In one of the quirks of assimilation, many Cambodians in Southern California have gone into the doughnut business, following the lead of a countryman whose success at the trade was widely publicized; some 500 doughnut shops in Los Angeles County are owned or operated by Cambodians.

18   Survivors of a genocidal war, Cambodians carry traumatic psychological burdens. Sometimes it seems as if the war has quite literally followed them across the sea. In the municipal cemetery in Stockton, Calif., a few graves are marked by odd, poignant gifts: plastic dolls, balloons, soft-drink cans, plates of fruit,

piles of pennies. They are the offerings of bereaved Cambodian parents to the spirits of four children who were murdered in last year's rampage by a mentally deranged drifter at the city's Cleveland elementary school. Though Stockton police maintain that the episode was not racially motivated, the Indochinese in California's Central Valley believe otherwise. Almost a year before the shooting, school officials had to paint over anti-Asian graffiti, including signs that said GOOKS GO HOME. Fights break out almost daily between Cambodian and Hispanic students at one high school. Says Sarmon Sor: "My daughter was shot, my son stabbed. I used to be happy here. Now all I do is worry. I worry all the time."

19   Whatever the cause, racism in one form or another, subtle or blatantly obvious, plagues many Asian Americans. Sometimes strong biases brought over by the immigrants themselves—including racial prejudice, clannishness and a reluctance to make problems public—hamper their assimilation into the majority. More often, however, Asians are the victims of discrimination. The very visible success of some Asian immigrants and the power of Asian finance have triggered a backlash.

20   In Los Angeles, as in other cities across the U.S., tension has arisen between Korean Americans and members of the black community, who resent the influx of "foreign" businesses that take money out of their neighborhoods. In a wider context, even though Canadians until recently owned more of California than Japanese did, it is the latter who are looked upon as encroachers. "I've heard more anti-Japanese sentiment in working-class bars than I can remember," says Richard Kjeldsen, a University of Southern California financial specialist of the Pacific Rim. Japan bashing easily becomes Asian bashing. The most famous case is the 1982 murder of Chinese American Vincent Chin by Detroit autoworkers who thought he was Japanese. As late as 1985 and 1986, violence against Asians jumped 50% in Los Angeles County. Says Henry Der of Chinese for Affirmative Action: "We're still vulnerable because of what we look like."

21   While Asians are often thoroughly assimilated into American culture after a generation, many say that no matter how integrated they become, they will never be considered bona fide Americans because of an "otherness" factor based entirely on race. The claims of an American meritocracy also ring hollow to some skilled immigrants. Says Dr. Jagjit Sehdeva, a member of the Los Angeles human-relations commission: "It is almost impossible for medical graduates from India to find residency positions in hospitals here. Many wind up in lower-paying jobs as lab technicians or hospital orderlies." Says Dr. Stanley Sue, director of the National Research Center on Asian American Mental Health: "Some people want you to be American, but then they treat you differently. Why, then, would you want to assimilate?"

22   Fitting in can be a traumatic, sometimes infuriating experience. Amy Tan, author of the best-selling novel *The Joy Luck Club*, recalls being ashamed that her homelife was not quite that of her white peers. "The Chinese food was wonderful when it was family," she remembers. "But when my friends came over, I was embarrassed." Selling movie projects in Hollywood, director Wayne Wang (*Chan Is Missing, Eat a Bowl of Tea*) finds some studio executives "patronizing or confused." Says he: "If you speak English with a French accent, they say, 'That's cute.' But if you speak it with a

Chinese accent, people say, 'That's awful. He's killing our language.'"

23 Asians also sense that a "glass ceiling" prevents them from rising to the top ranks in corporate America. To the extent that U.S. executives often equate leadership with assertiveness, Asians' traditional reticence and self-effacement have proved detrimental to corporate advancement. "We mind our own business and keep our noses to the grindstone," says David Lam, head of Expert Edge Technology in Palo Alto, Calif. "Doing a good job has turned into a bad thing." Now that Asians see themselves as players, they want to be a part of the corporate game. Says Harry Kitano, professor of social welfare at the University of California, Los Angeles: "Twenty or 30 years ago, we didn't expect to be promoted. A lot of people suffered in silence."

24 The retreat into silence also hampered the immigrants' quest for political influence. "All the things that are required in Western politics go against Asian culture," says Judy Chu, mayor pro tempore of Monterey Park. Asian Americans turn out at the voting booth even less frequently than whites or blacks: a 1986 study of Southern California voters showed that only 30% of eligible Asian voters registered, compared with 80% of whites.

25 Yet when Asians try out political roles, the "otherness" factor again comes into play. The family of Lon Hatamiya, a Japanese-American attorney, has lived in the agricultural region around Sacramento for more than 80 years. But when Hatamiya decided to run in next June's primary for a seat in California's 120-member state legislature, more voters seemed to regard him as an alien. "They look at us as if we're recent immigrants," he says. No one seemed to notice that the local roots of his white opponent do not go back as far as those of the Hatamiya clan.

26 Asians have made impressive forays into California politics. Since 1975, California's secretary of state has been March Fong Eu, a Chinese American. Two of the state's Congressmen are Norman Mineta and Robert Matsui, Japanese Americans. Another Japanese American, the noted philologist and educator S.I. Hayakawa, has served as U.S. Senator.

27 Still, the history of Asian settlement on the West Coast has been one of displacement and suppression. After completing the transcontinental railway in the 19th century, Chinese immigrants were rewarded with race riots, demagoguery and the Immigration Exclusion Act of 1882, which cut off the Chinese influx. Local hostility forced Asian Indians out of Washington State in 1907. During World War II, Japanese Americans were forced to liquidate their assets and relocate to detention camps, taking only the belongings they could carry by hand; a similar fate did not befall residents of German or Italian ancestry.

28 Today social and political integration remains fraught with ambiguity. Seen as a "model minority" rather than as a group of separate communities requiring specific kinds of help, Asian Americans are often shut out of affirmative-action programs. Asian Americans say the label is used to taunt blacks and Hispanics, that it implies, "The Asians have made it, so why can't you?" Says Reed Ueda, a Japanese-American professor of history at Tufts University in Massachusetts: "It's a way of manipulating other minorities. It tends to isolate Asians and brings resentment." Unfortunately, the typical response from Asian Americans to being held up as an example is to denigrate their own very real strengths—industriousness, perseverance, sacrifice—making it almost shameful for them to try to excel. Says Ueda: "It gets to the point where a lot of Asian-American leaders don't like to focus on success."

29   In the 16th century Chinese comic novel *Journey to the West*, a motley group of pilgrims, at the end of a magical, sometimes terrifying quest, arrives at the Western Paradise of Buddha to receive sacred books imparting enlightenment. To their chagrin, they discover that in order to secure their prize, they must grease the palms of Buddha's disciples. Buddha himself is rather condescending. Paradise has turned out to be less than perfect and more than a little disconcerting. What was it they set out to find, and why is it yet to be found? Even as their numbers and their influence expand, Asian Americans are pondering those very questions.

Howard E. Chua-Eoan's article was part of a cover story that appeared in *Time* magazine in 1990.

After You Read

Reading Journal

Dr. Stanley Sue, director of the National Research Center on Asian American Mental Health, is quoted as saying, "Some people want you to be American, but then they treat you differently. Why, then would you want to assimilate?" Comment on this dilemma, using your own experience as an ethnic American or non-native speaker of English.

Reading for Meaning

1. What does the author of this article mean when he says Asians are experiencing "the ambivalence of assimilation" and "the perils of prosperity"? Give specific examples to back up your answer.

2. Why does the author claim in paragraph 13 that "there is no such thing as an 'Asian American'"?

3. Why do Asian immigrants often feel a sense of "otherness," even after being thoroughly assimilated into American culture? In what areas of life is this particularly evident?

4. Find in the reading several examples of Asians who are stuck in the underclass and the reasons the author cites for this.

Exploring Further

Group Presentation

Do further research on one of the many Asian groups mentioned in the article. Assign each group member a different area such as (customs, clothing, food, religion, or politics) to research, write up and present to the class.

Timed Writing Exercise

In recent years, racial conflict between Korean Americans and African Americans has been particularly intense. This conflict has arisen, at least in part, from cross-cultural misunderstanding. African Americans interpret Korean reserve as rudeness. In your opinion, should American immigrants try harder to fit into the mainstream culture and its expectations for behavior? Why or why not?

Focused Essay Topics

1. According to the author, "There is no such thing as an Asian American." Is your native group lumped in or confused with a larger cultural group? (e.g., Hispanic for all Spanish-speaking groups) What characteristics particular to your group are lost as a result?

2. The article speaks about the drawbacks for Asian Americans of being labeled a "model minority." Write a personal essay in which you describe a time where you didn't live up to your cultural group's expectations. Describe the conflict and whether or not you were able to resolve it.

Before You Read

1. Examine the pictures below. Each represents a popular "look" worn by Americans at one time or another. Describe each one, paying particular attention to details of clothing, make-up and hair. What statement is the wearer trying to make?

2. Describe a manner of dress, personal appearance or habit that was in style when you were growing up. What did this represent to you and the youth culture of your day? Did you conform to this style or reject it? Why?

Hair
MALCOLM X

1   Shorty soon decided that my hair was finally long enough to be conked. He had promised to school me in how to beat the barbershops' three- and four-dollar price by making up congolene, and then conking ourselves.

2   I took the little list of ingredients he had printed out for me, and went to a grocery store, where I got a can of Red Devil lye, two eggs, and two medium-sized white potatoes. Then at a drugstore near the poolroom, I asked for a large jar of vaseline, a large bar of soap, a large-toothed comb and a fine-toothed comb, one of those rubber hoses with a metal spray-head, a rubber apron and a pair of gloves.

3   "Going to lay on that first conk?" the drugstore man asked me. I proudly told him, grinning, "Right!"

4   Shorty paid six dollars a week for a room in his cousin's shabby apartment. His cousin wasn't at home. "It's like the pad's mine, he spends so much time with his woman," Shorty said, "Now, you watch me—"

5   He peeled the potatoes and thin-sliced them into a quart-sized Mason fruit jar, then started stirring them with a wooden spoon as he gradually poured in a little over half the can of lye. "Never use a metal spoon; the lye will turn it black," he told me.

6   A jelly-like, starchy-looking glop resulted from the lye and potatoes, and Shorty broke in the two eggs, stirring real fast—his own conk and dark face bent down close. The congolene turned pale-yellowish. "Feel the jar," Shorty said. I cupped my hand against the outside, and snatched it away. "Damn right, it's hot, that's the lye," he said. "So you know it's going to burn when I comb it in—it burns *bad*. But the longer you can stand it, the straighter the hair."

7   He made me sit down, and he tied the string of the new rubber apron tightly around my neck, and combed up my bush of hair. Then, from the big vaseline jar, he took a handful and massaged it hard all through my hair and into the scalp. He also thickly vaselined my neck, ears and forehead. "When I get to washing out your head, be sure to tell me anywhere you feel any little stinging," Shorty warned me, washing his hands, then pulling on the rubber gloves, and tying on his own rubber apron. "You always got to remember that any congolene left in burns a sore into your head."

8   The congolene just felt warm when Shorty started combing it in. But then my head caught fire.

9   I gritted my teeth and tried to pull the sides of the kitchen table together. The comb felt as if it was raking my skin off.

10   My eyes watered, my nose was running. I couldn't stand it any longer; I bolted to the washbasin. I was cursing Shorty with every name I could think of when he got the spray going and started soap-lathering my head.

11   He lathered and spray-rinsed, lathered and spray-rinsed, maybe ten or twelve times, each time gradually closing the hot-water faucet, until the rinse was cold, and that helped some.

12   "You feel any stinging spots?"

13   "No," I managed to say. My knees were trembling.

14   "Sit back down, then. I think we got it all out okay."

15   The flame came back as Shorty, with a thick towel, started drying my head, rubbing hard. "*Easy, man, easy!*" I kept shouting.

16   "The first time's always worst. You get used to it better before long. You took it real good, homeboy. You got a good conk."

17   When Shorty let me stand up and see in the mirror, my hair hung down in limp, damp strings. My scalp still flamed, but not as badly; I could bear it. He draped the towel around my shoulders, over my rubber apron, and began again vaselining my hair.

18   I could feel him combing, straight back, first the big comb, then the fine-tooth one.

19   Then, he was using a razor, very delicately, on the back of my neck. Then, finally, shaping the sideburns.

20   My first view in the mirror blotted out the hurting. I'd seen some pretty conks, but when it's the first time, on your *own* head, the transformation, after the lifetime of kinks, is staggering.

21   The mirror reflected Shorty behind me. We both were grinning and sweating. And on top of my head was this thick, smooth sheen of shining red hair—real red—as straight as any white man's.

22   How ridiculous I was! Stupid enough to stand there simply lost in admiration of my hair now looking "white," reflected in the mirror in Shorty's room. I vowed that I'd never again be without a conk, and I never was for many years.

23   This was my first really big step toward self-degradation: when I endured all of that pain, literally burning my flesh to have it look like a white man's hair. I had joined that multitude of Negro men and women in America who are brainwashed into believing that the black people are "inferior"—and white people "superior"—that they will even violate and mutilate their God-created bodies to try to look "pretty" by white standards.

Malcolm X - Malcolm Little lived a life of street crime. He served six years in prison, during which he educated himself to become one of the most influential leaders of the civil rights movement of the 1960s. His life and his assassination in 1965 were portrayed in Spike Lee's recent film, *Malcolm X*. this excerpt is taken from *The Autobiography of Malcolm X* (1964), written in collaboration with Alex Haley.

After You Read

Reading Journal

Can you imagine tolerating intense pain in order to conform to a certain standard of beauty? Why or why not?

Reading for Meaning

1. What is a conk?

2. Why does Malcolm X say "my first view in the mirror blotted out the hurting"?

3. Why does the author describe the conking process in such detail? Which details do you find most effective and why?

Exploring Further

Research Project

In contrast to Malcolm X's experience, consider how many aspects of African-American culture (i.e., in the arts, music and style) have become part of mainstream contemporary American culture. Find examples in magazines and newspapers, and present your findings to the class.

Timed Writing Exercise

In the Black Power movement of the 1960's and 1970's, the popular motto, "Black is Beautiful" arose in reaction to the commonly accepted idea that anyone who looked different from the Caucasian "ideal" was unattractive. Is there an "ideal" form of beauty in your culture? If so, describe it. Then comment on whether or not those who do not conform to this ideal are devalued by the culture.

Focused Essay Topics

1. Malcolm X describes the step-by-step process of applying burning lye to his scalp and hair. Does he mean us to understand this as a folly of youth and an understandable need to conform, or as something more? Explain.

2. Malcolm X talks about how African Americans are "brainwashed" into accepting white standards of beauty. How does a culture accomplish this brainwashing? What other examples of this process can you point to in today's society?

Before You Read

1. Freewrite on the following: What comes to mind when you think of the term "American Indian"?

2. Get together in small groups to share your writing. As you listen to each other, try to identify the source(s) of your impressions. Ask yourselves the following questions: Has any member of the group actually met/known a Native American? Or, like many Americans, are your impressions based on film and TV images? How accurate do you think these are? For example, what stereotypes emerge from the group's writing? Are they primarily positive or negative? What consequences do you believe arise for Native Americans as a result of these stereotypes?

Blue Winds Dancing   THOMAS S. WHITECLOUD

1   There is a moon out tonight. Moon and stars and clouds tipped with moonlight. And there is a fall wind blowing in my heart. Ever since this evening, when against a fading sky I saw geese wedge southward. They were going home. . . . Now I try to study, but against the pages I see them again, driving southward. Going home.

2   Across the valley there are heavy mountains holding up the night sky, and beyond the mountains there is home. Home, and peace, and the beat of drums, and blue winds dancing over snow fields. The Indian lodge will fill with my people, and our gods will come and sit among them. I should be there then. I should be at home.

3   But home is beyond the mountains, and I am here. Here where fall hides in the valleys and winter never comes down from the mountains. Here where all in the trees grow in rows; the palms stand stiffly by the roadsides, and the groves the orange trees line in military rows and endlessly bear fruit. Beautiful, yes; there is always beauty in order, in rows of growing things! But it is the beauty of captivity. A pine fighting for existence on a windy knoll is much more beautiful.

4   In my Wisconsin, the leaves change before the snows come. In the air there is the smell of wild rice and venison cooking; and when the winds come whispering through the forests, they carry the smell of rotting leaves. In the evenings, the loon calls, lonely; and birds sing their last songs before leaving. Bears dig roots and eat late fall berries, fattening for their long winter sleep. Later, when the first snows fall, one awakens in the morning to find the world white and beautiful and clean. Then one can look back over his trail and see the tracks following. In the woods

there are tracks of deer and snowshoe rabbits and long streaks where partridges slide to alight. Chipmunks make tiny footprints on the limbs; and one can hear squirrels busy in hollow trees, sorting acorns. Soft lake waves wash the shores, and sunsets burst each evening over the lakes and make them look as if they were afire.

5   That land which is my home! Beautiful, calm—where there is no hurry to get anywhere, no driving to keep up in a race that knows no ending and no goal. No classes where men talk and talk, and then stop now and then to hear their own words come back to them from the students. No constant peering into the maelstrom[1] of one's mind; no worries about grades and honors; no hysterical preparing for life until that life is half over; no anxiety about one's place in the thing they call Society.

6   I hear again the ring of axes in deep woods, the crunch of snow beneath my feet. I feel again the smooth velvet of ghost-birch bark. I hear the rhythm of the drums. . . . I am tired. I am weary of trying to keep up this bluff of being civilized. Being civilized means trying to do everything you don't want to, never doing anything you want to. It means dancing to the strings of custom and tradition; it means living in houses and never knowing or caring who is next door. These civilized white men want us to be like them—always dissatisfied, getting a hill and wanting a mountain.

7   Then again, maybe I am not tired. Maybe I'm licked. Maybe I am just not smart enough to grasp these things that go to make up civilization. Maybe I am just too lazy to think hard enough to keep up.

8   Still, I know my people have many things that civilization has taken from the whites. They know how to give, how to tear one's piece of meat in two and share it with one's brother. They know how to sing—how to make each man his own songs and sing them; for their music they do not have to listen to other men singing over a radio. They know how to make things with their hands, how to shape beads into design and make a thing of beauty from a piece of birch bark.

9   But we are inferior. It is terrible to have to feel inferior, to have to read reports of intelligence tests and learn that one's race is behind. It is terrible to sit in classes and hear men tell you that your people worship sticks of wood—that your gods are all false, that the Manitou[2] forgot your people and did not write them a book.

10   I am tired. I want to walk again among the ghost-birches. I want to see the leaves turn in autumn, the smoke rise from the lodge-houses, and to feel the blue winds. I want to hear the drums; I want to hear the drums and feel the blue whispering winds.

11   There is a train wailing into the night. The trains go across the mountains. It would be easy to catch a freight. They will say he has gone back to the blanket; I don't care. The dance at Christmas. . . .

12   A bunch of bums warming at a tiny fire talk politics and women and joke about the Relief and the WPA[3] and smoke cigarettes. These men in caps and overcoats and dirty overalls living on the outskirts of civilization

---

[1] Maelstrom (māl' strəm): whirlpool.
[2] Manitou: Great Spirit.
[3] Relief . . . WPA: The WPA or Works Projects Administration was a Government agency organized in 1935 and designed to create jobs in order to relieve national unemployment.

are free, but they pay the price of being free in civilization. They are out-casts. I remember a sociology professor lecturing on adjustment to soci-ety; hobos and prostitutes and criminals are individuals who never adjusted, he said. He could learn a lot if he came and listened to a bunch of bums talk. He would learn that work and a woman and a place to hang his hat are all the ordinary man wants. These are all he wants, but other men are not content to let him want only these. He must be taught to want radios and automobiles and a new suit every spring. Progress would stop if he did not want these things. I listen to hear if there is any talk of communism or socialism in the hobo jungles. There is none. At best there is a sort of disgusted philosophy about life. They seem to think there should be a better distribution of wealth, or more work, or something. But they are not rabid about it. The radicals live in the cities.

13   I find a fellow headed for Albuquerque, and talk road-talk with him. "It is hard to ride fruit cars. Bums break in. Better to wait for a cattle car going back to the Middle West, and ride that." We catch the next east-bound and walk the tops until we find a cattle car. Inside, we crouch near the forward wall, huddle, and try to sleep. I feel peaceful and content at last. I am going home. The cattle car rocks. I sleep.

14   Morning and the desert. Noon and the Salton Sea, lying more lifeless than a mirage under a somber sun in a pale sky. Skeleton mountains rearing on the skyline, thrusting out of the desert floor, all rock and shadow and edges. Desert. Good country for an Indian reservation. . . .

15   Yuma and the muddy Colorado. Night again, and I wait shivering for the dawn.

16   Phoenix. Pima country. Mountains that look like cardboard sets on a forgotten stage. Tucson. Papago country. Giant cacti that look like petri-fied hitchhikers along the highways. Apache country. At El Paso my road-buddy decides to go on to Houston. I leave him and head north to the mesa[4] country. Las Cruces and the terrible Organ Mountains, jagged peaks that instill fear and wondering. Albuquerque. Pueblos along the Rio Grande. On the boardwalk there are some Indian women in colored sashes selling bits of pottery. The stone age offering its art to the twenti-eth century. They hold up a piece and fix the tourists with black eyes until, embarrassed, he buys or turns away. I feel suddenly angry that my people should have to do such things for a living. . . .

17   Santa Fe trains are fast, and they keep them pretty clean of bums. I decide to hurry and ride passenger coal tenders. Hide in the dark, judge the speed of the train as it leaves, and then dash out, and catch it. I hug the cold steel wall of the tender and think of the roaring fire in the engine ahead and of the passengers back in the dining car reading their papers over hot coffee. Beneath me there is a blur of rails. Death would come quick if my hands should freeze and I fall. Up over the Sangre De Cristo range, around cliffs and through canyons to Denver. Bitter cold here, and I must watch out for Denver Bob. He is a railroad bull who has thrown bums from fast freights. I miss him. It is too cold, I suppose. On north to the Sioux country.

18   Small towns lit for the coming Christmas. On the streets of one I see a beam-shouldered young farmer gazing into a window filled with shiny silver

4 Mesa (mā'sə): level-topped hill bounded wholly or in part by steep rock walls.

toasters. He is tall and wears a blue shirt, buttoned, with no tie. His young wife by his side looks at him hopefully. He wants decorations for his place to hang his hat to please his woman. . . .

19   Northward again. Minnesota, and great white fields of snow; frozen lakes and dawn running into dusk without noon. Long forests wearing white. Bitter cold, and one night the northern lights. I am nearing home.

20   I reach Woodruff at midnight. Suddenly I am afraid, now that I am but twenty miles from home. Afraid of what my father will say, afraid of being looked on as a stranger by my own people. I sit by a fire and think about myself and all other young Indians. We just don't seem to fit in anywhere—certainly not among the whites, and not among the older people. I think again about the learned sociology professor and his professing. So many things seem to be clear now that I am away from school and do not have to worry about some man's opinions of my ideas. It is easy to think while looking at dancing flames.

21   Morning, I spend the day cleaning up and buying some presents for my family with what is left of my money. Nothing much, but a gift is a gift, if a man buys it with his last quarter. I wait until evening, then start up the track toward home.

22   Christmas Eve comes in on a north wind. Snow clouds hang over the pines, and the night comes early. Walking along the railroad bed, I feel the calm peace of snowbound forests on either side of me. I take my time; I am back in a world where time does not mean so much now. I am alone; alone but not nearly so lonely as I was back on the campus at school. Those are never lonely who love the snow and the pines, never lonely when the pines are wearing white shawls and snow crunches coldly underfoot. In the woods I know there are the tracks of deer and rabbit; I know that if I leave the rails and go into the woods, I shall find them. I walk along feeling glad because my legs are light and my feet seem to know that they are home. A deer comes out of the woods just ahead of me and stands silhouetted on the rails. The North, I feel, has welcomed me home. I watch him and am glad that I do not wish for a gun. He goes into the woods quietly, leaving only the design of his tracks in the snow. I walk on. Now and then I pass a field, white under the night sky, with houses at the far end. Smoke comes from thecchimneys of the houses, and I try to tell what sort of wood each is burning by the smoke; some burn pine, others aspen, others tamarack. There is one from which comes black coal smoke that rises lazily and drifts out over the tops of the trees. I like to watch houses and try to imagine what might be happening in them.

23   Just as a light snow begins to fall, I cross the reservation boundary; somehow it seems as though I have stepped into another world. Deep woods in a white-and-black winter night. A faint trail leading to the village.

24   The railroad on which I stand comes from a city sprawled by a lake—a city with a million people who walk around without seeing one another; a city sucking the life from all the country around; a city with stores and police and intellectuals and criminals and movies and apartment houses; a city with its politics and libraries and zoos.

25   Laughing, I go into the woods. As I cross a frozen lake, I begin to hear the drums. Soft in the night the drums beat. It is like the pulse beat of the

world. The white line of the lake ends at a black forest, and above the trees the blue winds are dancing.

26 I come to the outlying houses of the village. Simple box houses, etched black in the night. From one or two windows soft lamplight falls on the snow. Christmas here, too, but it does not mean much; not much in the way of parties and presents. Joe Sky will get drunk. Alex Bodidash will buy his children red mittens and a new sled. Alex is a Carlisle man[5] and tries to keep his home up to white standards. White standards. Funny that my people should be ever falling farther behind. The more they try to imitate whites, the more tragic the result. Yet they want us to be imitation white men. About all we imitate well are their vices.

27 The village is not a sight to instill pride, yet I am not ashamed; one can never be ashamed of his own people when he knows they have dreams as beautiful as white snow on a tall pine.

28 Father and my brother and sister are seated around the table as I walk in. Father stares at me for a moment; then I am in his arms, crying on his shoulder. I give them the presents I have brought, and my throat tightens as I watch my sister save carefully bits of red string from the packages. I hide my feelings by wrestling with my brother when he strikes my shoulder in token of affection. Father looks at me, and I know he has many questions, but he seems to know why I have come. He tells me to go on alone to the lodge, and he will follow.

29 I walk along the trail to the lodge, watching the northern lights forming in the heavens. White waving ribbons that seem to pulsate with the rhythm of the drums. Clean snow creaks beneath my feet, and a soft wind sighs through the trees, singing to me. Everything seems to say, "Be happy! You are home now—you are free. You are among friends—we are your friends; we, the trees, and the snow, and the lights." I follow the trail to the lodge. My feet are light, my heart seems to sing to the music, and I hold my head high. Across white snow fields blue winds are dancing.

30 Before the lodge door I stop, afraid. I wonder if my people will remember me. I wonder— "Am I Indian, or am I white?" I stand before the door a long time. I hear the ice groan on the lake, and remember the story of the old woman who is under the ice, trying to get out, so she can punish some runaway lovers. I think to myself, "If I am white, I will not believe that story; if I am Indian, I will know that there is an old woman under the ice." I listen for a while, and I know that there is an old woman under the ice. I look again at the lights and go in.

31 Inside the lodge there are many Indians. Some sit on benches around the walls; others dance in the center of the floor around a drum. Nobody seems to notice me. It seems as though I were among a people I have never seen before. Heavy women with long black hair. Women with children on their knees—small children that watch with intent black eyes the movements of the dancers, whose small faces are solemn and serene. The faces of the old people are serene, too, and their eyes are merry and bright. I look at the old men. Straight, dressed in dark trousers and beaded velvet vests, wearing soft moccasins. Dark, lined faces intent on the music. I wonder if I am at all like them. They dance on, lifting their feet to

---

5 Carlisle man: graduate of the Carlisle School in Pennsylvania, the first reservation school, established by the Government in 1879.

the rhythm of the drums, swaying lightly, looking upward. I look at their eyes and am startled at the rapt attention to the rhythm of the music.

32   The dance stops. The men walk back to the walls and talk in low tones or with their hands. There is little conversation, yet everyone seems to be sharing some secret. A woman looks at a small boy wandering away, and he comes back to her.

33   Strange, I think, and then remember. These people are not sharing words—they are sharing a mood. Everyone is happy. I am so used to white people that it seems strange so many people could be together without someone talking. These Indians are happy because they are together, and because the night is beautiful outside, and the music is beautiful. I try hard to forget school and white people, and be one of these—my people. I try to forget everything but the night, and it is a part of me; that I am one with my people and we are all a part of something universal. I watch eyes and see now that the old people are speaking to me. They nod slightly, imperceptibly, and their eyes laugh into mine. I look around the room. All the eyes are friendly; they all laugh. No one questions my being here. The drums begin to beat again, and I catch the invitation in the eyes of the old men. My feet begin to lift to the rhythm, and I look out beyond the walls into the night and see the lights. I am happy. It is beautiful. I am home.

Thomas Whitecloud, M.D. was born in New York City but grew up on the Lac du Flambeau Chippewa Reservation in Wisconsin. He was a physician and helped to establish The American Association of Indian Physicians. He also wrote poetry throughout his life. This autobiographical essay won first prize in a college essay contest in 1938.

After You Read

Reading Journal

Now that you have read Whitecloud's story, have you changed your mind about any of the notions you held previously about Native Americans? Be specific. (Look back at your pre-reading ideas.)

Reading for Meaning

1. Compare Whitecloud's observations and images of his experience as a college student and those of his home in the Lac du Flambeau Chippewa Reservation in Wisconsin. How are the two sets of ideas in conflict?

2. What is Whitecloud saying about white men and white society? Find specific examples in the text.

3. When Whitecloud returns home to the lodge he says, "Everything seems to say 'Be happy'" (paragraph 29) What exactly is there in his native American culture that he finds so reassuring and joyous?

Exploring Further

Research Project

With a partner, research a Native American tribe, if possible, one that is native to your region. Prepare a short (one to three page) paper on major aspects of their culture and history to share with the class.

Timed Writing Exercise

Whitecloud focuses upon several aspects of white majority culture that he finds at odds with the native American experience and world view. In your writing, pinpoint an aspect of American culture that you have had difficulty adjusting to and explain.

Focused Essay Topics

1. Using the lists you compiled in question 1 of *Reading for Meaning*, write a narrative essay entitled "Going Home." Present at least three major differences between your native ethnic culture and mainstream American culture and what effect they would have on you.

2. Whitecloud, like most ethnic minority members, expresses pride in his heritage and tradition. Yet this pride is tempered by the shame he has been made to feel as an "inferior white." Using Whitecloud's story as a point of departure, discuss whether or not immigrants from your native cultural group have experienced a similar feeling of inadequacy when measured against the mainstream culture.

EXTENDING THE CONTEXT

> These questions are designed for further discussion or essay writing. Your responses should reflect the thinking, reading and writing you have done on the unit topic thus far.

1. Do a library search or ask your instructor for suggestions for a short story, poem or autobiographical essay written by an American of your native cultural background. Write an essay comparing/contrasting the author's experience with your own.

2. Helen Keller once said, "the highest result of education is tolerance." Examine a prejudice you had about someone whose cultural background and beliefs were different from your own which changed as a result of your knowing more about him/her.

3. What major literary work from your native culture do you think ought to be included in an American multicultural curriculum? How would it benefit American students?

4. There is great controversy surrounding the issue of bilingual education in America, particularly among the Spanish speaking population. Supporters say that children learn better when they are taught at least partially in their native language. Critics contend that since the official language of the United States is English, we are doing a disservice to our children not to require standard English fluency. Which side do you feel is right? Use your own experience as a guide.

5. Imagine a panel discussion on the value of stressing multicultural awareness whose participants were Malcolm X, Barbara Ehrenreich and Heather MacDonald. How do you think each would respond? Write an essay in which you summarize each position and then present your own opinion on the matter.

6. In his essay, *The Disuniting of America: Reflections on a Multicultural Society*, historian Arthur Schlesinger, Jr. writes, "Watching ethnic conflict tear one nation after another apart, one cannot look with complacency at proposals to divide the United States into distinct and immutable ethnic and racial communities, each taught to cherish its own apartness from the rest. One wonders: Will the center hold or will the melting pot give way to the Tower of Babel?" What is your opinion? (Use your native country or another country whose ethnic or religious diversity has caused conflict as support for your argument.)

7. In "Blue Winds Dancing," much of Thomas Whitecloud's ambivalence about his cultural identity arose as a result of his white education. How would Robert Lake ("An Indian Father's Plea") counsel Whitecloud? Write an imaginary dialogue in which Whitecloud presents his problem and Lake proposes a solution.

VIDEO SUGGESTIONS

The video selections are offered as suggestions for viewing in or out of class to enrich the unit topic.

America (PBS Series)   *The Joy Luck Club*
Hester Street   *Jungle Fever*
Do the Right Thing   *Straight out of Brooklyn*
Avalon   *Bronx Tale*
Far & Away   *Roots*
Dances with Wolves   *Green Card*
Black Robe

Unit Four

DEFINING GENDER: DIFFERENT BUT EQUAL

BARBARA KRUGER, *Untitled (We don't need another hero)*

Short Takes

Women have served all these centuries as looking-glasses possessing the power of reflecting the figure of man at twice its natural size.

Virginia Woolf

In our civilization, men are afraid that they will not be men enough and women are afraid that they might be considered only women.

Theodor Reik

Men build bridges and throw railroads across deserts, and yet they contend successfully that the job of sewing on a button is beyond them.

Heywood Broun

American women: How they mortify the flesh in order to make it appetizing! Their beauty is a vast industry, their enduring allure a discipline which nuns or athletes might find excessive.

Malcolm Muggeridge

A man is as old as he feels, a woman as old as she looks.

Proverb

Whatever women do they must do twice as well as men to be thought half as good. Luckily this is not difficult.

Charlotte Whitton

The allurement that women hold out to men is precisely the allurement that Cape Hatteras holds out to sailors: they are enormously dangerous and hence enormously fascinating.

H.L. Mencken

SUGGESTIONS FOR USING SHORT TAKES:

- Respond in writing to one of the quotations above. Then get together in groups and share what you have written.
- Work with a partner, small group or the entire class to discuss one or more quotations. You may want to agree, disagree, or compare it to similar expressions or sayings in your native language.

INTRODUCTION – DEFINING GENDER: DIFFERENT BUT EQUAL

Perhaps the greatest change in American society over the past fifty years is the change in women's lives, the relationship between the sexes, and by extension, the nature of the family.

The feminist, or women's liberation movement of the 1960s and 1970s is principally responsible for these changes, picking up where the first wave, or suffrage movement left off. But it took nearly a half a century, since women won the vote in 1918, for a feminist movement to take shape once again.

When it occurred, after the conservative, restrictive 1950s, most families fit a traditional model, with women caring for house and children and men working to support the family. However, given the affluence of the postwar years, more and more women became college-educated and entered professions. New economic self-sufficiency and personal empowerment spurred many to reassess society's expectations of them and of their roles. In so-called "consciousness-raising" groups, women all over the United States (and soon after in Europe) gathered to explore new ways of being, for themselves as individuals and in relationships with men, their families and other women. They examined the traditional roles and cultural expectations of femininity and femaleness, and questioned the equation of biology and destiny: that to be a woman necessarily meant motherhood and domestic life.

As a result of the women's movement, women have made enormous strides over the past twenty years. They have entered the work force in tremendous numbers, in part out of economic necessity. They are now freer to define themselves and their place in society—to choose, for example, to remain single or to raise a child alone. Nevertheless, there are still social sanctions against such anti-traditional behavior, particularly in conservative communities.

Most women today struggle to balance the traditional expectations of the past and the new demands and visions of the present. They also straddle two worlds—the private domain of home and family and the public domain of work. The resulting pressure to be "super-Mom" remains a concern, for wives are commonly the primary caretakers for children and home, even when their jobs are as demanding as those of their husbands.

In fact, the very belief that women's performance may be limited by these dual roles often hinders their professional advancement. This is evidenced by the fact that there are still proportionately fewer women in the most lucrative and traditionally male-dominated professions: in medical-surgical specialties, high-level government and university positions, and top management spots. Business analysts speak of the "glass ceiling," an invisible barrier to advancement and promotion. Despite the fact that women's salaries still lag behind those of men, some progress has been made. As of 1990, women between the ages of 24 and 35 earn 80 cents of every dollar earned by men of the same age, up from 69 cents in 1980.

Despite what some consider to be radical shifts in gender issues, the conservative Reagan and Bush years (1980-1992) brought a backlash against the gains accomplished in the 1970s. For example, the Equal Rights Amendment (ERA), that would have guaranteed women equality in many areas of legislation and policy, was not ratified by the House of Representatives in 1983.

More optimistically for women, however, 1992 was called "The Year of the Woman." Women were elected to seats in the House of Representatives and the Senate. It is quite likely that women's movement into government will bring policy changes that bolster the profound psychological and sociological changes already in place. The on-going evolution of gender roles will surely continue to modify the American cultural fabric in the century to come.

Before You Read

"We're pretty traditional around here. I handle everything on the domestic front except security."

1. Did you find this cartoon amusing? Why or why not?

2. Cartoonists often use a "truth" and then exaggerate it for comic effect. What "truth" about gender roles is exploited in this cartoon? What does it tell us about the way men and women view themselves?

3. As you read the article which follows, make a check in the margin next to any information or research findings which are new to you about gender.

Men vs. Women   MERRILL MCLOUGHLIN ET AL.

Biology may not be destiny, but these days researchers are finding some significant differences between the sexes—and, in many ways, women are coming out ahead

1   There was a time, not so long ago, when all the answers seemed clear. Everyone *knew* which was the weaker sex: Analyzed in terms of political power and bodily brawn, wasn't it obvious? Turn-of-the-century scientists produced learned tracts solemnly warning against an excess of exercise or education for girls: Too much activity—or thinking—would divert needed blood from their reproductive systems. Pseudoscientists meticulously

measured human brains and found women's wanting (along with those of blacks and Irishmen). And when the new science of intelligence testing turned up repeated and systematic superiority among girls, researchers kept tinkering with the tests until they produced the "right" results.

2   We've come a long way since those bad old days. We have also moved beyond a backlash of 1970s feminist scholarship, which insisted with equal ideological fervor that apart from the obvious dimorphism of human beings, there were *no* real differences between the sexes—that seeming disparities in mental abilities, emotional makeup, attitudes and even many physical skills were merely the product of centuries of male domination and male-dominated interpretation.

3   Lately, in bits and pieces that are still the subject of lively debate, science has been learning more about the fine points of how men and women differ—more about their physiology, their psychology, the interplay between the two and the subtle ways society influences both. Among the questions these studies may help answer:

4   • Are more women doomed to die of heart attacks as they rise to positions of power in the work world? Or are they peculiarly protected from the stresses that beleaguer modern men?

5   • Is there something to be learned from female longevity that might help improve and prolong the lives of men?

6   • Are boys always going to be better at math than girls? And why is it that there have been relatively few women of acknowledged artistic genius?

7   • Are men, by nature, better suited than women to lead and manage other people? Or is it possible that society would be better off with women's ways in the board rooms, female fingers near the nuclear buttons?

8   The old answers, once so sure, just won't do any more. In *The Myth of Two Minds*, her provocative 1987 book analyzing findings on sex differences, Beryl Lieff Benderly put the argument succinctly: "Who had the stronger shoulders, who might unpredictably become pregnant, clearly meant a great deal when work and warfare ran on muscle power and conception lay as far beyond human control as the weather. But now, when every American fingertip commands horsepower by the thousands, when the neighborhood drugstore and clinic offer freedom from fertility, those two great physical differences weigh very lightly indeed in the social balance."

9   While scientists still have a long way to go, research in a dozen disciplines—from neurology, endocrinology and sports medicine to psychology, anthropology and sociology—is beginning to point in the same direction: There are differences between the sexes beyond their reproductive functions, the pitch of their voices, the curves of elbows and knees, the fecundity of hair follicles. Many of these differences suggest that women are at least as well equipped as men for life in the modern world—and that in some ways they are, in fact, the stronger sex.

BODY

The distinctions are more than just skin-deep

10   If God created man first, He or She apparently took advantage of hindsight when it came to woman. Except for the moment of conception (when 13 to 15 males are conceived for every 10 females), the distaff side simply has a better chance at survival. Spontaneous abortions of boys outnumber those of girls. More males

than females die during infancy, youth and adulthood. In every country in the world where childbirth itself no longer poses mortal danger to women, the life expectancy of females exceeds that of males. And in the United States, the gap is growing. A baby girl born today can look forward to nearly 79 years—seven more than a baby boy.

11   Why? Some of the answers seem to lie deep in the genes. Others doubtless float in the hormones that carry messages from organ to organ, even, some researchers believe, "imprinting" each human brain with patterns that can affect the ways it responds to injury and disease. The research suggests that females start out with some distinct biological advantages. Among them:

12   ■ **The genetic code.** Genesis was wrong: Women came first—embryologically speaking, at least. Genetically, the female is the basic pattern of the species; maleness is superimposed on that. And this peculiarity of nature has the side effect of making males more vulnerable to a number of inherited disorders.

13   The reason lies in the way our genes determine who's a male and who's a female. A normal embryo inherits 23 chromosomes from the mother and 23 from the father. One of these chromosome pairs, the 23rd, determines what sex the baby will be. From the mother, the embryo always receives an X chromosome. From the father, it receives either an X, creating a female, or a Y, creating a male.

14   The Y chromosome carries little more than the genetic signal that, in the sixth week of development, first defeminizes the embryo, then starts the masculinization process. In a female, the X chromosome supplied by the father duplicates much of the genetic information supplied by the mother. Thus, if there are potentially deadly genetic anomalies on one of the female's X chromosomes, the other may cancel their effects. But the male embryo has no such protection: What's written on his sole X chromosome rules the day. Among the X-linked troubles he is more likely to inherit: Colorblindness, hemophilia, leukemia and dyslexia.

15   ■ **The estrogen factor.** The main task of the female sex hormones, or estrogens, is to keep the female body prepared to carry and care for offspring. But as it turns out, what's good for female reproduction is also good for the arteries. One effect of estrogens, for example, is to keep blood vessels pliable in order to accommodate extra blood volume during pregnancy. That also reduces the risk of atherosclerosis. And because a developing fetus needs lots of carbohydrates but is unable to use much fat, the mother's body must be able to break down the extra fat left behind after the fetus's demands are met. Estrogen makes this happen by stimulating the liver to produce high-density lipoproteins (HDL), which allow the body to make more efficient use of fat—and help to keep arteries cleared of cholesterol.

16   The male hormone testosterone, by contrast, causes men to have a far higher concentration of *low*-density lipoprotein. "LDL forms and fixes in large amounts to the lining of the blood vessels," explains endocrinologist Estelle Ramey. "They become narrower and more fragile." That didn't matter 2 million years ago, when men were far more physically active: Exercise lowers the LDL count.

17   Long after menopause, when estrogen production drops dramatically, women maintain the cardiovascular advantages built up during their childbearing years. The Framingham study, a 24-year examination of the health of almost 6,000 men and

women between the ages of 30 and 59, found approximately twice the incidence of coronary heart disease in men as in women, even in the upper age range. And in an analysis of the health patterns of 122,000 U.S. nurses, Graham Colditz, assistant professor at Harvard Medical School, has found that women who use estrogen supplements after menopause cut their risk of heart attacks by a third.

18   So—would men live longer if they took doses of estrogens? So far, the answer is a resounding no. In experiments where men received estrogen supplements, "they dropped like flies," says Elain Eaker, an epidemiologist at the National Institutes of Health—from heart attacks. Eaker speculates that men don't have the proper receptor sites for estrogen.

19   But there may be hope for greater longevity in highly experimental work on macrophages, cells that form part of the immune system. Macrophages, Ramey explains, "gobble up" unmetabolized glucose that randomly affixes itself to DNA—and would eventually cause damage. As people age, the macrophage system slows, and the damage gets worse. "Macrophage activity in females, because of estrogen, is much higher," says Ramey. It's the hope of researchers that they can find a way to increase and prolong that activity in both sexes.

20   ■ The stress syndrome. "Women," Ramey declares flatly, "respond better to stress." Although the evidence on how stress hurts the human body is still equivocal, there are two main hypotheses. The first is mechanical: Elevation of heart rate and blood pressure due to stress promotes damage to the inner lining of the artery wall, laying the groundwork for heart disease. The second is chemical: Increased production of stress hormones promotes arterial damage.

21   Ramey is one scientist who is convinced that stress does damage. And she puts the blame squarely on testosterone—and the fact that while the world has changed substantially, men's bodies have not. In the world where primitive man evolved, "testosterone is the perfect hormone." In effect, it orders neuroreceptors in the brain to drop everything else and react as quickly as possible to a release of stress hormones: This greater reaction to stress may be damaging in the long run, but the short-term benefits were much more important in an age when "the life expectancy was about 23," says Ramey. Today, when the average man is less likely to be threatened by a saber-toothed tiger than by a corporate barracuda, his stress reaction is exactly the same—and just as damaging to long-term health.

22   Perhaps because testosterone isn't egging them on, women seem to respond to stressful situations more slowly, and with less of a surge of blood pressure and stress hormones. Some researchers suspect that psychosocial factors also play a big role. Dr. Kathleen Light, a specialist in behavioral medicine at the University of North Carolina, thinks women may have a different perception of just what situations are threatening. Women show much less stress than men, for instance, when asked to solve an arithmetic problem. But Light's preliminary data in a study of public speaking show that women experience about the same surge in blood pressure as men. "Women may respond more selectively than men," she suggests. "We think this reflects learned experience."

23   But Karen Matthews is not so sure. Postmenopausal women, she observes, show higher heart rates and produce more stress hormones than women who are still menstruating. This leads her back to the reproductive hormones. One possible conclusion: Estrogens may be better adapted than

testosterone for the flight-or-fight situations of modern life.

24   ■ **The brain plan.** Men's and women's brains really are different. Over the last decade, researchers have discovered that in women, functions such as language ability appear to be more evenly divided between the left and right halves of the brain; in men, they are much more localized in the left half. After strokes or injuries to the left hemisphere, women are three times less likely than men to suffer language deficits.

25   What accounts for these differences in brain organization? One clue: The central section of the corpus callosum, a nerve cable connecting the left and right halves of the brain, seems to be thicker in women than in men, perhaps allowing more right-brain-left-brain communication.

26   Many researchers think that sex hormones produced early in fetal development—as well as after birth—literally "sex" the brain. In young animals, says neuroendocrinologist Bruce McEwen of New York's Rockefeller University, "the brain cells respond to testosterone by becoming larger and developing different kinds of connections."

27   These changes add up to big behavioral differences. Inject a female rat pup with testicular hormones, for instance, and it will mount other females just like a male. And it's not just a matter of mating. Male rat pups deprived of testicular hormones perform more poorly on maze tests than normal males; young females injected with testicular hormones do better. Many researchers are convinced that hormones have similar effects on human brains. Males produce testosterone from the third to the sixth month of gestation. Another burst is released just after birth, and then one final spurt at the onset of puberty—roughly coinciding with the time boys begin to surpass girls in

math. What's more, males with an abnormality that makes their cells insensitive to testosterone's effects have cognitive profiles identical to girls: Their verbal IQ is higher than in normal males and their "performance" IQ (correlated with mechanical ability) is inferior to that of normal males.

28   Such findings are highly controversial. Feminist scholars, in particular, fear that they will give new life to the notion that biology is destiny—and that females just aren't the equal of men at certain tasks. But biodeterminists tend to ignore a critical difference between humans and other animals: The hugely complex human brain is not simply the sum of its synapses. There are other factors at play.

MIND

Different ways of thinking, from math to morals

29   Declare that women are more sensitive to the color red, and you get a few raised eyebrows. Argue that females are—by nature—not as good as males at mathematics, and you'll get outrage. Not surprisingly, intellectual ability is the arena in which sex differences are most hotly disputed. The stakes are high: Research findings can influence funding and policy decisions in everything from education to employment.

30   Most of the controversy over sex differences has focused on the long-standing male edge on tests of math aptitude. And it was further fueled in 1980, when Johns Hopkins University researchers Camilla Benbow and Julian Stanley reported on a study of 10,200 gifted junior-high students who took the Scholastic Aptitude Test between 1972 and 1979. Their conclusion: Boys were far more likely than girls to be mathematically talented. The researchers went on to

speculate that there may be 13 male math geniuses for every female with such talent—and that the sex differences in math are the result of biological factors, perhaps exposure to the male sex hormone testosterone.

31   The Johns Hopkins studies were savagely attacked from the moment they were released. For one thing, the SAT's regularly have shown wider differences in male-female scores than other math tests. And the population that Benbow and Stanley studied is by definition exceptional: Its performance does not necessarily mean anything about boys and girls in general.

32   But many other tests have consistently turned up a male superiority in math as well. And the explanation of the results offered by critics—that boys traditionally have been *expected* to do better at math, so they got more encouragement from parents and teachers—doesn't quite wash, either. Girls get better average *grades* in math at every level.

33   Lately, some researchers have found hints that testosterone plays a role in enhancing math aptitude: Girls who have received abnormal doses of it in the womb seem to do better than average on the tests.

34   Whatever the explanation, however, the gap is narrowing. According to psychologist Janet Hyde of the University of Wisconsin, a preliminary analysis of dozens of studies of sex differences suggests that the gap has been cut in half in the past seven years.

35   But on another cognitive front—visual-spacial ability—males still hold an undisputed edge. The male advantage begins to show up around the age of 8, and it persists into old age.

36   Some simple explanations are tempting: A few researchers have even suggested that a single, sex-linked gene is responsible for the male edge in analyzing and mentally manipulating three-dimensional objects. Like hemophilia, such a sex-linked trait could be carried by both men and women but would become active in a woman only rarely—when both of her X chromosomes carried the gene. Men, who have only one X chromosome, would by contrast need only a single copy of the gene to acquire the ability.

37   But there are no rigorous data to support the idea: No gene has been identified, nor has anyone been able to trace the inheritance of an enhanced spatial ability from mothers to sons— as has been done extensively in the case of hemophilia. Moreover, most researchers are skeptical that such a complex ability as spatial reasoning could possibly rest in a single gene.

38   Many researchers are thus beginning to suspect that the male superiority is the product of a combination of factors—genetic, hormonal and cultural—with roots deep in humanity's hunting-gathering past.

■ Nature vs. nurture

39   Separating out those various factors is a daunting task. One promising approach is to study sex differences as they develop, rather than merely focusing on aptitude-test scores. Among the recent findings:

40   • Females are more attracted to people and males to objects.

41   Numerous studies show that girl infants between 5 and 6 months detect differences in photographs of human faces, while males of the same age do not. In addition, writes psychologist Diane McGuinness, studies on very young infants show that "females smile and vocalize only to faces, whereas males are just as likely to smile and vocalize to inanimate objects and blinking lights." McGuinness concludes that there probably is a biological predisposition in females to caretaking behavior that is later reinforced by observing adults.

42   • Boys have a shorter attention span.

43   McGuinness has conducted a series of studies of sex differences in preschool children. Her results are intriguing: In a given 20-minute interval, boys did an average of 4.5 different activities, while girls concentrated on 2.5. Girls started and finished more projects than the boys. Boys were more distractible, interrupting their play to look at something else almost four times as often as girls—and they also spent more time in general watching other kids. Why the difference? "Maybe boys are just more visually oriented, and they learn by watching," McGuinness suggests.

44   • Boys and girls differ in their approach to moral problems.

45   The pioneering work in the study of moral development was carried out 20 years ago by Harvard psychologist Lawrence Kohlberg. But as one of his former students, Carol Gilligan, notes, Kohlberg's research seemed to assume that "females simply do not exist": He studied 44 boys over 20 years, but no girls.

46   Gilligan has retraced some of Kohlberg's steps, including girls this time, and found some highly interesting differences between the sexes. One example: Gilligan posed one of the "moral dilemmas" Kohlberg used in his studies to a boy and a girl, both 11 years old. The dilemma involves the case of "Heinz," who faces the choice of stealing a drug his wife needs to say alive but which he cannot afford, or obeying the law and letting her die. Jake, the boy, thought Heinz should steal the drug because a life is worth more than property. Amy, the girl, argued that the problems was more complicated: "I think there might be other ways besides stealing it, like if he could borrow the money or make a loan or something. If he stole the drug, he might save his wife then, but if he did, he might have

to go to jail, and then his wife might get sicker again and he couldn't get more of the drug."

47   In Gilligan's analysis, Amy sees the moral problem in terms of "a narrative of relationships that extend over time." Jake, by contrast, sees a "math problem."

48   Even a few years ago, research on sex differences still met enormous resistance from feminists and others who believed that merely posing the question was unscientific at best, politically inspired at worst. Diane McGuinness recalls the rejection she received once from a scientific journal when she submitted a paper on cognitive processes in males and females. One of the scientific referees who reviewed the paper wrote: "The author *purports* to find sex differences. Who cares!"

49   That attitude is beginning to change. "As time passes, people are less frightened and less rigid," says Grace Baruch, associate director of the Center for Research on Women at Wellesley College. Scholars are finding that a focus on "female" psychology and behavior can add much to a body of knowledge built almost exclusively upon studies of males. And new statistical techniques have also made the investigation of sex differences more reliable.

50   The new wave of results has even made converts of researchers who were skeptical that sex differences existed. "I've had to revise my view considerably," confesses Purdue University social psychologist Alice Eagly. Still, she adds, "the public needs to be warned that knowing a person's sex doesn't allow you to predict much of anything about him or her." The overlap between men and women is still much greater than their average differences. There are males who are every bit as adept at verbal skills as even the best females—and

women who are better at math than most men.

ATTITUDE

In politics and management, the "gender gap" is real

51   There is one difference between the sexes on which virtually every expert and study agree: Men are more aggressive than women. It shows up in 2-year-olds. It continues through school days and persists into adulthood. It is even constant across cultures. And there is little doubt that it is rooted in biology—in the male sex hormone testosterone.

52   If there's a feminine trait that's the counterpart of male aggressiveness, it's what social scientists awkwardly refer to as "nurturance." Feminists have argued that the nurturing nature of women is not biological in origin, but rather has been drummed into women by a society that wanted to keep them in the home. But the signs that it is at least partly inborn are too numerous to ignore. Just as tiny infant girls respond more readily to human faces, female toddlers learn much faster than males how to pick up nonverbal cues from others. And grown women are far more adept than men at interpreting facial expressions: A recent study by University of Pennsylvania brain researcher Ruben Gur showed that they easily read emotions such as anger, sadness and fear. The only such emotion men could pick up was disgust.

53   What difference do such differences make in the real world? Among other things, women appear to be somewhat less competitive—or at least competitive in different ways—than men. At the Harvard Law School, for instance, female students enter with credentials just as outstanding as those of their male peers. But they don't qualify for the prestigious *Law Review* in proportionate numbers, a fact some school officials attribute to women's discomfort in the incredibly competitive atmosphere.

54   Students of management styles have found fewer differences than they expected between men and women who reach leadership positions, perhaps because many successful women deliberately imitate masculine ways. But an analysis by Purdue social psychologist Alice Eagly of 166 studies of leadership style did find one consistent difference: Men tend to be more "autocratic"—making decisions on their own—while women tend to consult colleagues and subordinates more often.

55   Studies of behavior in small groups turn up even more differences. Men will typically dominate the discussion, says University of Toronto psychologist Kenneth Dion, spending more time talking and less time listening.

■ Political fallout

56   The aggression-nurturance gulf even shows up in politics. The "gender gap" in polling is real and enduring: Men are far more prone to support a strong defense and tough law-and-order measures such as capital punishment, for instance, while women are more likely to approve of higher spending to solve domestic social problems such as poverty and inequality. Interestingly, there is virtually no gender gap on "women's issues," such as abortion and day care; in fact, men support them slightly *more* than women.

57   That fact might serve as a lesson in this year's election campaign. Alarmed at George Bush's low marks among women, his strategists have aimed their candidate directly at the "women's issues." It may be the wrong tactic. A close look at recent polls suggests that it's not the specifics of his programs, but a far bigger problem—his weak

image in terms of strength, compassion and vision—that bothers women voters about Bush. And there's a political footnote to the differences between the sexes in the Democratic camp. Veteran strategist Kirk O'Donnell, a top adviser to Michael Dukakis, says flatly that his is one of the best campaign organizations he has ever observed—with a remarkable lack of intramural squabbling, which O'Donnell attributes squarely to the unusually high number of women in senior positions.

58   Applied to the female of the species, the word "different" has, for centuries, been read to mean "inferior." At last, that is beginning to change. And in the end, of course, it's not a question of better or worse. The obvious point—long lost in a miasma of ideology—is that each sex brings strengths and weaknesses that may check and balance the other: each is half of the human whole.

> **Merrill McLoughlin**, along with Tracy Shryer, Erica Goode and Kathleen McAuliffe, wrote this article which appeared in *U.S. News & World Report* in 1988.

After You Read

Reading Journal

Were you surprised by any of the many scientific findings contained in this article? (Look at the check marks you made in the margin.) If so, which ones in particular? How did they contradict your previous beliefs about the differences between men and women?

Reading For Meaning

1. List the reasons why scientists are finding that women are physiologically "the stronger sex."

2. Why do some researchers claim that women are better adapted to the stresses of modern life than men?

3. Historically, theories and research findings about differences in male/female brains have changed from decade to decade, often to suit the scientists' biases. Summarize the latest findings about male/female brain differences. Why does the article say feminist scholars are wary of these findings?

4. Explain the controversy which has arisen over whether or not there is true male superiority in mathematics and higher level abstract thinking.

5. One psychologist, Carol Gilligan, found that girls tended to approach moral problems "in terms of a narrative of relationships that extend over time" whereas boys saw them as "math problems." How might this finding be significant?

6. Explain what the authors call an "aggression-nurturance gulf" between the sexes. What biological support is there for this? What are the effects of this gulf on American politics?

Exploring Further

Group Presentation

> This project can be extended outside of the classroom by interviewing one or two non-class members and returning with the data analyzed at the next class meeting.

1. Have group members fill in as many responses as they can to the following in five minutes. (Use adjectives or noun phrases only.)

Men are...

Women are...

2. Share all responses with the group, eliminating repetitions. Have the secretary make a master list in which each quality is labeled as being "positive" or "negative." Compare the two lists. Which gender had more positive associations? More negative? Attempt to arrive at an explanation for this. How do your findings confirm or contradict the research in the article you just read?

3. Write up your findings in a paragraph and share them with the rest of the class.

Timed Writing Exercise

Think back on your childhood and what was expected of you as a young girl or boy. How did your parents' and teachers' expectations differ according to whether you were male or female? (Compare yourself with other brothers or sisters, or classmates of the opposite sex.) How did it feel to be a member of your sex rather than the other?

Focused Essay Topics

1. Do you think, as the saying goes, that "biology is destiny"? For example, can women fight against being thought of as "intuitive" rather than "rational" or men as "aggressive" rather than "nurturing"? Should they?

2. Answer the following question posed by the authors: "Are men, by nature, better suited than women to lead and manage other people? Or is it possible that society would be better off with women's ways in the board rooms, female fingers near the nuclear buttons?" Use the research findings in the article to support your argument.

Before You Read

Freewrite on the following and share your response: Women's biological make-up, according to the author of the next article, makes them natural nurturers and gives them a kind of power which men do not possess. Do you think this is enough to satisfy most women? What evidence can you give to support your opinion?

Understanding the Difference   PHYLLIS SCHLAFLY

1   The first requirement for the acquisition of power by the Positive Woman is to understand the differences between men and women. Your outlook on life, your faith, your behavior, your potential for fulfillment, all are determined by the parameters of your original premise. The Positive Woman starts with the assumption that the world is her oyster. She rejoices in the creative capability within her body and the power potential of her mind and spirit. She understands that men and women are different, and that those very differences provide the key to her success as a person and fulfillment as a woman.

2   The women's liberationist, on the other hand, is imprisoned by her own negative view of herself and of her place in the world around her. This view of women was most succinctly expressed in an advertisement designed by the principal women's liberationist organization, the National Organization for Women (NOW), and run in many magazines and newspapers and as special announcements on many television stations. The advertisement showed a darling curlyheaded girl with the caption: "This healthy, normal baby has a handicap. She was born female."

3   This is the self-articulated dog-in-the-manger, chip-on-the-shoulder, fundamental dogma of the women's liberation movement. Someone—it is not clear who, perhaps God, perhaps the "Establishment," perhaps a conspiracy of male chauvinist pigs—dealt women a foul blow by making them female. It becomes necessary, therefore, for women to agitate and demonstrate and hurl demands on society in order to wrest from an oppressive male-dominated social structure the status that has been wrongfully denied to women through the centuries.

4   By its very nature, therefore, the women's liberation movement precipitates a series of conflict situations—in the legislatures, in the courts, in the schools, in industry—with man targeted as the enemy. Confrontation replaces cooperation as the watchword of all relationships. Women and men become adversaries instead of partners.

5   The second dogma of the women's liberationists is that, of all the injustices perpetrated upon women through the centuries, the most oppressive is the cruel fact that women have babies and men do not. Within the confines of the women's liberationist ideology, therefore, the abolition of this overriding inequality of women becomes the primary goal. This goal must be achieved at any and all costs—to the woman herself, to the baby, to the family, and to society. Women must be made equal to men in their ability *not* to become pregnant and *not* to be expected to care for babies they may bring into the world.

6   This is why women's liberationists are compulsively involved in the drive to make abortion and child-care centers for all women, regardless of religion or income, both socially acceptable and government-financed. Former Congresswoman Bella Abzug has defined the goal: "to enforce the constitutional right of females to terminate pregnancies that they do not wish to continue."

7   If man is targeted as the enemy, and the ultimate goal of women's liberation is independence from men and the avoidance of pregnancy and its consequences, then lesbianism is logically the highest form in the ritual of women's liberation. Many, such as Kate Millett,[1] come to this conclusion, although many others do not.

8   The Positive Woman will never travel that dead-end road. It is self-evident to the Positive Woman that the female body with its baby-producing organs was not designed by a conspiracy of men but by the Divine Architect of the human race. Those who think it is unfair that women have babies, whereas men cannot, will have to take up their complaint with God because no other power is capable of changing that fundamental fact. On some college campuses, I have been assured that other methods of reproduction will be developed. But most of us must deal with the real world rather than with the imagination of dreamers.

9   Another feature of the woman's natural role is the obvious fact that women can breast-feed babies and men cannot. This functional role was not imposed by conspiratorial males seeking to burden women with confining chores, but must be recognized as part of the plan of the Divine Architect for the survival of the human race through the centuries and in the countries that know no pasteurization of milk or sterilization of bottles.

10   The Positive Woman looks upon her femaleness and her fertility as part of her purpose, her potential, and her power. She rejoices that she has a capability for creativity that men can never have.

11   The third basic dogma of the women's liberation movement is that there is no difference between male and female except the sex organs, and that all those physical, cognitive, and emotional differences you *think* are there are merely the result of centuries of restraints imposed by a male-dominated society and sex-stereotyped schooling. The role imposed on women is, by definition, inferior, according to the women's liberationists.

12   The Positive Woman knows that, while there are some physical competitions in which women are better (and can command more money) than men, including those that put a premium on grace and beauty, such as figure skating, the superior physical strength of males over females in

---

[1] Kate Millett is a prominent member in the Women's Movement.

competitions of strength, speed, and short-term endurance is beyond rational dispute.

13   In the Olympic games, women not only cannot win any medals in competition with men, the gulf between them is so great that they cannot even qualify for the contests with men. No amount of training from infancy can enable women to throw the discus as far as men, or to match men in push-ups or in lifting weights. In track and field events, individual male records surpass those of women by 10 to 20 percent.

14   Female swimmers today are beating Johnny Weissmuller's records, but today's male swimmers are better still. Chris Evert can never win a tennis match against Jimmy Connors. If we removed lady's tees from golf courses women would be out of the game. Putting women in football or wrestling matches can only be an exercise in laughs.

15   The Olympic Games, whose rules require strict verification to ascertain that no male enters a female contest and, with his masculine advantage, unfairly captures a woman's medal, formerly insisted on a visual inspection of the contestants' bodies. Science, however, has discovered that men and women are so innately different physically that their maleness/femaleness can be conclusively established by means of a simple skin test of fully clothed persons.

16   If there is *anyone* who should oppose enforced sex equality, it is the women athletes. Babe Didrikson,who played and defeated some of the great male athletes of her time, is unique in the history of sports.

17   If sex equality were enforced in professional sports, it would mean that men could enter the women's tournaments and win most of the money. Bobby Riggs has already threatened: "I think that men 55 years and over should be allowed to play women's tournaments—like the Virginia Slims. Everybody ought to know there's no sex after 55 anyway."

18   The Positive Woman remembers the essential validity of the old prayer: "Lord, give me the strength to change what I can change, the serenity to accept what I cannot change, and the wisdom to discern the difference." The women's liberationists are expending their time and energies erecting a make-believe world in which they hypothesize that *if* schooling were gender-free, and *if* the same money were spent on male and female sports programs, and *if* women were permitted to compete on equal terms, *then* they would prove themselves to be physically equal. Meanwhile, the Positive Woman has put the ineradicable physical differences into her mental computer, programmed her plan of action, and is already on the way to personal achievement.

19   Thus, while some militant women spend their time demanding more money for professional sports, ice skater Janet Lynn, a truly Positive Woman, quietly signed the most profitable financial contract in the history of women's athletics. It was not the strident demands of the women's liberationists that brought high prizes to women's tennis but the discovery by sports promoters that beautiful female legs gracefully moving around the court made women's tennis a highly marketable television production to delight male audiences.

20   Many people thought that the remarkable filly named Ruffian would prove that a female race horse could compete equally with a male. Even

with the handicap of extra weights placed on the male horse, the race was a disaster for the female. The gallant Ruffian gave her all in a noble effort to compete, but broke a leg in the race and, despite the immediate attention of top veterinarians, had to be put away.

21   Despite the claims of the women's liberation movement, there are countless physical differences between men and women. The female body is 50 to 60 percent water, the male 60 to 70 percent water, which explains why males can dilute alcohol better than women and delay its effect. The average woman is about 25 percent fatty tissue, while the male is 15 percent, making women more buoyant in water and able to swim with less effort. Males have a tendency to color blindness. Only 5 percent of persons who get gout are female. Boys are born bigger. Women live longer in most countries of the world, not only in the United States where we have a hard-driving competitive pace. Women excel in manual dexterity, verbal skills, and memory recall.

22   Arianna Stassinopoulos in her book *The Female Woman* has done a good job of spelling out the many specific physical differences that are so innate and so all-pervasive that

> even if Women's Lib was given a hundred, a thousand, ten thousand years in which to eradicate *all* the differences between the sexes, it would still be an impossible undertaking. . . .
>
> It is inconceivable that millions of years of evolutionary selection during a period of marked sexual division of labor have not left pronounced traces on the innate character of men and women. Aggressiveness, and mechanical and spatial skills, a sense of direction, and physical strength—all masculine characteristics—are the qualities essential for a hunter; even food gatherers need these same qualities for defense and exploration. The prolonged period of dependence of human children, the difficulty of carrying the peculiarly heavy and inert human baby—a much heavier, clumsier burden than the monkey infant and much less able to cling on for safety—meant that women could not both look after their children and be hunters and explorers. Early humans learned to take advantage of this period of dependence to transmit rules, knowledge and skills to their offspring—women needed to develop verbal skills, a talent for personal relationships, and a predilection for nurturing going even beyond the maternal instinct.[2]

23   Does the physical advantage of men doom women to a life of servility and subservience? The Positive Woman knows that she has a complementary advantage which is at least as great—and, in the hands of a skillful woman, far greater. The Divine Architect who gave men a superior strength to lift weights also gave women a different kind of superior strength.

24   The women's liberationists and their dupes who try to tell each other that the sexual drive of men and women is really the same, and that it is only societal restraints that inhibit women from an equal desire, an equal enjoyment, and an equal freedom from the consequences, are doomed to frustration forever. It just isn't so, and pretending cannot make it so. The differences are not a woman's weakness but her strength.

2 Arianna Stassinopoulos, *The Female Woman* (New York: Random House, 1973), pp. 30-31.

25   Dr. Robert Collins, who has had ten years' experience in listening to and advising young women at a large eastern university, put his finger on the reason why casual "sexual activity" is such a cheat on women:

> A basic flaw in this new morality is the assumption that males and females are the same sexually. The simplicity of the male anatomy and its operation suggest that to a man, sex can be an activity apart from his whole being, a drive related to the organs themselves.
>
> In a woman, the complex internal organization, correlated with her other hormonal systems, indicates her sexuality must involve her total self. On the other hand, the man is orgasm-oriented with a drive that ignores most other aspects of the relationship. The woman is almost totally different. She is engulfed in romanticism and tries to find and express her total feelings for her partner.
>
> A study at a midwestern school shows that 80 percent of the women who had intercourse hoped to marry their partner. Only 12 percent of the men expected the same.
>
> Women say that soft, warm promises and tender touches are delightful, but that the act itself usually leads to a "Is that all there is to it?" reaction. . . .
>
> [A typical reaction is]: "It sure wasn't worth it. It was no fun at the time. I've been worried ever since. . . ."
>
> The new morality is a fad. It ignores history, it denies the physical and mental compositions of human beings, it is intolerant, exploitative, and is oriented toward intercourse, not love.[3]

26   The new generation can brag all it wants about the new liberation of the new morality, but it is still the woman who is hurt most. The new morality isn't just a "fad" —it is a cheat and a thief. It robs the woman of her virtue, her youth, her beauty, and her love—for nothing, just nothing. It has produced a generation of young women searching for their identity, bored with sexual freedom, and despondent from the loneliness of living a life without commitment. They have abandoned the old commandments, but they can't find any new rules that work.

27   The Positive Woman recognizes the fact that, when it comes to sex, women are simply not the equal of men. The sexual drive of men is much stronger than that of women. That is how the human race was designed in order that it might perpetuate itself. The other side of the coin is that it is easier for women to control their sexual appetites. A Positive Woman cannot defeat a man in a wrestling or boxing match, but she can motivate him, inspire him, encourage him, teach him, restrain him, reward him, and have power over him that he can never achieve over her with all his muscle. How or whether a Positive Woman uses her power is determined solely by the way she alone defines her goals and develops her skills.

28   The differences between men and women are also emotional and psychological. Without woman's innate maternal instinct, the human race would have died out centuries ago. There is nothing so helpless in all

---

[3] *Chicago Tribune*, 17 Aug., 1975.

earthly life as the newborn infant. It will die within hours if not cared for. Even in the most primitive, uneducated societies, women have always cared for their newborn babies. They didn't need any schooling to teach them how. They didn't need any welfare workers to tell them it is their social obligation. Even in societies to whom such concepts as "ought," "social responsibility," and "compassion for the helpless" were unknown, mothers cared for their new babies.

29   Why? Because caring for a baby serves the natural maternal need of a woman. Although not nearly so total as the baby's need, the woman's need is nonetheless real.

30   The overriding psychological need of a woman is to love something alive. A baby fulfills this need in the lives of most women. If a baby is not available to fill that need, women search for a baby-substitute. This is the reason why women have traditionally gone into teaching and nursing careers. They are doing what comes naturally to the female psyche. The schoolchild or the patient of any age provides an outlet for [the] woman to express her natural maternal need.

31   This maternal need in women is the reason why mothers whose children have grown up and flown from the nest are sometimes cut loose from their psychological moorings. The maternal need in women can show itself in love for grandchildren, nieces, nephews, or even neighbors' children. The maternal need in some women has even manifested itself in an extraordinary affection lavished on a dog, a cat or a parakeet.

32   This is not to say that every woman must have a baby in order to be fulfilled. But it is to say that fulfillment for most women involves expressing their natural maternal urge by loving and caring for someone.

33   The women's liberation movement complains that traditional stereotyped roles assume that women are "passive" and that men are "aggressive." The anomaly is that a woman's most fundamental emotional need is not passive at all, but active. A woman naturally seeks to love affirmatively and to show that love in an active way by caring for the object of her affections.

34   The Positive Woman finds somebody on whom she can lavish her maternal love so that it doesn't well up inside her and cause psychological frustrations. Surely no woman is so isolated by geography or insulated by spirit that she cannot find someone worthy of her maternal love. All persons, men and women, gain by sharing something of themselves with their fellow humans, but women profit most of all because it is part of their very nature.

35   One of the strangest quirks of women's liberationists is their complaint that societal restraints prevent men from crying in public or showing their emotions, but permit women to do so, and that therefore we should "liberate" men to enable them, too, to cry in public. The public display of fear, sorrow, anger, and irritation reveals a lack of self-discipline that should be avoided by the Positive Woman just as much as by the Positive Man. Maternal love, however, is not a weakness but a manifestation of strength and service, and it should be nurtured by the Positive Woman.

36   Most women's organizations, recognizing the preference of most women to avoid hard-driving competition, handle the matter of succession of officers by the device of a nominating committee. This eliminates the unpleasantness and the tension of a competitive confrontation every year or two. Many

women's organizations customarily use a prayer attributed to Mary, Queen of Scots, which is an excellent analysis by a woman of women's faults:

> Keep us, O God, from pettiness; let us be large in thought, in word, in deed. Let us be done with fault-finding and leave off self-seeking. . . . Grant that we may realize it is the little things that create differences, that in the big things of life we are at one.

37   Another silliness of the women's liberationists is their frenetic desire to force all women to accept the title *Ms* in place of *Miss* or *Mrs*. If Gloria Steinem and Betty Friedan[4] want to call themselves *Ms* in order to conceal their marital status, their wishes should be respected.

38   But that doesn't satisfy the women's liberationists. They want all women to be compelled to use *Ms* whether they like it or not. The women's liberation movement has been waging a persistent campaign to browbeat the media into using *Ms* as the standard title for all women. The women's liberationists have already succeeded in getting the Department of Health, Education and Welfare to forbid schools and colleges from identifying women students as *Miss* or *Mrs*.[5]

39   All polls show that the majority of women do not care to be called *Ms*. A Roper poll indicated that 81 percent of the women questioned said they prefer *Miss* or *Mrs*. to *Ms*. Most married women feel they worked hard for the *r* in their names, and they don't care to be gratuitously deprived of it. Most single women don't care to have their name changed to an unfamiliar title that at best conveys overtones of feminist ideology and is polemical in meaning, and at worst connotes misery instead of joy. Thus, Kate Smith, a very Positive Woman, proudly proclaimed on television that she is "Miss Kate Smith, not Ms." Like other Positive Women, she has been succeeding while negative women have been complaining.

40   Finally, women are different from men in dealing with the fundamentals of life itself. Men are philosophers, women are practical, and 'twas ever thus. Men may philosophize about how life began and where we are heading; women are concerned about feeding the kids today. No woman would ever, as Karl Marx did, spend years reading political philosophy in the British Museum while her child starved to death. Women don't take naturally to a search for the intangible and the abstract. The Positive Woman knows who she is and where she is going, and she will reach her goal because the longest journey starts with a very practical first step.

41   Amaury de Riencourt, in his book *Sex and Power in History*, shows that a successful society depends on a delicate balancing of male and female factors, and that the women's liberation movement, which promotes unisexual values and androgyny, contains within it "a social and cultural death wish and the end of the civilization that endorses it."

42   One of the few scholarly works dealing with woman's role, *Sex and Power in History* synthesizes research from a variety of disciplines—sociology, biology, history, anthropology, religion, philosophy, and psychology. De Riencourt traces distinguishable types of women in different

---

[4] Founding members of the Women's Movement.
[5] HEW—Regulation on Sex Discrimination in Schools and Colleges, effective 18 July, 1975, no. 86.21 (c)(4).

periods in history, from prehistoric to modern times. The "liberated" Roman matron, who is most similar to the present-day feminist, helped bring about the fall of Rome through her unnatural emulation of masculine qualities, which resulted in a large-scale breakdown of the family and ultimately of the empire.

43 De Riencourt examines the fundamental, inherent differences between men and women. He argues that man is the more aggressive, rational, mentally creative, analytical-minded sex because of his early biological role as hunter and provider. Woman, on the other hand, represents stability, flexibility, reliance on intuition, and harmony with nature, stemming from her procreative function.

44 Where man is discursive, logical, abstract, or philosophical, woman tends to be emotional, personal, practical, or mystical. Each set of qualities is vital and complements the other. Among the many differences explained in de Riencourt's book are the following:

> Women tend more toward conformity than men—which is why they often excel in such disciplines as spelling and punctuation where there is only one correct answer, determined by social authority. Higher intellectual activities, however, require a mental independence and power of abstraction that they usually lack, not to mention a certain form of aggressive boldness of the imagination which can only exist in a sex that is basically aggressive for biological reasons.
>
> To sum up: The masculine proclivity in problem solving is analytical and categorical; the feminine, synthetic and contextual. . . . Deep down, man tends to focus on the object, on external results and achievements; woman focuses on subjective motives and feelings. If life can be compared to a play, man focuses on the theme and structure of the play, woman on the innermost feelings displayed by the actors.[6]

45 De Riencourt provides impressive refutation of two of the basic errors of the women's liberation movement: (1) that there are no emotional or cognitive differences between the sexes, and (2) that women should strive to be like men.

46 A more colloquial way of expressing the de Riencourt conclusion that men are more analytical and women more personal and practical is in the different answers that one is likely to get to the question, "Where did you get that steak?" A man will reply, "At the corner market," or wherever he bought it. A woman will usually answer, "Why? What's the matter with it?"

47 An effort to eliminate the differences by social engineering or legislative or constitutional tinkering cannot succeed, which is fortunate, but social relationships and spiritual values can be ruptured in the attempt. Thus the role reversals being forced upon high school students, under which guidance counselors urge reluctant girls to take "shop" and boys to take "home economics," further confuse a generation already unsure about its identity. They are as wrong as efforts to make a left-handed child right-handed.

[6] Amaury de Riencourt, *Sex and Power in History* (New York: David McKay Co., Inc., 1974), p. 56.

> **Phyllis Schlafly**, author of the 1977 *The Power of The Positive Woman*, is a
> spokeswoman for the conservative, anti-feminist right that helped to defeat
> the Equal Rights Amendment (ERA) and continues to fight against abortion.
> Although a lawyer and activist herself, Schlafly maintains that a woman's place
> is in the home.

After You Read

Reading Journal

Phyllis Schlafly is an outspoken advocate for the conservative Right
and an opponent of feminist politics, notably the Equal Rights
Amendment (ERA) and abortion. Which view more clearly reflects your
view of what women should be, the "positive woman" or the "liberationist"? Explain.

Reading For Meaning

1. Paraphrase the three essential dogma of the "liberationist" according to Schlafly.

2. The author defines the "positive woman" by repeatedly contrasting
   her with the "liberationist." Write a one-paragraph description which
   illustrates the basic conflicts, according to Schlafly, between these
   two types of women. (Use your information from question 1.)

3. Schlafly uses many examples and quotes from other authors as support for her argument. Are there any examples which seem inap-
   propriate or unconvincing? Are any of her examples, presented as
   fact, which might be seen as *opinion* by those opposed to her argument? Do any of her conclusions seem illogical or extreme?
   Underline them in the text and say why.

Exploring Further

Debate

As more and more women enter the workforce, critics of the women's movement, like Phyllis Schlafly, blame women for giving up their maternal duties in favor of personal fulfillment. This, in turn, is viewed as contributing to the breakup of the American family. Do you agree or disagree? As you take sides, consider whether women should stay at home, and if they do, would the United States see a return of the nuclear family of the 1950s?

Timed Writing Exercise

In the mid 1970s, Gloria Steinem, one of the founders of the women's movement in America, is quoted as having said: "A woman needs a man like a fish needs a bicycle!" What fundamental belief about male-female relationships underlies this statement? Do you agree or disagree?

Focused Essay Topics

1. Some would argue that the "positive woman" uses indirect means (i.e., manipulation) to gain her power. Are there ever cases where women should use so-called "feminine charm"? Under what circumstances could feminine charm be more effective than a more direct route?

2. Schlafly asserts that it is part of a woman's essential nature to "love something alive. A baby fulfills this need in the lives of most women." Betty Rollins, a feminist writer, argues, on the other hand, in her article, "Motherhood: Who Needs It?" that "biological possibility and desire are not the same as biological need. Women have childbearing equipment. To choose not to use the equipment is no more blocking what is instinctive than it is for a man who, muscles or no, chooses not to be a weight lifter." Whose position do you support and why?

Before You Read

In the next essay, Susan Brownmiller recalls her childhood "lessons in femininity." Write a brief description of a childhood activity you remember being restricted to girls. What qualities made this "female"? What assumptions, if any, were made about boys who joined this activity? About girls who didn't?

Femininity   SUSAN BROWNMILLER

1   We had a game in our house called "setting the table" and I was Mother's helper. Forks to the left of the plate, knives and spoons to the right. Placing the cutlery neatly, as I recall, was one of my first duties, and the event was alive with meaning. When a knife or a fork dropped on the floor, that meant a man was unexpectedly coming to dinner. A falling spoon announced the surprise arrival of a female guest. No matter that these visitors never arrived on cue, I had learned a rule of gender identification. Men were straight-edged, sharply pronged and formidable, women were softly curved and held the food in a rounded well. It made perfect sense, like the division of pink and blue that I saw in babies, an orderly way of viewing the world. Daddy, who was gone all day at work and who loved to putter at home with his pipe, tobacco and tool chest, was knife and fork. Mommy and Grandma, with their ample proportions and pots and pans, were grownup soup spoons, large and capacious. And I was a teaspoon, small and slender, easy to hold and just right for pudding, my favorite dessert.

2   Being good at what was expected of me was one of my earliest projects, for not only was I rewarded, as most children are, for doing things right, but excellence gave pride and stability to my childhood existence. Girls were different from boys, and the expression of that difference seemed mine to make clear. Did my loving, anxious mother, who dressed me in white organdy pinafores and Mary Janes and who cried hot tears when I got them dirty, give me my first instruction? Of course. Did my doting aunts and uncles with their gifts of pretty dolls and miniature tea sets add to my education? Of course. But even without the appropriate toys and clothes, lessons in the art of being feminine lay all around me and I absorbed them all: the fairy tales that were read to me at night, the brightly colored advertisements I pored over in magazines before I learned to decipher the words, the movies I saw, the comic books I hoarded, the radio soap operas I happily followed whenever I had to stay in bed with a cold. I loved being a little girl, or rather I loved being a fairy princess, for that was who I thought I was.

3   As I passed through a stormy adolescence to a stormy maturity, femininity increasingly became an exasperation, a brilliant, subtle esthetic that was bafflingly inconsistent at the same time that it was minutely, demandingly concrete, a rigid code of appearance and behavior defined by do's and don't-do's that went against my rebellious grain. Femininity was a challenge thrown down to the female sex, a challenge no proud, self-respecting young woman could afford to ignore, particularly one with enormous ambition that she nursed in secret, alternately feeding or starving its inchoate life in tremendous confusion.

4   "Don't lose your femininity" and "Isn't it remarkable how she manages to retain her femininity?" had terrifying implications. They spoke of a bottom-line failure so irreversible that nothing else mattered. The pinball machine has registered "tilt," the game had been called. Disqualification was marked on the forehead of a woman whose femininity was lost. No records would be entered in her name, for she had destroyed her birthright in her wretched, ungainly effort to imitate a man. She walked in limbo, this hapless creature, and it occurred to me that one day I might see her when I looked in the mirror. If the danger was so palpable that warning notices were freely posted, wasn't it possible that the small bundle of resentments I carried around in secret might spill out and place the mark on my own forehead? Whatever quarrels with femininity I had I kept to myself; whatever handicaps femininity imposed, they were mine to deal with alone, for there was no women's movement to ask the tough questions, or to brazenly disregard the rules.

5   Femininity, in essence, is a romantic sentiment, a nostalgic tradition of imposed limitations. Even as it hurries forward in the 1980s, putting on lipstick and high heels to appear well dressed, it trips on the ruffled petticoats and hoopskirts of an era gone by. Invariably and necessarily, femininity is something that women had more of in the past, not only in the historic past of prior generations, but in each woman's personal past as well—in the virginal innocence that is replaced by knowledge, in the dewy cheek that is coarsened by age, in the "inherent nature" that a woman seems to misplace so forgetfully whenever she steps out of bounds. Why should this be so? The XX chromosomal message has not been scrambled, the estrogen-dominated hormonal balance is generally as biology intended, the reproductive organs, whatever use one has made of them, are usually in place, the breasts of whatever size are most often where they should be. But clearly, biological femaleness is not enough.

6   Femininity always demands more. It must constantly reassure its audience by a willing demonstration of difference, even when one does not exist in nature, or it must seize and embrace a natural variation and compose a rhapsodic symphony upon the notes. Suppose one doesn't care to, has other things on her mind, is clumsy or tone-deaf despite the best instruction and training? To fail at the feminine difference is to appear not to care about men, and to risk the loss of their attention and approval. To be insufficiently feminine is viewed as a failure in core sexual identity, or as a failure to care sufficiently about oneself, for a woman found wanting will be appraised (and will appraise herself) as mannish or neutered or simply unattractive, as men have defined these terms.

7   We are talking, admittedly, about an exquisite esthetic. Enormous pleasure can be extracted from feminine pursuits as a creative outlet or

purely as relaxation; indeed, indulgence for the sake of fun, or art, or attention, is among femininity's great joys. But the chief attraction (and the central paradox, as well) is the competitive edge that femininity seems to promise in the unending struggle to survive, and perhaps to triumph. The world smiles favorably on the feminine woman: it extends little courtesies and minor privilege. Yet the nature of this competitive edge is ironic, at best, for one works at femininity by accepting restrictions, by limiting one's sights, by choosing an indirect route, by scattering concentration and not giving one's all as a man would to his own, certifiably masculine, interests. It does not require a great leap of imagination for a woman to understand the feminine principle as a grand collection of compromises, large and small, that she simply must make in order to render herself a successful woman. If she has difficulty in satisfying femininity's demands, if its illusions go against her grain, or if she is criticized for her shortcomings and imperfections, the more she will see femininity as a desperate strategy of appeasement, a strategy she may not have the wish or the courage to abandon, for failure looms in either direction.

8   It is fashionable in some quarters to describe the feminine and masculine principles as polar ends of the human continuum, and to sagely profess that both polarities exist in all people. Sun and moon, yin and yang, soft and hard, active and passive, etcetera, may indeed be opposites, but a linear continuum does not illuminate the problem. (Femininity, in all its contrivances, is a very active endeavor.) What, then, is the basic distinction? The masculine principle is better understood as a driving ethos of superiority designed to inspire straightforward, confident success, while the feminine principle is composed of vulnerability, the need for protection, the formalities of compliance and the avoidance of conflict—in short, an appeal of dependence and good will that gives the masculine principle its romantic validity and its admiring applause.

9   Femininity pleases men because it makes them appear more masculine by contrast; and, in truth, conferring an extra portion of unearned gender distinction on men, an unchallenged space in which to breathe freely and feel stronger, wiser, more competent, is femininity's special gift. One could say that masculinity is often an effort to please women, but masculinity is known to please by displays of mastery and competence while femininity pleases by suggesting that these concerns, except in small matters, are beyond its intent. Whimsy, unpredictability and patterns of thinking and behavior that are dominated by emotion, such as tearful expressions of sentiment and fear, are thought to be feminine precisely because they lie outside the established route to success.

10   If in the beginnings of history the feminine woman was defined by her physical dependency, her inability for reasons of reproductive biology to triumph over the forces of nature that were the tests of masculine strength and power, today she reflects both an economic and emotional dependency that is still considered "natural," romantic and attractive. After an unsettling fifteen years in which many basic assumptions about the sexes were challenged, the economic disparity did not disappear. Large numbers of women—those with small children, those left high and

dry after a mid-life divorce—need financial support. But even those who earn their own living share a universal need for connectedness (call it love, if you wish). As unprecedented numbers of men abandon their sexual interest in women, others, sensing opportunity, choose to demonstrate their interest through variety and a change in partners. A sociological fact of the 1980s is that female competition for two scarce resources—men and jobs—is especially fierce.

11   So it is not surprising that we are currently witnessing a renewed interest in femininity and an unabashed indulgence in feminine pursuits. Femininity serves to reassure men that women need them and care about them enormously. By incorporating the decorative and the frivolous into its definition of style, femininity functions as an effective antidote to the unrelieved seriousness, the pressure of making one's way in a harsh, difficult world. In its mandate to avoid direct confrontation and to smooth over the fissures of conflict, femininity operates as a value system of niceness, a code of thoughtfulness and sensitivity that in modern society is sadly in short supply.

12   There is no reason to deny that indulgence in the art of feminine illusion can be reassuring to a woman, if she happens to be good at it. As sexuality undergoes some dizzying revisions, evidence that one is a woman "at heart" (the inquisitor's question) is not without worth. Since an answer of sorts may be furnished by piling on additional documentation, affirmation can arise from such identifiable but trivial feminine activities as buying a new eyeliner, experimenting with the latest shade of nail color, or bursting into tears at the outcome of a popular romance novel. Is there anything destructive in this? Time and cost factors, a deflection of energy and an absorption in fakery spring quickly to mind, and they need to be balanced, as in a ledger book, against the affirming advantage.

Susan Brownmiller became a major voice in the Women's Movement of the 1970s with her book, *Against Our Will: Men, Women and Rape* (1975), a radical feminist work that was serialized in popular magazines and became a bestseller and feminist classic. This reading is from her second book, *Femininity* (1984). Brownmiller has also written a novel, *Waverly Place* (1989).

After You Read

Reading Journal

Respond to one or more of Brownmiller's ideas about the concept of femininity. Think of examples from your own experience or, if you are male, of a woman or women you know well.

Reading For Meaning

1. Why does Brownmiller say that losing one's femininity has "terrifying implications"? (paragraphs 4-6)

2. Brownmiller views femininity as a trade-off between "little courtesies and minor privilege" extended women and a lifetime of compromises and restrictions. List several examples of this trade-off.

3. What reason does the author feel is responsible for a "renewed interest in femininity"?

Exploring Further

Research Project

Obtain several back and/or current issues of *Ms.*, a feminist magazine whose audience is primarily (although not exclusively) educated, liberal women. Skim through the magazine to familiarize yourself with its format. Make a list of "issues" which are addressed. Read an article which catches your interest and summarize the basic argument. Then write a short reaction to it to share with the class.

Timed Writing Exercise

Often students from other cultures find the concerns of the women's movement to be primarily an American preoccupation. Do you agree? Explain.

Focused Essay Topics

1. Imagine a debate between Phyllis Schlafly and Susan Brownmiller on the importance of femininity. Outline the two women's arguments on paper and then write a dialogue in which their essential areas of disagreement are highlighted.

2. Brownmiller claims that women have always had "a rigid code of appearance and behavior defined by do's and don't-do's that went against their rebellious grain." Compose a similar list of do's and don'ts based on your own childhood experience. Discuss whether or not any of the items listed went against *your* grain and why.

Before You Read

1. Examine the pictures below. What associations come to mind about men crying? What are your native culture's unwritten rules for the expression of grief? Do they differ for men and women? If so, in what respects?

2. Anthropologist Ashley Montagu argues in the next reading that "to be human is to weep." Do you agree?

Masculine Expression of Emotion   ASHLEY MONTAGU

1   American men don't cry because it is considered unmasculine to do so. Only sissies cry. Crying is a "weakness" characteristic of the female, and no American male wants to be identified with anything in the least weak or feminine. Crying, in our culture, is identified with childishness, with weakness and dependence. No one likes a crybaby, and we disapprove of crying even in children, discouraging it in them as early as possible. In a land so devoted to the pursuit of happiness as ours, crying really is rather un-American. Adults must learn not to cry in situations in

which it is permissable for a child to cry. Women being the "weaker" and "dependent" sex, it is only natural that they should cry in certain emotional situations. In women, crying is excusable. But in men, crying is a mark of weakness. So goes the American credo with regard to crying.

2   "A little man," we impress on our male children, "never cries. Only sissies and crybabies do." And so we condition males in America not to cry whenever they feel like doing so. It is not that American males are unable to cry because of some biological time clock within them which causes them to run down in that capacity as they grow older, but that they are trained not to cry. No "little man" wants to be like that "inferior creature," the female. And the worst thing you can call him is a sissy or crybaby. And so the "little man" represses his desire to cry and goes on doing so until he is unable to cry even when he wants to. Thus do we produce a trained incapacity in the American male to cry. And this is bad. Why is it bad? Because crying is a natural function of the human organism which is designed to restore the emotionally disequilibrated person to a state of equilibrium. The return of the disequilibrated organ systems of the body to steady states or dynamic stability is known as homeostatis. Crying serves a homeostatic function for the organism as a whole. Any interference with homeostatic mechanisms is likely to be damaging to the organism. And there is good reason to believe that the American male's trained incapacity to cry is seriously damaging to him.

3   It is unnecessary to cry whenever one wants to cry, but one should be able to cry when one ought to cry—when one needs to cry. For to cry under certain emotionally disequilibrating conditions is necessary for the maintenance of health.

4   On these matters we are strangely confused in our culture. Consider, for example, the behavior of husband and wife when a sudden catastrophe or bereavement befalls the family. The wife is likely to be prostrated with grief, shedding virtual waterfalls of tears. Having consumed all the linen in the household and having resorted to the bathroom mat, in the attempt to stanch the flood, she will furtively glance out of the corner of her eye admiringly at the heroic creature she married. So different from herself! There he stands, godlike, strong, silent, and with stiff upper lip, puffing away intrepidly at his pipe, without betraying a sign of the inner turmoil which is so outwardly visible in herself. What a noble creature is the male!

5   There indeed he may stand, but the truth is that he isn't standing the situation anywhere nearly as well as his wife is managing it horizontally. For in his marmoreal ineffectuality, not only is the male being useless to everyone for miles around, but he is also perhaps being most useless to himself. For while his wife is doing what she ought, weeping away and thus restoring herself to a state of equilibrium as soon as possible, her husband, being utterly incapable of expressing his emotions through tears, is nevertheless expressing his emotions in the manner to which he has been accustomed by those who have trained him in his incapacity to cry. He turns his emotions into his body. Instead of expressing them overtly, he expresses them covertly; he interiorizes them; he somatizes them—that is to say, he expresses them through his body. Instead of weeping through his lachrymal apparatus he now begins to weep vicariously, either through his skin in the form of some sort of dermatological eruption, such as urticaria, psoriasis, boils, and itching. Or he turns his

emotions into his respiratory system and comes up with a variety of asthmatoid conditions and begins to wheeze and whine and cough. Or he expresses himself through his gastrointestinal tract in the form of peptic ulcers of the stomach or duodenum or hyperirritability of the intestines or inflammation of the colon. Or he may express himself by expediting his emotions into his upper story and there begin to develop bats in his belfry in the form of a nervous breakdown. Or it may all go into his cardiovascular system, and there he may begin to develop heart or hypertensive symptoms. And so on most unmerrily, not to say unprofitably—except, of course, to the medical profession.

6   And there lies his grief-stricken wife, peeping worshipfully out of the corner of a moist eye at her seemingly composed husband, admiring him and depreciating herself for all the wrong reasons in the world. For it is he who is doing the wrong thing and she who is doing the right. The male by his stolid behavior is succeeding in damaging himself further, while the female is succeeding in restoring herself to a state of equilibrium and to continuing health. And this, supposedly, is why women are the weaker vessels and men are strong and resilient! The very opposite is the truth.

7   Women, by virtue of the availability of such outlets as crying for the expression of pent-up emotion, are likely to suffer from fewer psychosomatic disturbances than men.

8   I know of no studies on the expression of the emotions in businesswomen. But the increase in psychosomatic disorders among women in recent years—for example, the rise in the peptic ulcer rate—suggests that women in business may be attempting to restrain the normal expression of their emotions. If so, I would say that this is not good. Women in business who believe that in order to succeed, they must imitate men are barking up the wrong tree.

9   I am not suggesting that every time the boss bawls one out or every time one runs into a major frustration, one ought to assume the supine position and have a good cry. I think this would be silly. Crying should be reserved for the appropriate situation, and that is whenever one's organism indicates the necessity. In this respect the American male has a great deal to learn from the American female—whether in business or out of it. In business the emotions that are likely to be called into play are not those which usually lead to the desire to cry. On the contrary, they tend to be the angry emotions, and crying is not a natural way of expressing such emotions, nor is it being suggested that they should—even if they could—be so expressed. Opportunities to blow off steam in ways appropriate to the occasion should be provided until such time as we have contrived to produce human beings who have learned to deal with their frustrations in a constructive manner.

10   It would be absurd to suggest that the psychosomatic disorders from which men suffer in America are the result of the fact that they do not cry. The inability to cry is but one reflection of many indicating that the American male has not been taught how to use his emotions efficiently, and it is this general inefficient use of his emotions, rather than one particular expression of them, that is principally at fault. Nevertheless, it is agreed by most authorities that crying is a beneficial means of relieving the person of tensions which seek expression in this particular manner. It is far better that the energies which seek release in such emotional

expression find an outlet in weeping than that they should be pent up to seek adventitious expression through the body.

11   Tears have been likened to the clarifying and beneficent effects of the rain which comes after a thunderstorm on a sultry summer day. It was Charles Dickens, a man, who wrote: "Heaven knows we need never be ashamed of our tears, for they are rain upon the blinding dust of earth, overlying our hard hearts." Indeed, the evidence on all sides supports the view that under the conditions which call for it, a good cry is a wonderful restorative. Hence, it may be concluded that although crying would hardly be a solution to all the difficulties of the American male, it would certainly be a help in some.

12   Perhaps it would be helpful if instead of so wholeheartedly pursuing the ideals of life, liberty, and happiness, we modified our orientation in the direction of life, liberty, and the pursuit of homeostasis. Perhaps, also, the institution of the wailing wall is not such a bad idea. In any event, and quite seriatim, it is high time that parents realized that being a tender, gentle, warm, loving human being who can cry as well as laugh is not incompatible with being a man. The taboo on tenderness which is placed in the way of the American male's healthy development is something which we shall have to remove before American men are able to cry as and when they should. Italian and French men do not hesitate to cry whenever they feel like it, and I am sure that they are much the better off for being able to do so.

13   To be human is to weep. The human species is the only one in the whole of animated nature that sheds tears. The trained inability of any human being to weep is a lessening of his capacity to be human—a defect which usually goes deeper than the mere inability to cry. And this, among other things, is what American parents—with the best intentions in the world—have achieved for the American male. It is very sad. If we feel like it, let us all have a good cry—and clear our minds of those cobwebs of confusion which have for so long prevented us from understanding the ineluctable necessity of crying.

Ashley Montagu, trained in social biology and physical anthropology, has become one of the best known anthropologists in the world. He has taught at numerous American universities and is the author of more than fifty books, both popular and scholarly. His work explores the relation of cultural factors to the physical and behavioral evolution of man.

After You Read

Reading Journal

Do you agree with Montagu that men need to learn how to express grief? Or rather, do you feel there is something unmasculine, weak or childish about men who cry? (Use your pre-reading notes as a point of departure.)

Reading For Meaning

1. Why, according to Montagu, are American boys trained not to cry? Why does he disapprove of this practice?

2. Explain what Montagu means by "to be human is to weep."

3. What scientific explanation does Montagu give for the opinion he expresses in this article?

Exploring Further

Group Presentation

1. Often gender stereotypes embraced by a particular culture are reinforced through the media. In the United States, for example, one of the most recognizable models of "masculinity" is the cowboy, specifically the "Marlboro Man." As a group, make a list of as many qualities as you can which are associated with his image.

2. For the next class, bring in examples of advertisements using men and try to categorize them according to the criteria you established above. What other "types" of men are portrayed? What qualities are associated with them? What generalizations can you arrive at regarding the American male? Do you think his image has changed since Montagu wrote his book in the 1950s?

3. For your presentation, have your group design a poster (using the man/men you have selected) entitled "A Man of the 1990s." Decide what qualities he represents. Appoint a presenter to explain your choices to the entire class.

Timed Writing Exercise

Since Montagu's book was published in the 1950s, both the women's and men's movements have encouraged men to express grief and women to express anger openly. Yet cultural taboos continue to exist against the expression of these emotions. What reasons perpetuate our belief that men shouldn't cry and women shouldn't get angry?

Focused Essay Topics

1. Write a narrative essay which illustrates your culture's "rules" about crying. You may want to use your freewriting and journal entry as a point of departure.

2. In "Understanding the Difference," Phyllis Schlafly writes, "One of the strangest quirks of women's liberationists is their complaint that societal restraints prevent men from crying in public or showing their emotions, but permit women to do so, and that we should 'liberate' men to enable them, too, to cry in public. The public display of fear, sorrow, anger, and irritation reveals a lack of self-discipline that should be avoided by the Positive Woman just as much as the Positive Man." Write a short dialogue in which Schlafly and Montagu argue for or against displaying emotion. Then, in an argumentative essay, decide whom you agree with and why.

Before You Read

Imagine this situation: You and a friend of the opposite sex are in a restaurant. You have to wait 45 minutes to be seated and another half an hour for the waiter to take your order. When the food finally arrives, it is cold and not what you asked for. When you report this to the waiter he shrugs his shoulders and slams the check down on the table.

Which one of you is more likely to respond? Does being male or female influence your course of action. In what way? (For example: Do you believe that men are *expected* to handle situations involving anger? Are they taken more seriously? Would a woman handle this situation differently?

Sunday In The Park   BEL KAUFMAN

1   It was still warm in the late-afternoon sun, and the city noises came muffled through the trees in the park. She put her book down on the bench, removed her sunglasses, and sighed contentedly. Morton was reading the *Times Magazine* section, one arm flung around her shoulder; their three-year-old son, Larry, was playing in the sandbox; a faint breeze fanned her hair softly against her cheek. It was five-thirty on a Sunday afternoon, and the small playground, tucked away in a corner of the park, was all but deserted. The swings and seesaws stood motionless and abandoned, the slides were empty, and only in the sandbox two little boys squatted diligently side by side. *How good this is*, she thought, and almost smiled at her sense of well-being. They must go out in the sun more often; Morton was so city-pale, cooped up all week inside the gray factorylike university. She squeezed his arm affectionately and glanced at Larry, delighting in the pointed little face frowning in concentration over the tunnel he was digging. The other boy suddenly stood up and with a quick, deliberate swing of his chubby arm threw a spadeful of sand at Larry. It just missed his head. Larry continued digging; the boy remained standing, shovel raised, stolid and impassive.

2   "No, no, little boy." She shook her finger at him, her eyes searching for the child's mother or nurse. "We mustn't throw sand. It may get in someone's eyes and hurt. We must play nicely in the nice sandbox." The boy looked at her in unblinking expectancy. He was about Larry's age but perhaps ten pounds heavier, a husky little boy with none of Larry's quickness and sensitivity in his face. Where was his mother? The only other

people left in the playground were two women and a little girl on roller skates leaving now through the gate, and a man on a bench a few feet away. He was a big man, and he seemed to be taking up the whole bench as he held the Sunday comics close to his face. She supposed he was the child's father. He did not look up from his comics, but spat once deftly out of the corner of his mouth. She turned her eyes away.

3   At that moment, as swiftly as before, the fat little boy threw another spadeful of sand at Larry. This time some of it landed on his hair and forehead. Larry looked up at his mother, his mouth tentative; her expression would tell him whether to cry or not.

4   Her first instinct was to rush to her son, brush the sand out of his hair, and punish the other child, but she controlled it. She always said that she wanted Larry to learn to fight his own battles.

5   "Don't *do* that, little boy," she said sharply, leaning forward on the bench. "You mustn't throw sand!"

6   The man on the bench moved his mouth as if to spit again, but instead he spoke. He did not look at her, but at the boy only.

7   "You go right ahead, Joe," he said loudly. "Throw all you want. This here is a *public* sandbox."

8   She felt a sudden weakness in her knees as she glanced at Morton. He had become aware of what was happening. He put his *Times* down carefully on his lap and turned his fine, lean face toward the man, smiling the shy, apologetic smile he might have offered a student in pointing out an error in his thinking. When he spoke to the man, it was with his usual reasonableness.

9   "You're quite right," he said pleasantly, "but just because this is a public place. . . ."

10   The man lowered his funnies and looked at Morton. He looked at him from head to foot, slowly and deliberately. "Yeah?" His insolent voice was edged with menace. "My kid's got just as good right here as yours, and if he feels like throwing sand, he'll throw it, and if you don't like it, you can take your kid the hell out of here."

11   The children were listening, their eyes and mouths wide open, their spades forgotten in small fists. She noticed the muscle in Morton's jaw tighten. He was rarely angry; he seldom lost his temper. She was suffused with a tenderness for her husband and an impotent rage against the man for involving him in a situation so alien and so distasteful to him.

12   "Now, just a minute," Morton said courteously, "you must realize. . . ."

13   "Aw, shut up," said the man.

14   Her heart began to pound. Morton half rose; the *Times* slid to the ground. Slowly the other man stood up. He took a couple of steps toward Morton, then stopped. He flexed his great arms, waiting. She pressed her trembling knees together. Would there be violence, fighting? How dreadful, how incredible. . . . She must do something, stop them, call for help. She wanted to put her hand on her husband's sleeve, to pull him down, but for some reason she didn't.

15   Morton adjusted his glasses. He was very pale. "This is ridiculous," he said unevenly. "I must ask you. . . ."

16   "Oh, yeah?" said the man. He stood with his legs spread apart, rocking a little, looking at Morton with utter scorn. "You and who else?"

17   For a moment the two men looked at each other nakedly. Then Morton turned his back on the man and said quietly, "Come on, let's get out of here." He walked awkwardly, almost limping with self-consciousness, to the sandbox. He stooped and lifted Larry and his shovel out.

18   At once Larry came to life; his face lost its rapt expression and he began to kick and cry. "I don't *want* to go home, I want to play better, I don't *want* any supper, I don't *like* supper. . . ." It became a chant as they walked, pulling their child between them, his feet dragging on the ground. In order to get to the exit gate they had to pass the bench where the man sat sprawling again. She was careful not to look at him. With all the dignity she could summon, she pulled Larry's sandy, perspiring little hand, while Morton pulled the other. Slowly and with head high she walked with her husband and child out of the playground.

19   Her first feeling was one of relief that a fight had been avoided, that no one was hurt. Yet beneath it there was a layer of something else, something heavy and inescapable. She sensed that it was more than just an unpleasant incident, more than defeat of reason by force. She felt dimly it had something to do with her and Morton, something acutely personal, familiar, and important.

20   Suddenly Morton spoke. "It wouldn't have proved anything."

21   "What?" she asked.

22   "A fight. It wouldn't have proved anything beyond the fact that he's bigger than I am."

23   "Of course," she said.

24   "The only possible outcome," he continued reasonably, "would have been—what? My glasses broken, perhaps a tooth or two replaced, a couple of days' work missed—and for what? For justice? For truth?"

25   "Of course," she repeated. She quickened her step. She wanted only to get home and to busy herself with her familiar tasks; perhaps then the feeling, glued like heavy plaster on her heart, would be gone. *Of all the stupid, despicable bullies*, she thought, pulling harder on Larry's hand. The child was still crying. Always before she had felt a tender pity for his defenseless little body, the frail arms, the narrow shoulders with sharp, winglike shoulder blades, the thin and unsure legs, but now her mouth tightened in resentment.

26   "Stop crying," she said sharply. "I'm ashamed of you!" She felt as if all three of them were tracking mud along the street. The child cried louder.

27   *If there had been an issue involved,* she thought, *if there had been something to fight for. . . . But what else could he possibly have done? Allow himself to be beaten? Attempt to educate the man? Call a policeman? "Officer, there's a man in the park who won't stop his child from throwing sand on mine. . . ."* The whole thing was as silly as that, and not worth thinking about.

28   "Can't you keep him quiet, for Pete's sake?" Morton asked irritably.

29   "What do you suppose I've been trying to do?" she said.

30   Larry pulled back, dragging his feet.

31   "If you can't discipline this child, I will," Morton snapped, making a move toward the boy.

32   But her voice stopped him. She was shocked to hear it, thin and cold and penetrating with contempt, "Indeed?" she heard herself say. "You and who else?"

Bel Kaufman drew upon her twenty years' experience as a New York City public school teacher to write the best selling novel *Up The Down Staircase*, which was later made into a movie and a weekly television situation comedy. She is also the author of *Love, etc.* (1979). Her "Sunday in The Park" won the National Educational Association/PEN Short Story contest in 1983.

After You Read

Reading Journal

How would you have handled the situation in the park?

For male students: Would you have reacted as Morton did or would you have stood up to the other father? What would the consequences of your decision have been?

For female students: If Morton were your husband, would you, like his wife, have been disappointed in his avoidance of direct confrontation? Why or why not?

Reading For Meaning

1. Kaufman writes in paragraph 19: "She sensed that it was more than just an unpleasant incident, more than defeat of reason by force. She felt dimly it had something to do with her and Morton, something acutely personal, familiar, and important." What was it exactly that troubled the woman in the story?

2. How does Larry become the focus of his parents' anger and frustration as they leave the park? Why do you think this happens?

Exploring Further

Debate

Over the past twenty years, the American women's movement has encouraged women to become more assertive, particularly in the area of equal rights. Some critics of feminism, however, insist that American women have taken on the worst qualities of male aggressiveness, thereby alienating women who subscribe to more traditional gender roles. Use your personal experience, reading and examples from popular culture to argue whether or not American women today are too aggressive.

Timed Writing Exercise

In your native culture, is active confrontation encouraged? If not, explain why. In so doing, think back on the training you were given as a child about ways to solve conflict. Were boys and girls given different advice? (You might want to use a personal anecdote as support for your argument.)

Focused Essay Topics

1. At several points in the story, the couple justify Morton's behavior by saying that the issue (sand-throwing) was not worth fighting over, yet they are both left feeling angry and disappointed. What do you think Kaufman was trying to say about human nature and how we resolve conflict?

2. In Susan Brownmiller's essay, "Femininity," she defines femininity as designed "to avoid direct confrontation and to smooth over the fissures of conflict" and masculinity as "an effort to please women . . . by displays of mastery and competence." In what ways does Kaufman's story either support or refute this definition of gender roles? Use specific examples from the text in your argument.

EXTENDING THE CONTEXT

> These questions are designed for further discussion or essay writing. Your responses should reflect the thinking, reading and writing you have done on the unit topic thus far.

1. Several of the authors in this section present their definitions of masculinity and/or femininity. Write a definition essay of your own, using these readings as a point of departure. Consider as you write, the various cultural and social attitudes which have shaped your opinion.

2. Freewrite on the following question: "How would your life change if tomorrow morning you woke up as a member of the opposite sex?" Use your freewriting and the work you have done in this unit to write an essay in which you analyze the basic assumptions (and stereotypes) you make about gender.

3. What incentive do men have to make substantive changes in the ways in which they see and treat women if changes may result in a loss of male privilege? (In your essay you must define those privileges.)

4. There are an increasing number of American men, led by the poet Robert Bly, who see themselves as pro-feminist. Men's attempt to rethink gender stereotypes has even led to the formation of a men's movement. Research and report to the class the goals and philosophy of this group. Do you think this movement could gain a following in your native culture? Would any of its goals need to be modified?

5. Describe a world where women are the dominant sex. How would it differ? Would it be a better, more peaceful place, as some feminists suggest?

6. Interview an older woman in your family about her life. Ask her about opportunities to pursue an education and/or career, about childcare, housework, and marriage—in other words, the issues pertinent to a woman's life. Write up the interview and then write a commentary, explaining how your own life differs and how you feel about her story.

7. Phyllis Schlafly warned, nearly 20 years ago, that encouraging children to reverse traditional gender roles (i.e., boys learning to help with housework and childcare, and girls learning to work with tools and set career goals) "further confuse a generation already unsure about its identity." Using your experience and knowledge of American culture to date, do you think she was correct? What changes, if any, can you see around you as a result of this "re-education"?

VIDEO SUGGESTIONS

The video selections are offered as suggestions for viewing in or out of class to enrich the unit topic.

Kramer vs Kramer

Tootsie

Adam's Rib

The Secret of the Sexes (PBS video)

Mr. Mom

Baby Boom

Thelma and Louise

The Color Purple

The Good Mother

Roe v. Wade

The Accused

Unit Five

RIGHT AND WRONG IN AMERICA: EXAMINING MORAL VALUES

NORMAN
ROCKWELL,
The Golden Rule

Short Takes

The difference between a moral man and a man of honor is that the latter regrets a discreditable act, when it has worked and he has not been caught.

H.L. Mencken

Morals are an acquirement—like music, like a foreign language, like piety, poker, paralysis—no man is born with them.

Mark Twain

Man is the only animal who causes pain to others with no other object than wanting to do so.

Arthur Schopenhauer

We have, in fact, two kinds of morality side by side; one which we preach but do not practice, and another which we practice but seldom preach.

Bertrand Russell

It is often easier to fight for principles than to live up to them.

Adlai Stevenson

What is morality in any given time or place? It is what the majority then and there happen to like and immorality is what they dislike.

Alfred North Whitehead

You've go to be brave and you've go to be bold. Brave enough to take your chance on your own discrimination—what's right and what's wrong, what's good and what's bad.

Robert Frost

Do not be too moral. You may cheat yourself out of much life. So aim above morality. Be not simply good; be good for something.

Henry David Thoreau

SUGGESTIONS FOR USING SHORT TAKES:

- Respond in writing to one of the quotations above. Then get together in groups and share what you have written.
- Work with a partner, small group or the entire class to discuss one or more quotations. You may want to agree, disagree, or compare it to similar expressions or sayings in your native language.

INTRODUCTION – RIGHT AND WRONG IN AMERICA: EXAMINING MORAL VALUES

Americans everywhere are worried about the state of the nation. Worried about children who are as likely to carry a gun or a stash of drugs in their schoolbags as they are to carry books; worried about violent crime, no longer limited to urban areas; worried about domestic violence and the breakdown of the family. Worried that we have lost the moral and ethical guideposts that were once shared and taken for granted by the majority of Americans.

Speaking to these national concerns, *The Wall Street Journal* published an editorial in March 1993 entitled "The Decline of Self-Restraint." The article seemed to be so relevant that only twelve days later the *New York Times* reprinted it, asking its readers to respond. This editorial portrays a society that has lost sight of its moral and ethical standards as well as the institutions and habits by which to live them. The article further identifies the origins of America's troubles as the anti-war movement of the 1960s: "Those endless demonstrations were part of a much deeper shift in American culture—away from community and family rules of conduct and toward more autonomy, more personal independence." As to limits, "you set your own," the editorial states.

Following the 1950s, a decade of social repression and conformity, three social movements emerged that would alter long-entrenched patterns and would challenge power relations: the civil rights movement, the women's movement and the anti-war movement. Each in its own way brought profound changes to American life. In this upheaval, the family and the church, the two institutions which had set and enforced a moral code for most Americans—ceased to do so. The reasons behind these great social and political changes are undoubtedly much more complex than any single movement.

Neither church nor family stands at the heart of American experience as the forces of moral authority that they once were. Indeed, other forces, such as the media seem to have taken their place. Television, and the popular mass culture that it transmits into homes everywhere, present a set of values and models of behavior that often run counter to traditional notions of decency and morality. In fact, today the most frequently seen television image is that of violence, whether it be enacted as drama or reported as news.

Violence, drug use, disadvantaged children bearing and raising children on welfare rolls, increasing numbers of homeless Americans—these are our insoluble problems. It seems simplistic to place blame for this complex constellation of societal ills on one movement and on a single generation. More realistically, America's problems are the legacy of a political and social system that has not been able to provide equitably for all Americans—the urban and rural poor, and the disadvantaged ethnic and racial minorities. For many, legislation for affirmative action and equal opportunity offers too little, too late. It is clear that we must invent a politics of inclusion for all if American society is to cohere morally, socially and politically.

However, as always, there is no shortage of American citizens who are "part of the solution, not just part of the problem," to quote a 1960s motto. These Americans are to be found in schools and on school boards, in businesses, community centers and soup kitchens. They are heeding their conscience, much as anti-war protesters did 30 years ago; they are taking an ethical stand on the issues that concern them and their communities—and they are taking action. Perhaps they are the individuals who will help restore or reinvent an ethics that will carry us into the next century and make us a better America.

Before You Read

"I ran across something today you don't see much anymore—a guilty conscience."

1. What social issue is the cartoonist addressing?

2. The article you are about to read expresses a similar concern over America's "lack of a guilty conscience" and whether schools might be the best place to find one. What do you think? Can and should schools teach moral values?

Reading, Writing and Arithmetic and, Now, Right and Wrong   KATE STONE LOMBARDI

1   Forget for the moment why Johnny can't read. Consider instead why Johnny can't tell right from wrong. Can he be taught to make morally informed decisions? And should he be taught tolerance for those different from himself?

2   Mirroring a nationwide trend, many schools in Westchester County are grappling with these questions. Educators are studying and, in some cases, implementing a re-introduction of moral and democratic values into both the curriculum and the school setting.

3   For many parents and teachers, the focus represents a long-overdue recognition of the schools' critical role in combatting what they see as a deteriorating moral climate surrounding children. But others are balking at what they see as the schools' intrusion into what has historically been the role of the family. And some argue that an emphasis on values detracts from the schools' principal job of teaching academic subjects.

4   Critical to the debate, of course, is just what—or whose—values will be taught. Evelyn Stock, a former member of the Scarsdale School Board, described the quandary by recalling a retreat that board members took some years ago to study the issue.

'Core Values'

5   "It was easy to get the first few, like respect yourself, or respect others, but when we started to get into things like patriotism, we were still coming off the Vietnam War, and it was controversial. Charity was another one. It meant different things to different people," she said.

6   Despite the difficulty some communities have in coming to a consensus, many people argue that there are some basic principles almost everybody can agree on.

7   "People have become more comfortable talking about this," said Maureen Grolnick, principal of Bronxville High School. "One needn't be embarrassed by it; it's not a cliché value of 'law and order' or 'motherhood and apple pie.' There are some values around decency and responsibility toward oneself and others that we share pretty much across the board and that don't need to get us into a terribly painful conflict about what is the role of the school or the role of the family," she said.

8   The State Department of Education has held several conferences on values education. The most recent was last week in Albany, and several Westchester school districts were represented. The State Board of Regents has also taken a strong interest in the issue. It has identified what it calls "core values" on which it says there is universal agreement. These include responsibility, honesty, self-discipline, self-respect, respect for others, commitment to equality, justice, rule of law and the work ethic.

Reaction to New Focus is Mixed

9   "After four decades of neglect, values education is being emphasized again in many public schools of New York State," said Emlyn I. Griffith, a member of the State Board of Regents. "The Regents strongly support this initiative. The Regents have defined basic core values as principles of intrinsic enduring worth—the standards of conduct required of

everyone in a self-governing society," he said.

10   Values education can occur on two levels. First, children can be given moral or ethical guidance and taught critical thinking. Second, the atmosphere for learning can be one that underscores the importance of values. That is, not only should Johnny theoretically learn how to respect other people but he should also do so while not wearing a cap in class, putting his feet up on his desk or using abusive language toward the teacher.

11   The reaction to the new focus on values is mixed. For some it is a welcome relief.

12   "I'm finding that there is a visceral response to being given permission and validation for teaching values in the school," said Tom Laconna, a professor at the State University of New York at Cortland and a leading expert in the field. "There has been a mounting frustration in the face of a tidal wave of cultural and moral sleaze that has been washing over us, Madonna's sex book being the latest example. There is a deep anger on the part of parents and teachers that significant social institutions have not been able to address this."

Some Parental Opposition

13   While some administrators might welcome the license to re-emphasize values, parents are not always quite so sanguine. Mark Soss, principal at the Roaring Brook Elementary School in Chappaqua, described an incident where a fourth grader had come to school wearing a T-shirt that bore a statement that was blatantly sexual in nature. The principal asked the child to turn the shirt inside out and asked that he not wear it to school again. To his surprise, the child's parents objected to Mr. Soss's position, saying it was an infringement on their child's freedom of speech.

14   George Cohen, a human relations specialist for the White Plains Public Schools, has faced similar dilemmas. Mr. Cohen says he has seen a breakdown of discipline among students, with foul language used in the classrooms and a lack of respect for authority so basic that some children are willing to ignore direct requests from administrators and teachers. Children also show a lack of fear of any disciplinary action. Compounding the difficulty, he says, is the attitude of some parents.

15   "In the old days, if the school disciplined you, you were also going to get punished at home," Mr. Cohen said. "Now if the school punishes you, the parents run to the rescue. They keep the school from doing anything that sends the message that you have to be responsible for your own behavior," he said.

16   That is not to say that all parents oppose values in the schools. Many embrace the schools' interest in this area.

Values Start in the Family

17   "Our P.T.A. believes values should be a marriage of both the schools' responsibility and the family's. That way kids get the message louder and clearer," said Caren Fried, chairwoman of the parent education committee for the Chappaqua P.T.A. Mrs. Fried's committee is organizing a Parenting Symposium titled "Values Start in the Family . . . Then What?" for parents in the district next month.

18   The implementation of values education varies widely in the district. In White Plains, second graders are taught Socratic reasoning: they are given a text and are taught how to question its assumptions. At higher grade levels, in an attempt to reduce racial tension and promote tolerance, students with different backgrounds participate in ethnic sharing panels.

19   In Croton, students are trained in hands-on democracy. The traditional student council at Croton-Harmon High School has been replaced by a school governance congress, where various "stakeholders," that is, students, teachers, administrators, parent representatives and custodial and secretarial representatives, meet weekly to make decisions affecting the school community. The congress has decided a host of issues, including academic eligibility for participation in extracurricular activities and whether suspensions should take place in or out of the school building. The congress gives students the skills they need to participate in a democratic society, said Sherry King, Superintendent of the Croton Schools.

20   In Chappaqua, the district has developed what it calls standards of excellence, by which graduates of Horace Greeley High School will be evaluated. Students will be assessed in areas of "personal growth" and "responsible citizenship" as well as for academic excellence.

Values or Political Correctness?

21   But some parents are uncomfortable with the concept of giving equal weight to the more nebulous areas of personal growth and citizenship and believe that children will actually be evaluated for their "political correctness."

22   "The irony of this development is that you have a group of educational professionals whose left-of-center political orientation dominates the educational establishment, introducing a concept of 'growth of ethical reasoning' to an educational system which their liberal forefathers assured us needed to be free of any religious orientation to be truly liberal and democratic minded," said Paul Atkinson, a Chappaqua parent with two children in the school system.

"They're reintroducing school prayer on their terms."

23   Mr. Atkinson also said that he believed the central mission of the schools was becoming distorted by the emphasis on values. "It detracts both in time and in orientation from the teacher's basic role. It's a lot easier for a teacher to worry about a child's self-development than to sit down and work with a child who is having trouble learning some fundamental reading or writing skills," he said.

24   But proponents of values education are not discouraged by a certain amount of parental disapproval.

25   "Conflict is inherent in everything," said Georgine Hyde, vice president of the New York State School Board Association and area director for the region that includes Westchester. "I consider character development and values education a part of the educational sequence. Do we ask parents if we have to teach reading or writing? A child is not born with math skills or reading skills, and a child is not born with values. If you are not developing a whole child, you are only bringing him part of an education."

An Old Debate

26   The debate over the importance of values education is not a new one. Even Aristotle bemoaned the moral state of his day's youth. Like other educational trends, this one has come in and out of favor with administrators. It has also appeared in different guises.

27   In the 1970's, for instance, a program known as "values clarification" became popular. In this model, values were viewed to be relative. Students were given moral quandaries, and asked for their responses. There were no right or wrong responses, the point was simply that the students should "clarify" their positions, or know where they stood.

28   The current resurgence in values education follows a relatively dormant period in the 1980's, but in this incarnation, values are not a matter of opinion but clearly a matter of right and wrong.

29   "There is a tremendous amount of interest in this right now," said Tom Laconna. "What's different about the current scene is that values are seen as having objective worth. They are good for the individual, good for the whole human community and therefore they have a claim on our collective conscience."

Kate Stone Lombardi is a staff writer at *The New York Times*.

After You Read

Reading Journal

Reflecting back on your secondary school experience, do you remember efforts made to teach values? Were they implicit (role modeling of the teachers, values discussion in history or language class) or explicit (religious instruction or a "values" curriculum) or both? If your school did not address values, do you think it should have? Explain.

Reading For Meaning

1. What is the central conflict, according to the article, surrounding the teaching of moral values in the schools?

2. What are "core values"? What problems arise when people attempt to define these values? Do you agree with the list the Department of Education in New York came up with? Would you add to or remove anything from the list?

3. List several examples of how the Westchester, New York school system has implemented values education in their districts.

4. Define the parental opposition to explicit teaching of values in the school. How is this a different response than that of previous generations of parents?

5. Compare the "values clarification" model of the 1970s with that of the current "values education" model. What does it mean, as Professor Laconna says, that now "values are seen as having objective worth"?

Exploring Further

Group Presentation

In your group decide on a core value you feel has "objective worth." (See Question #5 in *Reading for Meaning* if you need further clarification on this term.) Then decide how you would try to "teach" this value in your English classroom. For example, if you decide that *honesty* is your core value, you might write up a policy concerning plagiarism and cheating. The policy should include (1) a definition of your policy, (2) the rationale for its necessity and (3) the consequences of violating it.

Timed Writing Exercise

Agree or disagree with the following statement: Asking teachers to transmit moral and ethical values "detracts both in time and in orientation from [their] basic role," which is to teach academic subjects. We cannot afford for this to happen, given the continued decline in American student performance.

Focused Essay Topics

1. A heated debate arose recently in New York City over whether to include in the elementary school curriculum a book called *Heather Has Two Mommies*. The book, which promotes acceptance of the homosexual lifestyle, is part of a larger initiative called the "Rainbow Curriculum" which stresses respect and tolerance of diversity. Opposition came from parents and educators who claimed that the book explicitly contradicted their personal and religious views on homosexuality. Write an essay in which you defend or oppose a school's right to transmit its own views on this or a similarly controversial moral issue, such as abortion, gun control or the right to die.

2. Write a personal essay in which you describe one "core value" which is essential to you. Be sure to use specific examples in your essay which will illustrate not only why the value is important to you but how you have chosen to incorporate it in your everyday life.

Before You Read

Freewrite on the following and share your response: The boy in the story you are about to read is called a "cipher." Check the meaning of this word in your dictionary if necessary. Why do you think he might be called this? Have you ever felt this way about yourself or about someone you knew well? Describe the circumstances surrounding these feelings.

Cipher in the Snow   JEAN E. MIZER

1   It started with tragedy on a biting cold February morning. I was driving behind the Milford Corners bus as I did most snowy mornings on my way to school. It veered and stopped short at the hotel, which it had no business doing, and I was annoyed as I had to come to an unexpected stop. A boy lurched out of the bus, reeled, stumbled, and collapsed on the snowbank at the curb. The bus driver and I reached him at the same moment. His thin, hollow face was white even against the snow.

2   "He's dead," the driver whispered.

3   It didn't register for a minute. I glanced quickly at the scared young faces staring down at us from the school bus. "A doctor! Quick! I'll phone from the hotel. . . ."

4   "No use. I tell you he's dead." The driver looked down at the boy's still form. "He never even said he felt bad," he muttered, "just tapped me on the shoulder and said, real quiet, 'I'm sorry. I have to get off at the hotel.' That's all. Polite and apologizing like."

5   At school, the giggling, shuffling morning noise quieted as the news went down the halls. I passed a huddle of girls. "Who was it? Who dropped dead on the way to school?" I heard one of them half-whisper.

6   "Don't know his name; some kid from Milford Corners," was the reply.

7   It was like that in the faculty room and the principal's office. "I'd appreciate your going out to tell the parents," the principal told me. "They haven't a phone and, anyway, somebody from school should go there in person. I'll cover your classes."

8   "Why me?" I asked. "Wouldn't it be better if you did it?"

9   "I didn't know the boy," the principal admitted levelly. "And in last year's sophomore personalities column I note that you were listed as his favorite teacher."

10   I drove through the snow and cold down the bad canyon road to the Evans place and thought about the boy, Cliff Evans. His favorite teacher! I

thought. He hasn't spoken two words to me in two years! I could see him in my mind's eye all right, sitting back there in the last seat in my afternoon literature class. He came in the room by himself and left by himself. "Cliff Evans," I muttered to myself, "a boy who never talked." I thought a minute. "A boy who never smiled. I never saw him smile once."

11   The big ranch kitchen was clean and warm. I blurted out my news somehow. Mrs. Evans reached blindly toward a chair. "He never said anything about bein' ailing."

12   His step-father snorted. "He ain't said nothin' about anything since I moved in here."

13   Mrs. Evans pushed a pan to the back of the stove and began to untie her apron. "Now hold on," her husband snapped. "I got to have breakfast before I go to town. Nothin' we can do now anyway. If Cliff hadn't been so dumb, he'd have told us he didn't feel good."

14   After school I sat in the office and stared bleakly at the records spread out before me. I was to close the file and write the obituary for the school paper. The almost bare sheets mocked the effort. Cliff Evans, white, never legally adopted by step-father, five young half-brothers and sisters. These meager strands of information and the list of D grades were all the records had to offer.

15   Cliff Evans had silently come in the school door in the mornings and gone out the school door in the evenings, and that was all. He had never belonged to a club. He had never played on a team. He had never held an office. As far as I could tell, he had never done one happy, noisy kid thing. He had never been anybody at all.

16   How do you go about making a boy into a zero? The grade school records showed me. The first and second grade teachers' annotations read "sweet, shy child"; "timid but eager." Then the third grade note had opened the attack. Some teacher had written in a good, firm hand, "Cliff won't talk. Uncooperative. Slow learner." The other academic sheep had followed with "dull"; "slow-witted"; "low I.Q." They became correct. The boy's I.Q. score in the ninth grade was listed at 83. But his I.Q. in the third grade had been 106. The score didn't go under 100 until the seventh grade. Even shy, timid, sweet children have resilience. It takes time to break them.

17   I stomped to the typewriter and wrote a savage report pointing out what education had done to Cliff Evans. I slapped a copy on the principal's desk and another in the sad, dog-eared file. I banged the typewriter and slammed the file and crashed the door shut, but I didn't feel much better. A little boy kept walking after me, a little boy with a peaked, pale face; a skinny body in faded jeans; and big eyes that had looked and searched for a long time and then had become veiled.

18   I could guess how many times he'd been chosen last to play sides in a game, how many whispered child conversations had excluded him, how many times he hadn't been asked. I could see and hear the faces and voices that said over and over, "You're dumb. You're dumb. You're nothing, Cliff Evans."

19   A child is a believing creature. Cliff undoubtedly believed them. Suddenly it seemed clear to me: When finally there was nothing left at all for Cliff

Evans, he collapsed on a snowbank and went away. The doctor might list "heart failure" as the cause of death, but that wouldn't change my mind.

20   We couldn't find ten students in the school who had known Cliff well enough to attend the funeral as his friends. So the student body officers and a committee from the junior class went as a group to the church, being politely sad. I attended the services with them, and sat through it with a lump of cold lead in my chest and a big resolve growing through me.

21   I've never forgotten Cliff Evans nor that resolve. He has been my challenge year after year, class after class. I look up and down the rows carefully each September at the unfamiliar faces. I look for veiled eyes or bodies scrounged into a seat in an alien world. "Look, kids," I say silently, "I may not do anything else for you this year, but not one of you is going to come out of here a nobody. I'll work or fight to the bitter end doing battle with society and the school board, but I won't have one of you coming out of here thinking himself into a zero."

22   Most of the time—not always, but most of the time—I've succeeded.

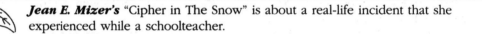

Jean E. Mizer's "Cipher in The Snow" is about a real-life incident that she experienced while a schoolteacher.

After You Read

Reading Journal

Do you believe, along with the author, that Cliff could have been saved if only someone had paid him sufficient attention? Why or why not?

Reading For Meaning

1. Sketch a brief portrait of Cliff, the circumstances of his life, both at home and at school.

2. What was the cause of Cliff's death, according to the author?

3. Whom does the author blame for his death?

4. What personal vow did Mizer make after learning of Cliff's tragedy? Was she successful?

Exploring Further

Debate

Argue for or against the following: Given the complexity of modern society and the imperfect nature of humankind, tragedies like the death of Cliff Evans are unavoidable.

Timed Writing Exercise

Write an essay in which you outline the problem of children like Cliff and then propose at least one concrete solution for what can be done to help them.

Focused Essay Topics

1. In your opinion, who should bear the greatest responsibility for what happened to Cliff? Society at large? His family and friends? The school? His teachers? Explain.

2. Describe a teacher you remember who held either a particularly good or particularly bad opinion of you and/or your work. In the body of your essay be sure to talk about how this made you feel and what impact it had on your performance. (Use your notes from the *Before You Read* section, if applicable.) Does your experience seem to support or refute Mizer's story?

Before You Read

In the article "How About a Swift Kick?" the author describes an unusual method for teaching young people at risk to take responsibility for their lives. Write a personal anecdote about a person you know—a family member, friend, teacher, coach or clergyman—who taught you an important moral or ethical lesson. How did s/he accomplish this?

How About a Swift Kick? JOE KLEIN

1   Last week I read James Q. Wilson's formidable new book, "The Moral Sense," and thought of Geoffrey Canada. Wilson has taken a daring leap, even for a sociologist of his stature: he has come out for virtue. He proposes—and endeavors to prove, citing a mountain of recent behavioral studies—that morality is innate and has evolved over the millenniums, rooted in the very qualities that enable us to succeed as social animals: sympathy, fairness, self-control and sense of duty (or conscience). He argues that the moral sense is fragile, varying in intensity, subject to buffeting by more elemental instincts—survival, greed, passion—but persistent nonetheless, very much like our sense of beauty. "My interest in this. . . grew out of my studies of crime," he writes. "What needed explanation, it seemed to me, was not why some people are criminals, but why most people are not."

2   The question seems especially relevant in communities like Harlem, where (the argument too often goes) antisocial behavior is a consequence of hopelessness—and where Geoff Canada has been cultivating virtue, and hope, in children for the past 10 years. He has done this in a variety of ways, as the president of the Rheedlen Centers for Children and Families, but most creatively in a way that might tickle James Q. Wilson: he teaches a karate class. His methods are unrelenting and unpatronizing. He expects, in return for the skills he teaches, a strict standard of moral behavior. His students stay in school. They don't break the law. They don't have children out of wedlock (not one in 10 years, he insists).

3   The penalty for breaking the rules is harsh, and immediate: "I saw it happen once," says Alex Echevarria, who began the program seven years ago and has now become an instructor. "Two people were caught dealing drugs. Geoff went to their houses, stripped them of their belts and, in front of the rest of us, cut the belts in two with scissors. These people had invested *years* in getting those belts. I was maybe 15 at the time. I decided that I could not afford to lose what I was working toward." What he was working toward, what Canada really teaches, was self-control (a far more practical virtue than "self-esteem"). "You can apply karate to everything else you do in life," says Alex François, another Canada student who has now become an instructor (and, like Echevarria, gone on to college). "It gives you the discipline to follow up on your plans."

4   What Canada does is not unique. Time and again, strong authority figures with strict disciplinary regimes have proven that they can inspire kids growing up in the most desperate circumstances. The question is, why do these programs remain isolated, relatively rare—and mostly private? With even most liberals now paying lip service to the importance of personal responsibility, why haven't these principles become public policy? Why does the stray tough-guy math teacher—whose story inevitably becomes a stirring made-for-TV movie—always wind up *in trouble* with the authorities? And why will Wilson's book—posing an idea that most people consider basic common sense—be seen as controversial in academic and policy circles?

5   Wilson argues that we are paying the price for a century of intellectual wrongheadedness. The legatees of Marx, Freud and Darwin argued that morality was a chimera; it had "no basis in science and logic." Moralists were forced to flee to the musty backwaters of philosophy and theology; the barbarians took hold of public policy. "It is difficult to say what effects have followed [our] effort to talk ourselves out of having a moral sense," Wilson writes. "We may have harmed vulnerable children who ought to have received surer guidance from family and neighborhoods; we may have promoted self-indulgence when we thought we were only endorsing freedom."

6   It is impossible, of course, to pinpoint the precise moment when moral relativism became acceptable public policy—but in the '60s, the structures of moral authority were systematically removed from the poorest neighborhoods. A series of legal judgments made it harder for teachers to discipline their students and for housing projects to screen their tenants; the cop on the beat was seen as an occupying force and removed. The moral consequences of programs like welfare were never considered. Instead of nurturing virtue, popular culture celebrated intemperance—and intemperance, as Adam Smith pointed out 200 years ago, may addle the rich, but it devastates the poor.

7   The effects of virtue-free social policy have been devastating—but we don't seem quite ready to accept the alternative. Few politicians are comfortable about using words like "right" and "wrong," especially when the subject is sexual irresponsibility (which remains the surest predictor of criminality, ill health and welfare dependency among the poor). Last week's census report announcing a continuing trend toward out-of-wedlock births across society was greeted by total silence from public figures—including the president, who seems to have forgotten about "personal responsibility" since the campaign.

8   In fact, it *isn't* easy. It requires the fortitude to sometimes cast people into the outer darkness—as Canada did when he stripped the belts from the two drug dealers. It has become nearly impossible for a polity as rights-conscious, and tolerant, as ours to admit that some people who behave badly, if not quite criminally, aren't worthy of our support—to kick them off welfare, or out of schools and housing projects. But it is inescapable; the system can't work without sanctions—even if they require the sort of stiff, humorless, *un-American* propriety that gave morality such a bad name.

Joe Klein's piece appeared on the *Public Lives* page of *Newsweek* in 1993.

After You Read

Reading Journal

Describe someone you knew who was considered a troublemaker. Do you feel she or he could have profited from joining Canada's karate class? Why or why not?

Reading For Meaning

1. Klein uses several abstract terms and phrases which you will need to look up in order to fully understand your reading. Use the dictionary to explain the following:

   a. *Moral relativism*

   b. *Morality is a chimera.*

   c. *Intemperance may adle the rich, but it devastates the poor.*

2. What is the thesis behind James Wilson's book, *The Moral Sense?* How does this relate to Geoff Canada's unique approach to morality?

3. What is the operating principle of Canada's technique? Explain how karate can "apply to everything else you do in life," as one of his instructors claims.

4. Both Wilson and Klein blame the moral relativism of the 1960s for removing "moral authority" from society. What does this mean? What do they feel are the consequences of this policy for American society today?

5. What does Klein suggest may be a better way of reinforcing moral values in America? Why does he call this "un-American"?

Exploring Further

Group Presentation

1. Tough disciplinary approaches and strong role modeling, like Canada's program, have been the subjects of several American films. Divide the class into small sections. Have each rent a different film, such as *Stand and Deliver*, *The Prime of Miss Jean Brodie*, *Dead Poets' Society* (or any other film which deals with student-teacher issues).

2. Each section will then write a critique of the method(s) used to influence students to present to the class. In so doing, consider the following:
   (a) What specific techniques were used by the teacher involved?
   (b) What problems were they designed to help?
   (c) How effective were they?
   (d) Do you think these techniques could easily be used by others?
   (e) What, if any, drawbacks are there to this approach?

Timed Writing Exercise

Until recently corporal (physical) punishment like spanking was used in the schools to discipline students. Today, however, this method is rarely used. Do you believe this method is effective? Use your own experience as a point of departure.

Focused Essay Topics

1. Write an essay in which you discuss the attitude of your native culture toward authority and discipline. How, for example, would your culture regard a program such as Canada's? Would there be a need for his program? Why or why not?

2. How would you respond to the thesis which prompted Wilson's book, *The Moral Sense*, that "what needed explanation . . . was not why some people are criminals, but why most people are not."?

Before You Read

The next reading discusses a basic lack of trust expressed by American institutions. (For example, the use of surveillance cameras in banks and stores.) Do you think this distrust is justified? Give examples from your experience in and observation of the U.S.

Severing the Human Connection   H. Bruce Miller

1   Went down to the local self-serve gas station the other morning to fill up. The sullen cashier was sitting inside a dark, glassed-in, burglar-proof, bullet-proof, probably grenade-proof cubicle covered with cheerful notices. "NO CHECKS." "NO CREDIT." "NO BILLS OVER $50 ACCEPTED." "CASHIER HAS NO SMALL CHANGE." And the biggest one of all: "PAY BEFORE PUMPING GAS." A gleaming steel box slid out of the wall and gaped open. I dropped in a $20 bill. "Going to fill 'er up with no-lead on Number 6," I said. The cashier nodded. The steel box swallowed my money and retracted into the cubicle. I walked back to the car to pump the gas, trying not to slink or skulk. I felt like I ought to be wearing striped overalls with a number on the breast pocket.

2   The pay-before-you-pump gas station (those in the trade call it a "pre-pay") is a response to a real problem in these days of expensive gas and cut-rate ethics: people who fill their tanks and then tear out of the station without paying. Those in the business call them "drive-offs." The head of one area gasoline dealers' association says drive-offs cost some dealers $500 to $600 a month. With a profit margin of only about a nickel a gallon, a dealer has to sell a lot of gallons to make up that kind of loss. The police aren't much help. Even if the attendant manages to get a license plate number and description of the car, the cops have better things to do than tracking down a guy who stole $15 worth of gas. So the dealers adopt the pre-pay system.

3   Intellectually, I understand all of this, yet I am angry and resentful. Emotionally I cannot accept the situation. I understand the dealers' position, I understand the cops' position. But I cannot understand why I should be made to feel like John Dillinger every time I buy a tank of gasoline. It's the same story everywhere. You go to a department store and try to pay for a $10.99 item with a check and you have to pull out a driver's license, two or three credit cards and a character reference from the pope—and then stand around for 15 minutes to get the manager's approval. Try to pay with a credit card and you have to wait while the cashier phones the central computer bank to make sure you're not a deadbeat or the Son of Sam[1] or something. It's not that we don't trust you, they smile. It's just that we have to protect ourselves.

[1] David Berkowitz, who called himself "Son of Sam," murdered several people in the New York City area in the 1970's.

4   Right. We all have to protect ourselves these days. Little old ladies with attack dogs and Mace and 12-gauges, shopkeepers with closed-circuit TVs and electronic sensors to nab shoplifters, survivalists storing up ammo and dehydrated foods in hope of riding out Armageddon, gas station owners with pay-before-you-pump signs and impenetrable cashiers' cages—all protecting themselves. From what? From each other. It strikes me that we are expending so much time, energy and anguish on protecting ourselves that we are depleting our stock of mental and emotional capital for living. It also strikes me that the harder we try to protect ourselves, the less we succeed. With all the home burglar alarms and guard dogs and heavy armament, the crime rate keeps going up. With all the electronic surveillance devices, the shoplifters' take keeps climbing. The gas chiselers haven't figured out a way to beat the pre-pay system yet, but they will.

5   Is it that the people are simply incorrigibly dishonest, that the glue of integrity and mutual respect that holds society together is finally dissolving? I don't know, but I suspect that if something like this really is going on, our collective paranoia contributes to the process. People, after all, tend to behave pretty much the way other people expect them to behave. If the prevailing assumption of a society is that people are honest, by and large they will be honest. If the prevailing assumption is that people are crooks, more and more of them will be crooks.

6   What kind of message does a kid get from an environment where uniformed guards stand at the entrance of every store, where every piece of merchandise has an anti-shoplifting tag stapled to it, where every house has a burglar alarm and a .38, where the gas station cashiers huddle in glass cages and pass your change out through a metal chute? What can he conclude but that thievery and violence are normal, common, expected behaviors?

7   A society which assumes its members are honest is humane, comfortable, habitable. A society which treats everyone like a criminal becomes harsh, unfeeling, punitive, paranoid. The human connection is severed; fear of detection and punishment becomes the only deterrent to crime, and it's a very ineffective one. Somehow, sometime—I don't know when, but it was within my lifetime—we changed from the first type of society to the second. Maybe it's too late to go back again, but the road we are now on is a dark and descending one.

H. Bruce Miller wrote "Severing the Human Connection" while a staff reporter on the *San Jose Mercury News.*

After You Read

Reading Journal

Imagine that you are the owner of a small store. Do you think that you would set things up in such a way that you relied on the honesty of your customers or would you protect yourself by using the various means described in Miller's essay? Be specific.

Reading For Meaning

1. What does Miller mean when he says in paragraph 1 that he felt he "ought to be wearing striped overalls with a number on the breast pocket"?

2. Make a list of examples from the article Miller cites that indicate Americans' distrust of their fellow man. Try to add a few of your own. Are these measures truly necessary?

3. What does Miller mean when he says in paragraph 5 that "our collective paranoia contributes to the process"? What process is he referring to? Do you agree?

4. How does the title, "Severing the Human Connection," express Miller's basic view of American society today?

Exploring Further

Debate

Argue for or against the following: Many people believe that we tend to behave the way others expect us to. Sociologists call this principle the *self-fulfilling prophecy*. Do you agree with Miller's claim that, "If the prevailing assumption of a society is that people are honest, by and large they will be honest. If the prevailing assumption is that people are crooks, more and more of them will be crooks."?

Timed Writing Exercise

Discuss how trusting your native culture appears in comparison with that of the United States. In your response, be sure to include specific ways in which one might measure this trust or lack of it. (For example, in some cultures, a handshake alone is sufficient to close a business transaction, rather than an exchange of money or a credit check.)

Focused Essay Topics

1. In his second-to-last paragraph, Miller poses a question about the impact on young people of a society which operates on distrust. Do you agree with his conclusion? Why or why not?

2. Using Miller's thesis, discuss how your college or university could encourage trust and honesty. (For example, you might argue whether or not cheating would be reduced by instituting an honor code.)

Before You Read

Freewrite on the following and share your response: In his piece, "I Find the Homeless Hateful," the author expresses his despair about the American homeless situation. Explore your feelings toward the homeless and detail any encounters you may have had with them.

I Find the Homeless Hateful   DALE MAHARIDGE

1   Four months ago, I moved from California to New York City to take a teaching job. I soon became acquainted with many beggars in my Upper West Side neighborhood.

2   There's the tattered entertainer who cheerfully sings "I Love New York." There was the 90-pound man, with a cancerous whisper, absent lately; perhaps with the onset of winter he is dead from AIDS. The other day, I came upon a woman sitting on a ledge. As I passed, she said softly she was starving. She spoke so quietly that her words could have been my conscience talking. When I kept moving, she let out a tubercular cough, deep and wrenching.

3   I hate her. I hate them all.

4   It didn't start this way. At first I dug into my pockets. Liberal companions laughed at such stupidity, or looked oddly as I put money in cups. In the last two months or so, I haven't given a thing to anyone. I will take a cab on the short trip home, which costs four bucks—more than I might give—just to avoid running the gantlet of outstretched hands.

5   And I'm a liberal. How do the conservatives feel?

6   Despite the holiday season, now that New York has begun a crackdown on the homeless in the subways and the Port Authority bus terminal, how do we all feel? When others come upon a panhandler, are they a bit uneasy? If they give, how do they react to the eighth panhandler in two blocks, or the aggressive one who won't take no for an answer?

7   I'm not going to offer any excuse about "compassion fatigue," a bit of rot coined by San Francisco's Mayor, Art Agnos. The result of doing nothing is the same as hatred.

8   I did not confront these feelings until I came here. There was no shortage of panhandlers near my home in Sacramento, Calif. When I did see them I usually gave. When I did not want to see them, I changed my walking route or drove my car. In New York, you cannot avoid them.

9   The panhandlers are just the outcropping of a greater problem of general poverty. They are the most visible reminders of the nightmare where they came from—tenements in Harlem or the Bronx. They drift down like messengers to remind us that all is not well, each representing hundreds or thousands of shattered lives hidden from our view.

10   I wonder if things are any different now than on a cold, windy day in

December 1881, when Leo Tolstoy descended into the heart of the destitution of Moscow, the Khitrov market. Horrified by the condition of the group of beggars, he emptied his pockets, and a minor riot ensued. He went to a friend's home seeking solace. The friend told Tolstoy that the poor were an "inevitable condition of civilization." Tolstoy, with tears in his eyes, cried out: "One cannot live so; one cannot; one cannot!"

11   Tolstoy eventually wrote "What Then Must We Do?" In that book, he asked what a society can and should do about poverty. The question is as valid today: what then must we do?

12   But what does society do? We sweep the homeless from the subways. Our liberal Mayor, David Dinkins, supports the plan. So do many otherwise progressive citizens. Only the most ardent friends of the homeless oppose it.

13   I have a file, now two inches thick, documenting sweeps all over the country. I've stopped adding to it because sweeps are no longer news. We do not stop the problem. We sweep it from sight.

14   The solutions are obvious: increasing the minimum wage, housing, mental health facilities, education, etc., etc. You know the answers.

15   Yet liberals and conservatives alike condone an intolerant society. The police, at the request of liberals and conservatives, tear down shantytowns; at least in the 1930's, we let the homeless have their Hoovervilles. Our elected officials, at the request of liberals and conservatives, oppose shelters or low-cost housing to the battlecry of "not in my backyard!"

16   We all hate them, as a society.

17   When we close our eyes at night we sweep them from our sight. But they will not go away.

Dale Maharidge's piece appeared on *The New York Times* Op-Ed page. He is a co-author of *And Their Children After Them*, a Pulitzer Prize-winning book about Southern sharecroppers, and of *Yosemite – A Landscape of Life* (1990).

After You Read

Reading Journal

In the essay, Maharidge gradually justifies the rather bold statement "I hate them" (the homeless). In your own words, sketch out his argument and compare it with your own feelings stated in the pre-reading exercise.

Reading For Meaning

1. What is the importance of the author's repeated distinction between liberal and conservative attitudes toward the homeless?

2. Why did Maharidge experience a change in attitude when he came to New York?

3. Maharidge calls the expression "*compassion fatigue*, a bit of rot coined by San Francisco's mayor, Art Agnos." How does he support his view that Agnos' position toward the needy and unfortunate is unacceptable?

Exploring Further

Interview/Questionnaire

Make up a questionnaire that explores attitudes and reactions to the homeless. The questionnaire should have at least five questions. Then distribute it to a sample of 5 Americans and 5 immigrants or foreigners. When you collate your responses, look for any patterns which show differences in the way the two groups view the homeless.

Sample questions:

a. How many encounters with homeless people do you have each week, on average?
    (1) none (2) 1-5 (3) 5-10 (4) more than 10

b. How do you feel about this?
    (1) no reaction (2) angry (3) frustrated (4) guilty (5) fearful

c. My encounters are primarily. . .
    (1) on the street (2) on public transportation (3) in public spaces such as buildings, doorways, parks (4) other

d. My typical reaction when encountering a homeless person is. . .
    (1) to ignore him/her (2) to speak to him/her (3) to offer money, food or other help (4) to avoid contact

Timed Writing Exercise

Agree or disagree with the following: As members of a truly civilized society, we have a moral duty to help those less fortunate than ourselves.

Focused Essay Topics

1. Often students from other countries are shocked by the numbers of homeless people on the streets of American cities. How are the poor and disenfranchised handled in your native country? Be as specific as you can. (Identify who those people are, the nature of their problems, what resources are available for helping them and, lastly, how well this system appears to work.)

2. Research the "Hoovervilles" of the 1930s which Maharidge refers to in the article. Write a short essay incorporating your research with an argument as to whether or not this would be a workable solution today.

Before You Read

The short story which follows deals with a young man's decision not to go to war and the family conflict that arises as a result. Do you think one should be permitted to refuse to serve in the military during wartime on moral or philosophical grounds? (This protest is called *conscientious objection*.) You may want to discuss how this issue is dealt with in your country or culture as a point of comparison.

El Patrón   NASH CANDELARIA

1   My father-in-law's hierarchy is, in descending order: Dios, El Papa, y el patrón. It is to these that mere mortals bow, as in turn el patrón bows to El Papa, and El Papa bows to Dios.

2   God and the Pope are understandable enough. It's this el patrón, the boss, who causes most of our trouble. Whether it's the one who gives you work and for it pay, the lifeblood of hardworking little people, or others: our parents (fathers affectionately known as "jefe," mothers known merely as "Mamá"), military commanders ("el capitán"), or any of the big shots in the government ("el alcalde," "el gobernador," "el presidente," and never forget "la policía"). It was about some such el patrón trouble that Señor Martínez boarded the bus in San Diego and headed north toward L.A.—and us.

3   Since I was lecturing to a midafternoon summer school class at Southwestern U, my wife Lola picked up her father at the station. When I arrived home, they were sitting politely in the living room talking banalities: "Yes, it does look like rain. But if it doesn't rain, it might be sunny. If only the clouds would blow away."

4   Lola had that dangerous look on her face that made me start talking too fast and too long in hope of shifting her focus. It never worked. She'd sit there with a face like a brown-skinned kewpie doll whose expression was slowly turning into that of an angry maniac. When she could no longer stand it, she'd give her father a blast: "You never talk to me about anything important, you macho, chauvinist jumping bean!" Then it would escalate to nastiness from there.

5   But tonight it didn't get that far. As I entered, Señor Martínez rose, dressed in his one suit as for a wedding or a funeral, and politely shook my hand. Without so much as a glance at Lola he said, "Why don't you go to the kitchen with the other women."

6   "There are no other women," Lola said coldly. She stood and belligerently received my kiss on the cheek before leaving.

7   Señor Martínez was oblivious to her reaction, sensing only the absence of "woman," at which he visibly relaxed.

8   "Rosca," he said, referring to me as he always did by my last name. "Tito is in trouble with the law."

9   His face struggled between anger and sadness, tinged with a cross-current of confusion. Tito was his pride and joy. His only son after four daughters. A twilight gift born to his wife at a time when he despaired of ever having a son, when their youngest daughter Lola was already ten years old and their oldest daughter twenty.

10   "He just finished his examinations at the state university. He was working this summer to save money for his second year when this terrible thing happened."

11   I could not in my wildest fantasies imagine young Vicente getting into trouble. He impressed me as a bright, polite young man who would inspire pride in any father. Even when he and old Vicente had quarreled about Tito going to college instead of working full time, the old man had grudgingly come around to seeing the wisdom of it. But now. The law! I was stunned.

12   "Where is he?" I asked, imagining the nineteen-year old in some filthy cell in the San Diego jail.

13   "I don't know." Then he looked over his shoulder toward the kitchen as if to be certain no one was eavesdropping. "I think he went underground."

14   Underground! I had visions of drug crazed revolutionary zealots. Bombs exploding in Federal Buildings. God knows what kind of madness.

15   "They're probably after him," he went on. Then he paused and stared at me as if trying to understand. "Tito always looked up to you and Lola. Of all the family it would be you he would try to contact. I want you to help me." Not help Tito, I thought, but help *me*.

16   I went to the cabinet and poured from the bottle that I keep for emergencies. I took a swallow to give me courage to ask the question. "What . . . did . . . he do?"

17   Señor Martínez stared limply at the glass in his hand. "You know," he said, "my father fought with Pancho Villa."

18   Jesus! I thought. If everyone who told me his father had fought with Pancho Villa was telling the truth, that army would have been big enough to conquer the world. Besides—what did this have to do with Tito?

19   "When my turn came," he continued, "I enlisted in the Marines at Camp Pendleton. Fought los japoneses in the Pacific." Finally he took a sip of his drink and sat stiffly as if at attention. "The men in our family have never shirked their duty!" He barked like the Marine corporal he had once been.

20   It slowly dawned on me what this was all about. It had been *the* topic during summer school at Southwestern U. Registration for the draft. "No blood for mideast oil!" the picket signs around the campus post office had shouted. "Boycott the Exxon army!"

21   "I should never have let him go to college," Señor Martínez said. "That's where he gets such crazy radical ideas. From those rich college boys whose parents can buy them out of all kinds of trouble."

22   "So he didn't register," I said.

23   "The FBI is probably after him right now. It's a Federal crime, you know. And the Canadians don't want draft dodgers either."

24   He took a deep swallow, polishing off the rest of his drink, and put the empty glass on the coffee table. There, his gesture seemed to say, now you know the worst.

25   Calmer now, he went on to tell me more. About the American Civil War; a greater percentage of Spanish-speaking men of New Mexico had joined the Union Army than the men from any other group in any other state. About the Rough Riders, including young Mexican-Americans, born on horseback, riding roughest of all over the Spanish in Cuba. About the War-to-End-All-Wars, where tough, skinny, brown-faced doughboys from farms in Texas, New Mexico, Arizona, Colorado, and California gave their all "Over There." About World War II, from the New Mexico National Guard captured at Bataan to the tough little Marines whom he was proud to fight alongside; man for man there were more decorations for bravery among Mexican-Americans than among any other group. Then Korea, where his younger brother toughed it out in the infantry. Finally Vietnam, where kids like his nephew, Pablo, got it in some silent, dark jungle trying to save a small country from the Communists.

26   By now he had lost his calm. There were tears in his eyes, partly from the pride he felt in this tradition of valor. But partly for something else, I thought. I could almost hear his son's reply to his impassioned call to duty: "Yes, Papá. So we could come back, if we survive, to our jobs as busboys and ditch diggers; that's why I have to go to college. I don't want to go to the Middle East and fight and die for some oil company when you can't even afford to own a car. If the Russians invaded our country, I would defend it. If a robber broke into our house, I would fight him. If someone attacked you, I would save you. But this? No, Papá."

27   But now Tito was gone. God knows where. None of his three sisters in San Diego had seen him. Nor any of his friends in the neighborhood or school or work.

28   I could hear preparations for dinner from the kitchen. Señor Martínez and I had another traguito while Lolita and Junior ate their dinner early, the sounds of their childish voices piercing through the banging of pots and pans.

29   When Lola called me Emiliano instead of by my nickname, Pata, I knew we were in for a lousy meal. Everything her father disliked must have been served. It had taken a perverse gourmet expending a tremendous amount of energy to fix such rotten food. There was that nothing white bread that presses together into a doughy flat mess instead of the tortillas Papá thrived on. There was a funny little salad with chopped garbage in it covered by a blob of imitation goo. There was no meat. *No meat!* Just all those sliced vegetables in a big bowl. Not ordinary vegetables like beans and potatoes and carrots, but funny, wiggly long things like wild grass—or worms. And quivering cubes of what must have been whale blubber. But enough. You get the idea.

30   Halfway through the meal, as Señor Martínez shuffled the food around his plate like one of our kids resisting what was good for them, the doorbell rang.

31   "You'd better get that, Emiliano," Lola said, daring me to refuse by her tone of voice and dagger-throwing glance.

32   Who needs a fight? In a sense I was lucky because I could leave the table and that pot of mess-age. When I opened the door, a scraggly young man beamed at me. "I hitchhiked from San Diego," Tito said.

33   Before I could move onto the steps and close the door behind me, he stumbled past into the house. Tired as he was, he reacted instantly to seeing his father at the table. "You!" he shouted, then turned and bolted out the door.

34   Even tired he could run faster than me, so I hopped into the car and drove after him while Lola and Señor Martínez stood on the steps shouting words I couldn't hear.

35   Two blocks later Tito climbed into the car when I bribed him with a promise of dinner at McDonald's. While his mouth was full, I tried to talk some sense into him, but to no avail. He was just as stubborn as his father and sister. Finally, I drove him to the International House on campus where the housing manager, who owed me a favor, found him an empty bed.

36   "You should have made him come back with you," Lola nagged at me that night.

37   "He doesn't want to be under the same roof with his father." From her thoughtful silence I knew that she understood and felt the same way. When I explained to her what it was all about—her father had said nothing to her—it looked for a moment as if she would get out of bed, stomp to the guest room, and heave Señor Martínez out into the street.

38   The next day was an endless two-way shuttle between our house and the I House. First me. Then Lola. If Señor Martínez had had a car and could drive, he would have followed each of us.

39   Our shuttle diplomacy finally wore them down. At last there were cracks in father's and son's immovable positions.

40   "Yes. Yes. I love my son."

41   "I love my father."

42   "I know. I know. Adults should be able to sit down and talk about their differences, no matter how wrong he is."

43   "Maybe tomorrow. Give me a break. But definitely not at mealtime. I can't eat while my stomach is churning."

44   The difficulty for me, as always, was in keeping my opinions to myself. Lola didn't have that problem. After all, they were her brother and father, so she felt free to say whatever she pleased.

45   "The plan is to get them to talk," I said to her. "If they can talk, they can reach some kind of understanding."

46   "Papá has to be set straight," she said. "As usual, he's wrong, but he always insists it's someone else who messed things up."

47   "He doesn't want Tito to go to jail."

48   "That's Tito's choice!" Of course she was right; they were both right.

49   The summit meeting was set for the next afternoon. Since I had only one late morning lecture, I would pick up Tito, feed him a Big Mac or two, then bring him to the house. Lola would fix Señor Martínez some nice tortillas and chili, making up for that abominable dinner of the night before last. Well fed, with two chaperones mediating, we thought they could work something out.

50   When Tito and I walked into the house, hope started to tremble and develop goose bumps. It was deathly silent and formal. Lola had that dangerous look on her face again. The macho, chauvinist jumping bean

sat stiffly in his suit that looked like it had just been pressed—all shiny and sharply creased, unapproachable and potentially cutting, warning of what lay behind Señor Martínez's stone face.

51 Tito and I sat across from the sofa and faced them. Or rather I faced them. Both Tito and Señor Martínez were looking off at an angle from each other, not daring to touch glances. I smiled, but no one acknowledged it so I gave it up. Then Lola broke the silence.

52 "What this needs is a woman's point-of-view," she began.

53 That's all Señor Martínez needed. The blast his eyes shot at her left her open-mouthed and silent as he interrupted. "I don't want you to go to jail!" He was looking at Lola, but he meant Tito.

54 Tito's response was barely audible, and I detected a trembling in his voice. "You'd rather I got killed on some Arabian desert."

55 The stone face cracked. For a moment it looked as if Señor Martínez would burst into tears. He turned his puzzled face from Lola toward his son. "No," he said. "Is that what you think?" Then, when Tito did not answer, he said, "You're my only son. Damn it! Sons are supposed to obey their fathers!"

56 "El patrón, El Papa, and Dios," Tito said with a trace of bitterness.

57 But Lola could be denied no longer. "Papá, how old were you when you left Mexico for the U.S.?" She didn't expect an answer, so didn't give him time to reply. "Sixteen, wasn't it? And what did your father say?"

58 Thank God that smart-ass smile of hers was turned away from her father. She knew she had him, and he knew it too, but he didn't need her smirk to remind him.

59 He sighed. The look on his face showed that sometimes memories were best forgotten. He shook his head but did not speak. Lola had seen her father's reaction, and her voice lost its hard edge and became more sympathetic.

60 "He disowned you, didn't he? Grandpa disowned you. Called you a traitor to your own country. A deserter when things got tough."

61 "I did not intend to stay in Mexico and starve," he said. He looked around at us one by one as if he had to justify himself. "He eventually came to Los Estados Unidos himself. He and Mamá died in that house in San Diego."

62 "What did you think when Grandpa did that to you?"

63 No answer was necessary. "Can't you see, Papá?" Lola pleaded.

64 Meanwhile Tito had been watching his father as if he had never seen him before. Only the older children had heard Papá's story of how he left Mexico.

65 "I don't intend to go to jail, Papá," Tito said. "I just have to take a stand along with thousands of others. In the past old men started wars in which young men died in order to preserve old men's comforts. It just has to stop.

66 "There's never been a war without a draft. Never a draft without registration. And this one is nothing but craziness by el patrón in Washington, D.C. If enough of us protest, maybe he'll get the message."

67 "They almost declared it unconstitutional," I said. "They may yet."

68 "Because they aren't signing women," Papá said in disgust. But from the look on Lola's face, I'd pick her over him in any war.

69 "If they come after me, I'll register," Tito said. "But in the meantime I have to take this stand."

70   There. It was out. They had had their talk in spite of their disagreements.

71   "He's nineteen," Lola said. "Old enough to run his own life."

72   Señor Martínez was all talked out. He slumped against the back of the sofa. Even the creases in his trousers sagged. Tito looked to his sister, and his face brightened.

73   "Papá," Tito said. "I—I'd like to go home if you want me to."

74   On Papá's puzzled face I imagined I could see the words: "My father fought with Pancho Villa." But it was no longer an accusation, only a simple statement of fact. Who knows what takes more courage: to fight or not to fight?

75   "There's a bus at four o'clock," Señor Martínez said.

76   Later I drove them in silence to the station. Though it was awkward, it wasn't a bad silence. There are more important ways to speak than with words, and I could feel that sitting shoulder to shoulder, father and son had reached some accord.

77   Papá still believed in el patrón, El Papa, and Dios. What I hoped they now saw was that Tito did too. Only in his case, conscience overrode el patrón, maybe even El Papa. In times past, Popes too declared holy wars that violated conscience. For Tito, conscience was the same as Dios. And I saw, in their uneasy truce, that love overrode their differences.

78   I shook their hands as they boarded the bus, and watched the two similar faces, one old, one young, smile sadly at me through the window as the Greyhound pulled away.

79   When I got back home, Junior and Lolita were squabbling over what channel to watch on TV. I rolled my eyes in exasperation, ready to holler, but Lola spoke first.

80   "I'm glad Papá got straightened out. The hardest thing for parents is to let go of their children."

81   Yeah, I started to say, but she stuck her head into the den and shouted at Junior and Lolita to stop quarreling or they were going to get it.

> **Nash Candelaria** is the author of a trilogy of novels about New Mexico, *Memories of the Alhambra, Not by The Sword* and *Inheritance of Strangers*. His ancestors were among the founders of Albuquerque, New Mexico. "El Patrón" is from his collection of stories, *The Day the Cisco Kid Shot John Wayne.*

After You Read

Reading Journal

Write about a time in your life when your own desires or ideas clashed with those of an authority figure—a parent, teacher or clergy member. Discuss how you resolved the conflict.

Reading For Meaning

1. Why do you think Candelaria begins his story "My father-in-law's hierarchy is, in descending order: Dios, El Papa, y el patrón"? How does the first paragraph set up and emphasize the themes of the story?

2. How does Señor Martínez's relationship with his daughter contrast with his relationship with his son? How does his family hierarchy affect the resolution of the conflict?

3. Summarize Señor Martínez's secret history, which is revealed at the end of the story. Why is it important?

4. Do you think the author wants to present Tito as essentially different from his father? Explain.

Exploring Further

Research Project

Research the issue of conscientious objection/draft dodging in an American war fought during this century. In so doing, look for information about how the American public at large viewed this issue. (You might, in addition interview several Americans about how they feel now or felt then about fighting for their country.)

Timed Writing Exercise

In some cultures, obedience to those above one in the social hierarchy goes unquestioned. In American culture, however, individual rebellion against authority is often considered—as in the case of teenagers—a natural stance of growing up. Discuss these two differing attitudes toward hierarchy and obedience. Which comes closer to your own personal experience?

Focused Essay Topics

1. Reread the story. Then analyze the conflict between the father and the son from a generational, cultural and historical perspective. How do these elements contribute to the attitudes of the elder and younger Martínez men?

2. Define your personal hierarchy. Compare it with that of Señor Martínez. Does your hierarchy reflect that of your native culture or is it unique to you? Explain.

EXTENDING THE CONTEXT

> These questions are designed for further discussion or essay writing. Your responses should reflect the thinking, reading and writing you have done on the unit topic thus far.

1. There are numerous practices that, while accepted by some cultures, are denounced by others. For example, many Americans find the ancient Chinese practice of footbinding, initiation rites which involve body mutilation, or the use of rape as a weapon of war unacceptable. Do you believe we have the right to judge another culture's values? Use specific examples to support your essay.

2. Choose one of the quotations in the *Short Takes* of this unit with which to agree or disagree.

3. Given the increase in violent crime in America, many believe that capital punishment is the best deterrent. Where do you stand on this controversial issue?

4. Choose any single moral value such as honesty, patriotism, or respect for human rights and write a brief definition essay. Draw on any appropriate articles in the unit to expand your discussion. (For example: respect for authority in "El Patrón.")

5. Choose a controversial moral issue such as abortion or euthanasia and take a stand. Be certain you address those arguments which the opposition would use to discredit your argument.

6. In moral issues, do the ends ever justify the means? (For example, a man stealing bread to feed his starving family?) Write a personal essay in which you relate an incident which supports your point of view.

7. Read the newspapers for the current week. Choose one news item which is noteworthy for its moral or ethical controversy. In your essay, define the issue, state why it is controversial, and lastly, discuss your personal feelings on the matter.

8. It is easy to cite evidence that moral values are in decline—from the violent crime in the streets to political scandals in the White House. Not as frequently, however, we hear a story which renews our faith in human nature—the fireman who risks his life to save a child or a stranger who returns a wallet with cash inside. Do you think there is evidence that Americans are becoming less and less moral? Give examples to support your position.

VIDEO SUGGESTIONS

The video selections are offered as suggestions for viewing in or out of class to enrich the unit topic.

Do the Right Thing	*Mr. Smith Goes to Washington*
Crimes and Misdemeanors	*The Long Walk Home*
The King of Comedy	*To Sir with Love*
Wall Street	*Eyes on the Prize*

Unit Six

POPULAR CULTURE: THE IMAGE SHAPERS

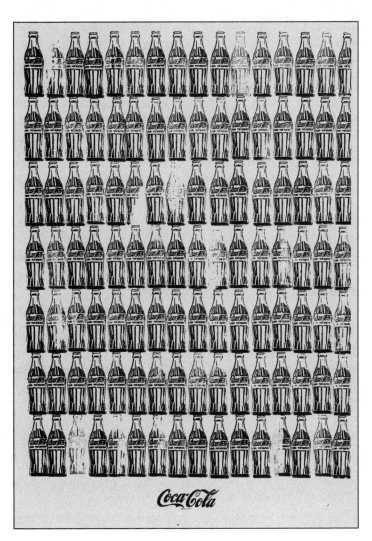

ANDY WARHOL,
*Green Coca-Cola
Bottles*

Short Takes

The hand that rules the press, the radio, the screen and the far-spread magazine, rules the country.

Learned Hand

In an automobile civilization, which was one of constant motion and activity, there was almost no time to think; in a television one, there is small desire.

Louis Kronenberger

It is not enough to show people how to *live* better: there is a mandate for any group with enormous powers of communication to show people how to *be* better.

Marya Mannes

News is the rough draft of history.

Benjamin Bradlee

Television is the literature of the illiterate, the culture of the low-brow, the wealth of the poor, the privilege of the underprivileged, the exclusive club of the excluded masses.

Lee Loevinger

Newspapers have developed what might be called a vested interest in catastrophe. If they can spot a fight, they play up that fight. If they can uncover a tragedy, they will headline that tragedy.

Henry A. Overstreet

Television is chewing gum for the eyes.

Frank Lloyd Wright

The media of communications on which people depend for facts and information—the press, the movies, radio and television—have been used to reduce the people to conformity and dumb acquiescence. They bear a large share of the responsibility for the climate of fear and hysteria which has enveloped our country and which has become such a threat to our freedom.

William T. Evjue

The television commercial is the most efficient power-packed capsule of education that appears anywhere on TV.

G.L. Gray

SUGGESTIONS FOR USING SHORT TAKES:

- Respond in writing to one of the quotations above. Then get together in groups and share what you have written.
- Work with a partner, small group or the entire class to discuss one or more quotations. You may want to agree, disagree, or compare it to similar expressions or sayings in your native language.

INTRODUCTION – POPULAR CULTURE: THE IMAGE SHAPERS

Before the average immigrant ever arrives on American soil, she is likely to be familiar with much of American popular culture, for the culture that we export internationally is indeed *popular* or mass culture. It would probably be fair to say that most of what passes today for international popular culture is American in origin: from icons such as the Coca Cola trademark and McDonald's golden arches, to performers Madonna and Michael Jackson, or Sylvester Stallone's *Rambo*, all are products "made in the United States" but exported far and wide.

Why is American popular culture so widespread and well-loved in so many parts of the world? The answer probably lies in economics and the power behind our entertainment industries and institutions. Hollywood, for example, produces more movies each year than all the European countries put together. In addition, the huge budgets behind most Hollywood films buy top talent, not only in terms of actors and directors, but also in the less visible but essential arts of lighting, cinematography, sound, and special effects. Put together, these magical ingredients create the American "blockbuster" movies that gross billions of dollars in the foreign market alone.

American television programs, too, have had a widespread success in many foreign countries. "Colombo," the tough New York detective who starred in a series of the same name, was a household word in Japan as well as the United States. TV characters like Edith and Archie Bunker, the husband and wife in the most popular sitcom of the 1970s, "All in the Family," and J.R., the powerful and conniving Texan who starred in "Dallas," are known to television viewers half the world over.

Likewise the American music industry wields tremendous power internationally. Young people all over the globe share a passion for leading American pop stars like Michael Jackson and Madonna, to name only two examples. We, too, import foreign music, mainly from England, perhaps because there is no language barrier. But the language barrier doesn't seem to dampen the foreign taste for American pop music. Music may even be one of the ways that many foreigners begin to acquire a knowledge of English, or the desire to learn it.

"Highbrow" culture—classical dance, music, visual arts and literature—that comes out of the European tradition is viewed as the province of the middle and elite classes. Popular culture, on the other hand, appeals to the masses. Although "highbrow" culture has been generally considered more serious, valuable and worthy of study, recently popular culture has also become a focus of scholarship. Students of culture now believe that any cultural artifact or representation can yield relevant information about who and what we are.

However, the worldwide export of American pop culture is not celebrated by all. Around the world, some feel that America's cultural imports overwhelm indigenous forms of culture. Huge budgets guarantee that American products will be sold in promotions and advertising campaigns that can't be matched by competing foreign products. Good old American "hype" goes far in selling pop culture overseas as well as at home.

But popular culture is often as harshly criticized by Americans as it is by foreigners. Most recently "gangsta rap," which glorifies violence, guns, gender discrimination and racial hatred, has been surrounded by controversy; critics say it gives a dangerous message to impressionable young people. Similarly, the preoccupation with violence in both entertainment and news programs has been called into question by the U.S. Attorney General and by critics in and out of the media industry.

But like it or not, popular culture is an international multi-billion dollar industry because it speaks not only to Americans but to people all over the world about common fears, visions and realities. We must admit that, if nothing else, pop culture is a reflection of ourselves and of our increasingly complex and changing societies.

Before You Read

Freewrite on the following and share your response: In this article about the opening of Euro Disney in France, the author argues that American pop culture is the closest thing we have to an international culture. What do you think about this? What did you know about American pop culture before you came to this country? How much has American pop culture become part of your own national culture? (If you haven't lived in your native country for a long enough time to answer this, discuss the importance of your native popular culture in the lives of your ethnic community here in the U.S.)

World Leaders: Mickey, Et Al.   TODD GITLIN

1   A few years ago, an amazed Japanese girl asked an American visitor, "Is there really a Disneyland in America?"

2   That should be music to the mouse ears of Euro Disneyland's management, beleaguered by charges that they are defiling the Frenchness of France. Ah, to convince the French that Mickey and Donald belong to Marne-la-Vallée as they do to Anaheim, Orlando and Tokyo. Sensitive to the charge that Euro Disneyland amounts to what the theater director Ariane Mnouchkine, in a widely quoted assessment, called a "cultural Chernobyl," the company tried for months to persuade Europeans that, in the words of Disney spokesman, "It's not America, it's Disney."

3   On opening day last month, Disney's chairman Michael Eisner stressed, like a guest too eager to please, that the company had repackaged original European characters: the French Cinderella, the Italian Pinocchio, the German Snow White. More truculently, a Euro Disneyland spokeswoman said: "Who are these Frenchmen, anyway? We offer them the dream of a lifetime and lots of jobs. They treat us like invaders."

4   Beyond the cultural battle of the moment, both sides can agree on one thing: American popular culture is the closest approximation there is today to a global lingua franca, drawing urban classes in most nations into a federated culture zone. In one month, "Terminator 2" sold five million tickets in France. It is possible to see a Donald Duck decal on a wall in a village in the middle of a Greek island, hear country-western music on the radio in Ireland, buy a Woodie Guthrie tribute tape at a gas station in Norway. Charles Bronson, Clint Eastwood, Arnold Schwarzenegger and Coke are, thanks to the multinational corporation, the icons of a global semiculture, helping to integrate at least the plugged-in classes of most nations into a single cultural zone. Entertainment is America's largest export—after weaponry. The question is what this means.

5   Protectionists, such as the French Minister of Culture, Jack Lang, fear that America's marketing clout will succeed in paving over the profuse variety of global cultures. Once it is overstated, the fear is easy to sweep aside. Obviously, American popular culture does not erase all the vernacular alternatives. The new semiculture coexists with local cultures more than it replaces them.

6   As the Norwegian media researcher Helge Ronning suggests, it is plausible to suppose that global, largely American popular culture is becoming everyone's second culture. It doesn't necessarily supplant local traditions, but it does activate a certain cultural bilingualism. People from Australia to Zimbabwe acquire a second cultural membership, switching with ease from local news to the American Oscar ceremonies, and back again.

7   As his Americophile enemies love to point out, even Jack Lang recently conferred France's highest honor in the arts on Sylvester Stallone.

8   Why were "Dallas" and "Dynasty" at their peaks, on television in 100 countries—popular in all but Japan and Brazil? Indisputably, economies of scale are one reason. The United States can simply undersell other suppliers. A programmer in Copenhagen can lease an hourlong episode of "Dallas" or "Miami Vice" for under $5,000, less than the cost of producing one original minute of Danish drama. American formulas have also helped establish the conventions— the slickness, the melodrama, the cuteness, the glibness, the uplift— that imitators around the world aim to match.

9   There is evidence that if Europeans had a choice, they would prefer programs produced in their own countries. But in the end, no one is forcing the Danes to watch American shows. In "Dallas" and its ilk they must be attracted by a range of pleasures comparable to those Americans find.

10   Scholars have demonstrated that when people watch the same program they see the program they are disposed to see. For instance, studies of "All in the Family" in Canada and Holland showed that the audience was divided between those who thought Edith, Gloria and Meathead won the arguments and those who believed that Archie regularly gave them their comeuppance.

11   Likewise, Tamar Liebes and Elihu Katz, sociologists at the Hebrew University in Jerusalem, have shown that Israeli families of Russian, American and Moroccan provenance interpret the same "Dallas" episode in different ways and like it for different reasons. Indeed, the commercial strength of many American television programs in particular lies in their capacity to speak out of several sides of their mouths at once, enabling, to cite an example, teen-age girls to watch "Beverly Hills 90210" for both its good-looking guys and its "relevance."

12   Another explanation for the success of American culture is that it has been driven by a single overriding purpose: to entertain. For this reason, it is easy to see why American series have outdone British programs developed in large part for cultural elevation and erstwhile Soviet programs developed for didactic purposes. As a Euro Disneyland official protested last fall, "We're not trying to sell anything but fun, entertainment."

13   Moreover, as the British sociologist Jeremy Tunstall has observed, by the time it leaves our shores, much American popular culture has been pre-tested in a large internal market that incorporates elements of foreign tastes. America's music derives from the rhythms and songs of African slaves and their descendants. Its comic sense comes principally from

English settlers, East European Jews and, again, blacks. By the time commercial work comes out of Hollywood or New York or Nashville, it has already been certified as widely marketable to a diverse population. No competitor from the monocultures of Europe and Asia can make this claim.

14   In popular music, where production costs are low, multinationals, ever thirsting for novelty, frequently import and reprocess styles from abroad, replenishing the stock of American music and giving something back to the global mix.

First the Bad News
Cultural Fast Food Goes Global

15   Frequently in movies and television, global semi-Americanization has the effect of withering much of the foreign competition. Hollywood's principal style has narrowed the cultural repertory of film makers and audiences alike. America's so-called high production values, often mechanistic and mindless, have become the fast food of global culture.

16   The pressure to make films exportable further degrades them into entertainment machines. Many of today's major films are made to open in Paris and Peoria simultaneously and to sell on videocassette everywhere else a few weeks later. "Terminator 2," with its Austrian-born star, its French co-financing and its Spanish-language gags, might as well come from the moon or the Cayman Islands.

17   The English language, with its vast ready-made market on every continent, boosts the export prospects of these hybrids. Monosyllables help, too, because they are easily grasped and dubbed. To appeal to crowds from Copenhagen to Calcutta, "Terminator 2" and other mainstream Hollywood movies today use words as captions for pictures, which in turn are stripped to their most banal common denominators. Not only is American

politics dragged down to the level of "Make my day," "Read my lips" and "Hasta la vista, baby," but many literate young screenwriters in America and elsewhere aspire to write at the primitive level of Steven Spielberg and George Lucas.

18   Melodrama and comics have long been American specialties, of course, and one could argue that crude cartoon style is America's most potent export. Euro Disneyland may not be all-American—there are European grace notes—but it is Disney, with its squeaky-clean appeal to innocence. Last summer, the author and illustrator Maurice Sendak protested that Disney's cartoon version of Hans Christian Andersen's "Little Mermaid" was "a total contradiction of the original . . . the tale is about sacrifice. The little mermaid doesn't even get what she wants . . . that's a hard lesson. This movie is about getting married, having cupcakes for bras and going to live in White Plains somewhere."

19   The flip side of Disney cuteness is Hollywood brutishness. In the name of improving the balance of payments, Hollywood sends its most primitive goods abroad. The "Diehard" and "Lethal Weapon" movies reportedly brought in $1 billion worldwide. The glitzier the technology, the more American movies acquire a reputation for speed, savagery, ethical emptiness and smug surface. Fueled partly by the promise of global markets, the industry is in the grip of inner forces whose cynicism is so deep as to defy parody. Driven by economic incentives and a perverse pride in what they consider craft, movie makers concentrate on new ways to savage and kill. Once hooked, viewers everywhere require steadily increasing doses.

20   The predilections of financiers, directors, writers, makeup artists and teen-age audiences come together to

ratchet up the frequency and magnitude of violence. Directors draw pride from their ability to surpass the previous round of abominations. Studio bosses, bankers and distributors see no reason to temper the cycle as long as it pays off. Everyone takes the loop of least resistance, doing more of what they already know how to do.

21   The secret of the global box-office success of these films is that they evoke a forbidden pleasure in the victim's pain and paranoia. The viewer is not drawn to identify with the victim, who is barely on the screen long enough to warrant a second thought. Instead, there is a delirium of delight in the perpetrator's ability to get away with murder. Freedom becomes another word for no one left to kill.

22   In the movies, Gresham's law, that most relentless of free-market principles, comes into play. Primitive entertainment drives out the local and complicated, which don't travel well. Local film industries usually cannot compete with Hollywood, much as they may try. Producers in central Europe are in a state of collapse. Small countries like Norway and Switzerland, which make a handful of films a year, drown in American movies, and young film makers in Europe and the third world find it hard to make careers amid the pressure of American imports.

23   Indeed, the ascendancy of Hollywood exports, along with most Americans' dislike of foreign films and television shows (Americans are allergic to sub-titles, and barely 1 percent of American prime-time television comes from abroad), helps explain why the great European film-making generation of Bergman, Fellini, Antonioni, Godard, Truffaut, Rohmer and Resnais seems largely barren of successors.

24   As for Hollywood importing foreigners to make its movies, this does not represent so much an openness to foreign styles as the capacity to buy film makers into submission. The usual American mode is to take promising film makers from around the world and process them into banality. The Hollywood-financed work of the Australian Fred Schepisi ("A Cry in the Dark") and the Indian Mira Nair ("Mississippi Masala") is the exception. Closer to the rule, unfortunately, is the more-Hollywood-than-Hollywood Americanization of film makers like the Dutch director Paul Verhoeven ("Total Recall," "Basic Instinct") and directors with excellent credits abroad, like the New Zealander Roger Donaldson ("White Sands"), the Englishman Roland Joffe ("City of Joy") and the Australian Peter Weir ("Green Card").

Now the Good News
We're Not So Bad After All

25   Fortunately, American entertainment has another side. About 10 years ago, a Hungarian media researcher, asked what were the most popular shows on Hungarian television, answered "Kojak" and "The Streets of San Francisco," because Hungarians had good reason to appreciate, even love, the casual, approachable American cops.

26   Five years ago, with much fanfare, a galaxy of rock stars including Michael Jackson and Bruce Springsteen recorded "We Are the World." Hip critics said it was arrogant and sentimental. Then a multicolored group of South African protesters marched into an all-white neighborhood singing "We Are the World."

27   Two years ago, the American historian Paul Buhle, visiting East Berlin just after the wall came down, was told by a student: "Last night I dreamed of Route 66." The route she dreamed of, of course, was the one immortalized on the television series of the early 60's.

28   A year ago, according to an account in *The Observer* of London, several Serbian students arrested by the Belgrade riot police after an opposition rally were beaten with truncheons, fists and walkie-talkies, "then forced to stand with their hands up against a wall for the next four hours. When anyone dropped their hands, they were kicked in the knees. Then the policemen forced them to stand on tiptoe. Students who disobeyed were beaten. The tip-toe torture was followed by a mock-ery of a trial. When one student asked for a defense lawyer, he was told: 'You have been watching too many American films!'"

29   It's all American pop culture: the coupling of irreverence and brutal-ity; intimations of freedom alongside the worship of power; the exaltation of the proverbial little guy alongside technological elephantiasis; the love of the road alongside the degradation of dialogue; the lyrical spunk of R.E.M. alongside the racket of Megadeth. This curious compound will continue to flow into the world for worse, and for better. It will invite immigration, emulation, amusement and revulsion.

30   Meanwhile, outside our vision, Mexican and Brazilian tele-novelas, Hong Kong kung fu, Finnish-English comedy, Senegalese drama, Polish-French existentialism and the world's other currents swirl into the leftover niches. No other super culture has the capital, organization and ambi-tion to break the world into inter-changeable parts. Americans may not feel the need to know what the rest of the world is imagining, but we would do well to open our eyes and see what's happening outside our theme park.

> *Todd Gitlin* is Professor of Sociology and Mass Communication at the University of California, Berkeley. He is the author of numerous books, including *Inside Prime Time* (1983), *The Sixties: Years of Hope, Days of Rage* (1987) and a forthcoming novel.

After You Read

Reading Journal

Do you think that American global pop culture has suppressed other countries' film or music production, as some believe? (Look back at your pre-reading notes, if applicable.) What talent or tradition from your own or other national culture(s) do you think could have global appeal if it had the financial backing and publicity behind it?

Reading For Meaning

1. What objections are raised, particularly by the French, to the infil-tration of American pop culture in France? Explain why this senti-ment led to calling Euro Disney a "cultural Chernobyl."

2. What primary reasons does the author give for the success of American pop culture in the world market?

3. What evidence is there, as Jeremy Tunstall suggests in paragraph 13, that American pop culture "has been pre-tested in a large internal market that incorporates elements of foreign tastes" before it is shipped abroad? Why is this not possible for most other cultures?

4. What two genres of films are the most successful American exports? What accounts for this success, according to the article?

5. The author concludes his piece by dividing it into a "bad news/good news" format. Summarize the basic arguments of each section, making sure to include supporting examples.

Exploring Further

Group Presentation

Divide into small groups based on shared ethnic background.
Prepare a short oral presentation in which you discuss a form of entertainment (such as film or music) or an aspect of popular culture (like a celebration) commonly known and enjoyed by members of your national ethnic group. Try to bring in audio or video examples to supplement your presentation.

Timed Writing Exercise

Take an example of American popular culture, like fast food, Disneyland or rap music, and argue that it represents either a positive or a negative contribution to global culture.

Focused Essay Topics

1. The writer of this article is quite critical of many aspects of American entertainment or popular culture produced with worldwide export in mind. Discuss two or three of his points and agree or disagree with his conclusion. (You may want to use your notes from *Reading for Meaning,* question 5 as a basis for your discussion.)

2. Gitlin claims in paragraph 29 that American pop culture is a curious mixture which "will invite immigration, emulation, amusement and revulsion." Reread the paragraph in question to make sure you understand his definition of this mixture, then choose one of these four abstract nouns to argue for or against his conclusion. Use examples from your knowledge of American pop culture and your own experience as support.

Before You Read

The author of the next reading argues that most "pop culture" is empty and superficial when compared to "high culture." In a paragraph, write a definition of these two terms and list several examples of each to distinguish them from one another.

Popular Culture Leaves Its Mark on the 20th Century

JON MARGOLIS

1   Bill Clinton is the first president of the 21st Century.

2   No, that's not a prediction that he'll be re-elected in 1996. When he took office he became the first president of the 21st Century, which has already begun.

3   The 20th Century is over. Historian John Lukacs, one of the first to notice, said the "main political and social phenomenon" of the 20th Century was nationalism.

4   But it was also the century of democracy and consumer technology, and through them the century of popular culture. The 20th was the American Century. The 21st may not be.

5   The 21st Century is likely to be dominated by electronic technology, which rejects national boundaries. It allows people to live farther away from each other, and also provides more ways to have fun. Individualism gives everyone the right to have fun. Mass affluence, an invention of the 20th Century, enables most people to have fun.

6   Thus, popular culture. At one of those symposiums that serious intellectuals attend, Saul Bellow complained recently that "the prevailing culture is what we see on television," that "our mental life is being taken over by [popular culture's] powers," and that "there seems to be a collective turning away from the arts."

7   Well, serious intellectuals are always complaining like this, and in some ways, "the arts," measured by concert audiences, book sales and university theater departments, have never been healthier. "Serious" culture has so far survived popular culture, but in diluted form.

8   The dilution results not because popular culture exists but because it is taken seriously. There are sociologists of football. A certified college professor has written a book about Madonna, whose only talent is self-promotion. Three new books are about to appear on the topic of Hunter Thompson, the "gonzo"[1] journalist who has little to say and doesn't say it

---

[1] Gonzo journalism: form of journalism which mocks the conventions of serious journalism.

very well, perhaps because he doesn't know much. He writes about political campaigns without knowledge of politics, history, economics or how society works. He has insights, some wit and no restraint.

9   That's how popular culture has diluted everything around it. Insight and passion are sufficient to win a hearing. Even to inquire about other credentials is deemed undemocratic. Were someone to come along now and say, "a fair and open field is not to be refused to any speaker, but this solemn way of heralding him is quite out of place, unless he has . . . some significance," he would be derided as elitist and reactionary. In fact, Matthew Arnold, who said that some 120 years ago, was a liberal. He was an elitist, though, and part of an educated elite.

10   As he knew, that elite could be snobbish and empty-headed. But at least most of its members knew things. Nor was it necessary to have been born into the elite. Robert Burns, 100 years earlier, was a poor Scottish farmboy who never went to a university. He had insight and passion, but he also knew a great deal—the Bible, Greek mythology, the history of his country, Shakespeare and Milton, a foreign language. An ignoramus could not be a great poet.

11   Popular culture means democratic culture, in which every idea is equal to every other idea, as long as it is fervently held and boldly stated. An important point of view in the finest universities holds that all works are simply "text"—Danielle Steele no less than Shakespeare. No wonder there's a book about Madonna.

12   The democratization of culture and politics has enormous benefits. Modern America is the first place in the history of the world where almost everyone can go to college. This gives unprecedented access to both economic opportunity and great skill.

13   But there is a danger in learning skills without learning content. Oliver Stone is an extraordinarily skilled moviemaker, and an extraordinarily ignorant man. His movies are good, in the way a Buick commercial is good. But because their technique is superb, their content becomes influential.

14   There is probably nothing to be done about this. As Neil Postman points out in his book, "Amusing Ourselves to Death," a society that gets its knowledge through television differs from one that gets its knowledge through books. Even their concepts of "knowledge" differ.

15   "We have so thoroughly accepted [television's] definitions of truth, knowledge and reality," Postman said, "that irrelevance seems to us to be filled with import, and incoherence seems eminently sane." The result, he said, is that "much of our public discourse has become dangerous nonsense."

16   So it's interesting, and perhaps important, that Clinton reads a lot and immerses himself in the details of policy. The first president of the 21st Century is in some ways a 19th Century person.

17   Maybe what 21st Century America needs is a 19th Century president. After all, America is an 18th Century idea.

Jon Margolis wrote this piece for *The Chicago Tribune,* where he is a staff writer.

After You Read

Reading Journal

Do you consider yourself to be a "cultured" person in the nineteenth century sense of the term? Why or why not?

Reading For Meaning

1. In your own words, describe the primary characteristics Margolis uses to distinguish the 20th from the 21st century.

2. What criticism is frequently voiced by intellectuals concerning the growing influence of popular culture? What is Margolis's attitude toward this concern?

3. What point is the author making about the 18th and 19th century conception of culture when he cites the examples Matthew Arnold and Robert Burns?

4. What advantages and disadvantages does the author see in the democratization of culture? What examples does he cite to prove his case?

5. What does Margolis mean by his last paragraph? What is a 19th century president? Why is America an 18th century idea?

Exploring Further

Debate

Argue for or against the following: Popular culture is as important to society as "high culture."

Timed Writing Exercise

To what extent do you believe, as New York University professor Neil Postman does, that America gets its knowledge, truth and reality from television rather than books? You may use your personal experience to support your argument.

Focused Essay Topics

1. Respond to the idea mentioned in paragraph 11 that "every idea is equal to every other idea, as long as it is fervently held and boldly stated." For example, in your English class, would you choose to read a popular, so-called "dimestore" book (i.e. a Danielle Steele romance) rather than a literary classic? Defend your choice.

2. Describe a typical day in the 21st century as Margolis imagines it. What will the consequences be if society is dominated by electronic technology?

Before You Read

In "Media Courtesans" Ted Koppel, an ABC news commentator, laments the lowering of broadcast media standards. Before you begin his piece, plan to watch two evening news programs on television— one a local news program and the other national news. As you watch, jot down the topics covered on each. On a separate piece of paper, write a brief critical reaction to the two programs. Discuss differences in format, content and presentation.

Media Courtesans   TED KOPPEL

1   I don't know what's happened to our standards. I fear that we in the mass media are creating such a market for mediocrity that we've diminished the incentive for excellence. We celebrate notoriety as though it were an achievement. Fame has come to mean being recognized by more people who don't know anything about you. In politics, we have encouraged the displacement of thoughtfulness by the artful cliché.

2   Which brings me to my own profession, indeed, my very own job and that of several of my distinguished colleagues here. Overestimated, overexposed—and by reasonable comparison with any job outside sports and entertainment, overpaid. I am a television news anchor—role model for Miss America contestants and tens of thousands of university students in search of a degree without an education. How does one live up to the admiration of those who regard the absence of an opinion as objectivity or (even more staggering to the imagination) as courage?

3   How does one grapple with a state of national confusion that celebrates questions over answers? How does one explain or, perhaps more relevant, guard against the influence of an industry which is on the verge of becoming a hallucinogenic barrage of images, whose only grammar is pacing, whose principal theme is energy?

4   We are losing our ability to manage ideas; to contemplate, to think. We are in a constant race to be first with the obvious. We are becoming a nation of electronic voyeurs whose capacity for dialogue is a fading memory, occasionally jolted into reflective life by a one-liner: "New ideas." "Where's the beef?" "Today is the first day of the rest of your life." "Window of vulnerability." "Freeze now." "Born again." "Gag me with a spoon." "Can we talk?"

5   No, but we can relate. Six-year-olds want to be stewardesses. Eight-year-olds want to be pilots. Nineteen-year-olds want to be anchorpersons. Grown-ups want to be left alone, to interact in solitary communion with the rest of our electronic global village.

6   Consider this paradox: Almost everything that is publicly said these days is recorded. Almost nothing of what is said is worth remembering. And what *do* we remember? Thoughts that were expressed hundreds or even thousands of years ago by philosophers, thinkers, and prophets whose ideas and principles were so universal that they endured without videotape or film, without the illustrations or photographs or cartoons— in many instances even without paper, and for thousands of years without the easy duplication of the printing press.

7   What is largely missing in American life today is a sense of context, of saying or doing anything that is intended or even expected to live beyond the moment. There is no culture in the world that is so obsessed as ours with immediacy. In our journalism, the trivial displaces the momentous because we tend to measure the importance of events by how recently they happened. We have become so obsessed with facts that we have lost all touch with truth.

8   As broadcast journalists, it's easy to be seduced into believing that what we're doing is just fine; after all, we get money, fame, and to a certain degree even influence. But money, fame, and influence without responsibility are the assets of a courtesan. We must accept responsibility for what we do, and we must think occasionally of the future.

Ted Koppel began his career in radio. He later moved to television as head of the Miami and Hong Kong bureaus. His career took off after he anchored "America Held Hostage," nightly news updates on the 1979 Iranian siege of the American embassy in Tehran. By 1980 Koppel had his own evening news show, ABC's *Nightline*, which is still being broadcast.

After You Read

Reading Journal

Look back over your notes from the pre-reading exercise. How do you think Ted Koppel would have reacted to the two programs you watched? Why?

Reading For Meaning

1. What is Koppel's thesis in this piece?

2. List in your own words the lowered "standards" Koppel feels America is experiencing. Do you agree with his charges ?

3. Paraphrase paragraph 3. Then explain what principal criticism Koppel is putting forth here about the media.

4. Look at paragraph 4. How many of the one-liners are familiar to you? Write down a cultural context for those you know.

5. How do you interpret the phrase "media courtesan"? Is this title unnecessarily harsh? Why or why not?

Exploring Further

Debate

Argue for or against the following: "Almost everything that is publicly said these days is recorded. Almost nothing of what is said is worth remembering."

Timed Writing Exercise

Koppel claims that "there is no culture in the world that is so obsessed as ours with immediacy" and that we are a "nation of electronic voyeurs." Explain what he means by this and give your own opinion. (You may refer to the article if you wish.)

Focused Essay Topics

1. Write an essay in which you either support or refute Koppel's contention that "what is largely missing in American life today is a sense of context, of saying or doing anything that is intended or even expected to live beyond the moment." (Use specific examples from the pre-reading assignment and/or watch additional broadcasts with this question in mind.)

2. Compare an English language newspaper to a newspaper written in your native language for differences and similarities of style and content. What conclusions can you draw from the way the news is presented? Would Koppel's criticisms be valid for your native language paper as well? Explain.

Before You Read

1. Freewrite on the following: "Teenagers don't invent violence, they learn it."

2. Speculate on what the author means by that sentence. Then share your response.

The Violence in Our Heads   By David Gelman

The culture of aggression shows up in our speech, our play and our entertainment. It's better than hip, it's commercial.

1   Teenagers don't invent violence, they learn it. To a considerable extent, they act out the attitudes and ethics of the adults closest to them. Thus any study of the causes of teen crime might look first at the violence grown-ups have been carrying in their heads. In the last 30 years, Americans have developed a culture of violence surpassing in its pervasiveness anything we experienced before. It shows up in our speech, in our play, more than ever in the entertainments we fashion and fancy, in business style. "There's an extraordinary degree of violence in the language, and it's the window to the actual feelings and mores of the culture," says Dr. Robert Phillips, director of forensic services for the Connecticut Department of Public Health. "You get a sense of how the social fabric is beginning to wear thin— a lot of it is directed at minorities."

2   Everyone seems aggressively on the defensive these days. A rampant "make my day" ethic expressed at various levels of the culture may be largely to blame for both the rise in teen crime

and its increasing callousness, says Deborah Prothrow-Stith, an assistant dean at the Harvard School of Public Health. Our national icons tend to be men who excel at violence, from John Wayne to Clint Eastwood. When President Clinton ordered a retaliatory airstrike on Baghdad because of an alleged plot against George Bush, his popularity rating took a leap, just as Bush's had when, as president, he ordered up the gulf war, in which an estimated 100,000 Iraqi civilians were killed by bombs and missiles.

3   Ironically, a quarter century of feminist consciousness-raising has managed, among worthier achievements, to bring us back to a macho mystique. Meanwhile the Schwarzenegger generation is pumping iron and signaling "Don't mess with me." T shirts are broadcasting more direct messages— and so are rap lyrics: "Beat that bitch with a bat," one of them urges. "Violence is hip right now," says Jack Levin, a professor of sociology and criminology at Northeastern University. Better than hip: it's commercial.

4   In her 1991 book, "Deadly Consequences," Prothrow-Stith says that, for adolescents, an attraction to violence is developmentally normal. But what accounts for adults' voyeuristic fascination with it? Are Rambo and RoboCop our surrogate avengers, as one psychologist suggests? It's not only teenagers who flock to the latest kung fu epic. It's certainly not teenagers alone who are guzzling beer and starting brawls at sports contests that are themselves turning ever more violent.

5   With new, improved technology, films grow more and more like demolition derbies. Trailers for these movies are edited to breathtaking montages of blazing guns, exploding cars and heads, and bodies hurtling out of windows. The destruction is cartoonish, but the shattered glass and bodies look real enough to leave disturbing afterimages. On the tube, growly-voiced promos whip up viewers' lust for bone-crunching, blood-letting sports contests to come. Videos capture football's hardest hits, complete with spliced-in grunts and groans. On the field, despite a belated ban, players still dance the obscene little touchdown shimmy that is intended to add manly insult to injury. If that doesn't sate your appetite, you can always attend the fights, at the hockey game—and, lately, at basketball and baseball games as well. Fans seem to love them. The danger, psychiatrists say, is that the constant repetition of violence and violent imagery desensitizes us in much the same way a therapist desensitizes a phobia patient: by deliberate exposure to what's scary.

6   Images are not reality, but they feed into the perception many people have of an inescapable, "out of control" violence in the country. And it would be a mistake to think this sensory inundation doesn't have an impact on the young. By now, the media-violence relationship is one of the best-researched connections in social science, says Myriam Miedzian, author of "Boys Will Be Boys: Breaking The Link Between Masculinity and Violence." But it is also, she adds, one of the best-kept secrets. "There's been an enormous reluctance to deal with this. Mothers will still say, 'Oh, I took the kids to see the Slasher, and they came home and had milkshakes and cookies.'"

7   In fact, milkshakes and cookies may not be such a bad idea. The impact of violent movies and TV—almost impossible to put off-limits since the advent of VCRs—can be mitigated by a caring parent who sits down with the children and helps put things in perspective. That, of course, assumes a caring parent is available. "It's virtually impossible when the parent is working 50 or 60 hours a week," says Stephen Klineberg, a professor of sociology at Rice University, in Texas. In 1974, for the first time, 50 percent of American children had nobody at home when school let out at 3 o'clock. Now, it's closer to 80 percent, but schools still kick kids out at 3. "While the family has undergone a revolution, there's been a failure of these other structures to change accordingly," says Klineberg. "It's what sociologists call a cultural lag."

8   The failure of schools to adapt is only one example of what social analysts believe is a general failure of will, a kind of paralysis in the face of the growing dimensions of the problem. The token gesture of the TV networks in volunteering parental-guidance labels for certain shows scarcely changes the picture. There are obvious dangers in imposing more aggressive restraints and flinging the doors open wider to censorship. But meanwhile, the levels of tolerated violence in the media, in sports and in the real world keep

ratcheting upward. When do we stop feeling helpless and start doing something? "The surgeon general's reports for years have said that violence on television is related to violence in children," says Carol Nagy Jacklin, dean of the division of social science and communication at the University of Southern California. "It's so upsetting that, on the one hand, we seem to deplore this violence but, on the other, we are not stopping it in the ways that we know it needs to be stopped."

9   Taken down to cases, there are more proximate causes of adolescent crime in this country—guns and drugs, to name just two. But in the longer view, they may be no more responsible than the cultural violence of which we are the principal makers and consumers, and which we still hesitate to bring under effective control.

David Gelman's "The Violence in Our Heads" appeared on *Newsweek's* Society page in 1993.

After You Read

Reading Journal

Look back at your pre-reading response. Did the article confirm or change your opinion about the nature and causes of teenage violence? In what way(s)?

Reading for Meaning

1. List the primary causes, according to the article, of "learned" violence in American culture and give at least one concrete example of each.

2. What is a "make my day" ethic? (paragraph 2) What are the possible consequences of subscribing to such an ethic?

3. Summarize the research findings of the relationship between media violence and violent behavior.

4. Gelman describes what he calls a "general failure of will" when it comes to curbing the problem of violence in America. Explain in your own words what he means by this and the possible solutions he proposes.

Exploring Further

Interview/Questionnaire

In your group design a short questionnaire to test how tolerant people are of various forms of "culturally approved" violence. You might begin by listing the areas mentioned in the article such as music lyrics, television programs, films, sports, and political events. For each area, write up three or four questions with which respondents can agree or disagree. Tabulate your findings and present them to the rest of the class.

Sample questions for music lyrics:	Agree	Disagree
1. I would buy a recording if I liked the music, even if the lyrics were violent.		
2. The violence in many rap lyrics is justified because it reflects real life situations.		
3. A store's refusal to sell recordings with violent lyrics is censorship.		
4. Listening to violent lyrics does not make a person violent.		

Timed Writing Exercise

Write about your personal tolerance for violence in everyday life. For example, do you feel yourself to be desensitized to the violent imagery in popular culture by having been exposed to so much of it, or do you try to avoid films and television programs which are especially violent?

Focused Essay Topics

1. Discuss your native culture's attitude toward media violence. Is it more or less tolerant than Gelman's assessment of mainstream America's? Why do you think this is so?

2. "The Violence in Our Heads" concludes by urging Americans to control both the production and the consumption of cultural violence. Write an essay in which you outline the problem and then make at least two specific suggestions for helping to solve it.

Before You Read

1. Read the following biblical passages and translate them into standard conversational English. (The first is taken from *The King James Version,* the most commonly read English version of the *Bible.* The second version, written for African Americans, is taken from *The Black Bible Chronicles.)*

> "Thou shalt not take the name of the Lord thy God in vain; for the Lord will not hold him guiltless that taketh his name in vain."

> "You shouldn't diss the Almighty's name, usin' it in cuss words or rappin' with one another. It ain't cool, and payback's a monster."

2. Which of the first two versions seemed more difficult for you to understand? Why?

3. Now exchange your translation with a classmate. How do they compare with each other?

"Diss" Is the Word of the Lord

By Sophfronia Scott Gregory

Profits being honorable, Bible merchants serve up market-driven Scriptures

1   Remember the temptation of Eve in Eden? Here's how it goes in one new version of *Genesis.* Eve: "Yeah, snake, I can eat of these trees, just not the tree of knowledge or the Almighty said I'd be knocked off." Snake: "Nah, sister, he's feeding you a line of bull. You won't die. The Almighty just knows that if you eat from the tree you'll be hipped to what's going down." Say what?

2   That snatch of conversation from *Black Bible Chronicles* is just one of many new attempts to make the Bible get with the program. One-third of American adults today have trouble decoding the King James Version, and 70% of teenagers in a typical week do not even bother to try, according to Barna Research Group, a religious polling firm. So religious publishers, eager to expand a $400 million Bible industry, are out peddling niche-oriented Bibles in a Babel of new interpretations and formats—or, to paraphrase Shakespeare, quoting Scripture for their own purposes. "In a Baskin-Robbins society, people don't want chocolate or vanilla. They want a special flavor that really suits their needs," says Bill Anderson, president of the Christian Booksellers Association.

3   The International Bible Society, for example, has published *Path to Victory* ($2.25), a New Testament that includes profiles of such sports stars as Michael Chang, Orel Hershiser and Evelyn Ashford discussing their favorite scriptural sayings. Blank pages in the back are for autographs. Readers used to *USA Today* will get into the spirit of Thomas Nelson Publishers *The Word in Life Study Bible* ($19.99), which is highlighted with sidebars, graphs and charts on topics such as "Does God Work on Sundays?" For those for whom seeing is believing, there is *The Bible Alive* (Harper Collins; $25), which is illustrated by 250 photo re-enactments of biblical scenes shot in the Middle East and manipulated by computer photography technology for a you-are-there feel.

4   But *Black Bible Chronicles* (African American Family Press; $14.95) remains the most striking and the most controversial of the lot. The God here is one mean dude, sounding at times more like a gang leader than the Lord. Warning Noah of the Flood, he says, "I'm fed up with what's happenin' 'round here. These folks ain't what's happenin' anymore, so I'm gonna do what I gotta do, and end things once and for all. Man, I'm gonna blow the brothers clear outta the water."

5   The *Leviticus* chapter includes a section on sex straightforwardly called "All About Getting Down." It solemnly notes, "It was a bad thing to do the wild thing without the blessing from the Almighty. You had to be hitched." And, in *Genesis*, Joseph rejects Potiphar's wife because he "couldn't betray a homeboy that way. Also, he couldn't jock the Almighty either, 'cuz it wouldn't be right sleeping with somebody else's ol' lady."

6   "There is way too much street language," Says Gleason Ledyard, a Christian book publisher. He says some people will be offended. Journalist P.K. McCary, who translated the first five books of the Old Testament into slang, insists that she is not "dissin' the Almighty." She has written biblical poetry and essays and developed the book by telling stories to children in Atlanta and Houston. The 39-year-old single mother believes she's filling a void. "While this is slang, it is not irreverent," she says. "It's a dramatic, colorful way of speaking. I think teenagers are going to like reading it because it gives them that Afrocentric flavor they can relate to."

7   McCary intends to carry on her work by slangifying the four Gospels in *Rapping About Jesus*, due out before Christmas. "All I want to do is introduce kids to Jesus," she says. "It doesn't matter how you get it."

8   For some, there is another avenue to the way, the truth and the life. *The African Heritage Study Bible* (Winston-Derek Publishers; $39.95) keeps to the King James Version and adds scholarly chapters on such topics as ancient Black Christians and "African Edenic Women and the Scriptures." It also features 25 original slave songs and 57 pages of photos and artwork in which all the biblical characters are black—and never lose their dignity.

Sophronia Scott Gregory's article appeared on the religion page of *Time* Magazine in 1993.

After You Read

Reading Journal

Respond to the following quotation in light of the article you have just read: "In a Baskin-Robbins society, people don't want chocolate or vanilla. They want a special flavor that really suits their needs." Would you characterize your native culture as a "Baskin-Robbins society" as well? Explain.

Reading For Meaning

1. According to the article, what has prompted religious publishers to revise the standard version of the Bible?

2. Find specific examples of the innovative presentations mentioned in the article which are aimed at increasing readership. Would you like to see a creative version of your own religious text? Why or why not?

3. How does P.K. McCary defend her use of street slang? Do you agree with her rationale?

Exploring Further

Group Presentation

Decide as a group on a passage from a well-known English literary classic. (The "To be or not to be" speech from Shakespeare's *Hamlet*, or Psalm 23 from the *Bible*, for example.) Rewrite the passage in conversational English and present it to the class. Ask the class to identify the passage as soon as they are able.

Timed Writing Exercise

Some people might argue that "translating" a classical text for any one group, no matter how well-intended, carries with it the risk of distorting certain historical "truths." (Consider for example a Bible in which all characters are black, or Hispanic.) Do you think that the end (getting more people to read the *Bible*) justifies the means (slanting history)? Why or why not?

Focused Essay Topics

1. Imagine that you are in charge of curriculum development for your college English department. The issue of "translating" Shakespeare into idiomatic, modern English has been raised. Present your argument as you might for the faculty and students for or against the use of such material.

2. Agree or disagree with the following statement: Rewriting classical works, and the *Bible* in particular, is nothing more than a simplification of culture for the sake of publisher profits. At worst, it is demeaning to those it would claim to serve—African Americans—by implying that they are unable to relate to a world not their own.

Before You Read

"How I Write My Songs by Bill B. White" promises to enlighten readers on the process of song writing. What contemporary musician(s) or
songwriter(s) would you like to know more about in terms of artistic
process? Explain.

How I Write My Songs
by Bill B. White

DONALD BARTHELME

1   Some of the methods I use to write my songs will be found in the following examples. Everyone has a song in him or her. Writing songs is a
basic human trait. I am not saying that it is easy; like everything else
worthwhile in this world it requires concentration and hard work. The
methods I will outline are a good way to begin and have worked for me
but they are by no means the only methods that can be used. There is no
one set way of writing your songs, every way is just as good as the other
as Kipling said. (I am talking now about the lyrics; we will talk about the
melodies in a little bit.) The important thing is to put true life into our
songs, things that people know and can recognize and truly feel. You
have to be open to experience, to what is going on around you, the things
of daily life. Often little things that you don't even think about at the time
can be the basis of a song.

2   A knowledge of all the different types of songs that are commonly
accepted is helpful. To give you an idea of the various types of songs
there are I am going to tell you how I wrote various of my own, including
"Rudelle," "Last Night," "Sad Dog Blues," and others—how I came to
write these songs and where I got the idea and what the circumstances
were, more or less, so that you will be able to do the same thing. Just
remember, *there is no substitute for sticking to it* and listening to the work
of others who have been down this road before you and have mastered
their craft over many years.

3   In the case of "Rudelle" I was sitting at my desk one day with my pen-
cil and yellow legal pad and I had two things that were irritating me. One
was a letter from the electric company that said "The check for $75.60
sent us in payment of your bill has been returned to us by the bank
unhonored etc. etc." Most of you who have received this type of letter
from time to time know how irritating this kind of communication can be
as well as embarrassing. The other thing that was irritating me was that
I had a piece of white thread tied tight around my middle at navel height
as a reminder to keep my stomach pulled in to strengthen the abdomi-
nals while sitting—this is the price you pay for slopping down too much

beer when your occupation is essentially a sit-down one! Anyhow I had these two things itching me, so I decided to write a lost-my-mind song.

4   I wrote down on my legal pad the words:

> When I lost my baby
> I almost lost my mine

5   This is more or less a traditional opening for this type of song. Maybe it was written by somebody originally way long ago and who wrote it is forgotten. It often helps to begin with a traditional or well-known line or lines to set a pattern for yourself. You can then write the rest of the song and, if you wish, cut off the top part, giving you an original song. *Songs are always composed of both traditional and new elements.* This means that you can rely on the tradition to give your song "legs" while also putting in your own experience or particular way of looking at things for the new.

6   Incidentally the lines I have quoted may look pretty bare to you but remember you are looking at just one element, the words, and there is also the melody and the special way various artists will have of singing it which gives flavor and freshness. For example, an artist who is primarily a blues singer would probably give the "when" a lot of squeeze, that is to say, draw it out, and he might also sing "baby" as three notes, "bay-ee-bee," although it is only two syllables. Various artists have their own unique ways of doing a song and what may appear to be rather plain or dull on paper becomes quite different when it is a song.

7   I then wrote:

> When I lost my baby
> I almost lost my mine
> When I lost my baby
> I almost lost my mine
> When I found my baby
> The sun began to shine

You will notice I retained the traditional opening because it was so traditional I did not see any need to delete it. With the addition of various material about Rudelle and what kind of woman she was, it became gold in 1976.

8   Incidentally while we are talking about use of traditional materials here is a little tip: you can often make good use of colorful expressions in common use such as "If the good Lord's willin' and the creek don't rise" (to give you just one example) which I used in "Goin' to Get Together" as follows:

> Goin' to get to-geth-er
> Goin' to get to-geth-er
> If the good Lord's willin' and the creek don't rise

These common expressions are expressive of the pungent ways in which most people often think—they are the salt of your song, so to say. Try it!

9   It is also possible to give a song a funny or humorous "twist":

Show'd my soul to the woman at the bank
She said put that thing away boy, put that thing away
Show'd my soul to the woman at the liquor store
She said put that thing away boy, 'fore it turns the wine
Show'd my soul to the woman at the 7-Eleven
She said: Is that all?

Copyright © 1974 by Rattlesnake Music, Inc.

You will notice that the meter here is various and the artist is given great liberties.

10   Another type of song which is a dear favorite of almost everyone is the song that has a message, some kind of thought that people can carry away with them and think about. Many songs of this type are written and gain great acceptance every day. Here is one of my own that I put to a melody which has a kind of martial flavor:

How do you spell truth? L-o-v-e is how you spell truth
How do you spell love? T-r-u-t-h is how you spell love
Where were you last night?
Where were you last night?

Copyright © 1975 by Rattlesnake Music/A.I.M. Corp.

When "Last Night" was first recorded, the engineer said "That's a keeper" on the first take and it was subsequently covered by sixteen artists including Walls.

11   The I-ain't-nothin'-but-a-man song is a good one to write when you are having a dry spell. These occur in songwriting as in any other profession and if you are in one it is often helpful to try your hand at this type of song which is particularly good with a heavy rhythm emphasis in the following pattern:

Da da da da *da*
Whomp, whomp

where some of your instruments are playing da da da da *da*, hitting that last note hard, and the others answer whomp, whomp. Here is one of my own:

I'm just an ordinary mane
Da da da da *da*
Whomp, whomp
Just an ordinary mane
Da da da da *da*
Whomp, whomp
Ain't nothin' but a mane
Da da da da *da*
Whomp, whomp
I'm a grizzly mane
Da da da da *da*
Whomp, whomp
I'm a hello-goodbye mane
Da da da da *da*
Whomp, whomp
I'm a ramblin'-gamblin' mane

Da da da da *da*
Whomp, whomp
I'm a *mane's* mane
I'm a woeman's mane
Da da da da *da*
Whomp, whomp
I'm an upstairs mane
Da da da da *da*
Whomp, whomp
I'm a today-and-tomorrow mane
Da da da da *da*
Whomp, whomp
I'm a Freeway mane
Da da da da *da*
Whomp, whomp

12   Well, you see how it is done. It is my hope that these few words will get you started. Remember that although this business may seem closed and standoffish to you, looking at it from the outside, inside it has some very warm people in it, some of the finest people I have run into in the course of a varied life. The main thing is to persevere and to believe in yourself, no matter what the attitude of others may be or appear to be. I could never have written my songs had I failed to believe in Bill B. White, not as a matter of conceit or false pride but as a human being. I will continue to write my songs, for the nation as a whole and for the world.

> ***Donald Barthelme*** began his writing career as a journalist before he became a leading practitioner of experimental fiction, which dispenses with traditional fictional elements, like plot and character. He won many awards for his writing before his death in 1989.

After You Read

Reading Journal

Agree or disagree, citing examples and/or exceptions: Some critics of pop and rock music claim much of the music today is banal and undistinctive; in fact, the top 100 of any particular season are quickly replaced by a new crop of uninspired songs and forgotten.

Reading For Meaning

1. What sort of character do you think Barthelme wants to portray in this story?

2. Describe the style and tone of Barthelme's story. What is its effect?

3. "How I Write My Songs by Bill B. White" is a "how-to" piece of writing that intends to instruct readers on the craft of songwriting. Is it informative and instructive? Why or why not?

4. How do you imagine the music that accompanies Bill White's lyrics? Describe it.

Exploring Further

Group Presentation

Choose one of the songs in the Barthelme story and describe how you would design a video of it. Include details of costumes, hairstyles, action, choreography, special camera work (angles or close-ups). What attitude or message do you want to convey? Present your plans to the class.

Timed Writing Exercise

Certain kinds of music, like "gangsta rap" or "heavy metal," and the videos that go along with them, have been criticized for having a negative influence on teenagers. Critics say that these lyrics encourage young adults to act violently. One solution that has been suggested is to issue a warning label on all tapes and CDs with explicitly violent or sexual lyrics. In your opinion, is this a good or even workable solution? Explain.

Focused Essay Topics

1. According to Bill B. White "everyone has a song in him or her. Writing songs is a basic human trait." In a personal essay, extend the meaning of the word song to include other forms of creative expression (writing, art, dance, etc.) Describe your "song" and the ideas/feelings it conveys.

2. Compare and/or contrast the clichés (commonly shared images, phrases, etc.) that Bill B. White presents in his songs with those which appear in the folk or pop music of your native country or culture. What conclusions can you draw from their differences or similarities?

EXTENDING THE CONTEXT

> These questions are designed for further discussion or essay writing. Your responses should reflect the thinking, reading and writing you have done on the unit topic thus far.

1. "Gangsta rap," according to its musicians, producers and fans, reflects the brutal conditions of life in the inner city and the rage of minority youth today. However, according to opponents of this music, it incites and glamorizes the violence of these communities. Some radio stations have gone so far as to ban this music. Should stations continue to do this? Why or why not?

2. As all advertising executives know, "sex sells." Nearly naked men and women are used to sell everything—from winter vacations to jeans, perfume and beer. But recent protests from feminists and others have forced advertisers to tone down the ads and make them less obvious. How do you feel about using sexual imagery to sell a product? Use specific examples to support your thesis.

3. Television and video technology is becoming more and more advanced and sophisticated every year, yet television is criticized for reducing information to banal "sound bites." Explore ways in which we might harness this electronic technology to educate and inform.

4. Critics of network news claim that these news programs have become increasingly sensational and trivial in their coverage. Agree or disagree, using specific examples.

5. Discuss a film or television show which informed you about something important or made a lasting impression on you.

6. Children today often have little exposure to high culture (classical music, theater, art and dance). There are many probable causes ranging from increased television and video exposure and cuts in educational budgets for culture in the schools to the breakup of the nuclear family. Whatever the causes, there is a fear that high culture will die out without the support and interest of the upcoming generations. Do you feel that this is a legitimate cause for concern? Why or why not?

7. Choose one of the quotations from the Short Takes section at the beginning of this unit and write an essay supporting or refuting it.

8. Many Americans are angered over the fact that any public figure's private life is open to scrutiny. Argue for or against a public figure's right to privacy from the media, using specific examples.

VIDEO SUGGESTIONS

The video selections are offered as suggestions for viewing in or out of class to enrich the unit topic.

Cross-Over Dreams
Truth or Dare
Broadcast News
Network
Mambo Kings

THE WRITER'S GUIDE

EXPLORING AMERICAN CULTURE IN WRITING

PART ONE
A GUIDE TO WRITING ASSIGNMENTS

This brief guide to the writing assignments in *Explorations in American Culture* is followed by more detailed explanations of the reading, thinking, and writing processes you may want to use as you respond to the reading selections your instructor assigns.

BEFORE YOU READ

The questions in *Before You Read* are intended to help you focus on the subject or theme of the reading selection that follows. Keeping a written copy of your responses may prove helpful later; you will be able to see how your viewpoint has changed or how it has been confirmed after reading other people's ideas.

AFTER YOU READ

A variety of questions for writing and assignments for informal research follows each reading selection. These questions help you focus on the author's main ideas, connect the author's ideas with your own, and give you ideas for writing essays that explore these connections.

Reading Journal   Throughout this book, you will be asked to write your first responses to reading selections in your journal. Be sure to think about and answer *all* the parts of the journal questions. For example, the question "Do you think being married or living with someone can increase one's happiness? Describe your own living situation and how satisfying it is," requires a three-part response. In your journal you would note (1) whether you believe living with a partner can increase happiness, and why; (2) a description of your living situation (Are you married? Do you live with another person?); and (3) to what degree you are satisfied or dissatisfied with your living situation? You may want to read *Strategies for Developing Essays and Paragraphs* on page 263 for further guidance.

Reading for Meaning   The *Reading for Meaning* section is designed to test your understanding of a given writer's ideas. These are short answer questions which may ask you to restate or summarize an author's main points, explain a passage of the text in your own words or list examples which support the author's thesis.

One strategy for approaching these questions is called "mapping" the text. This means, quite simply, that you make notes, underline and annotate the reading as you go. Follow these guidelines for writing as you read:

• Underline the thesis statement and/or the topic sentences.

• If the thesis is not stated directly but only implied, write the thesis statement in the margin.

- Bracket the introduction and conclusion.
- Make brief notes in the margins on the major details the author uses to support the thesis statement.
- Star or number the most important examples.
- Note questions when you are unsure of the author's meaning so that you can reread a section more carefully once you've finished reading the first time.

See *Analyzing Others' Ideas* on page 237 to become a more critical reader, and *Writing Essays* on page 255 to learn about the major parts of an English essay.

EXPLORING FURTHER

Exploring Further assignments ask you to do one of the following projects: (1) conduct informal research on a subject by surveying other people's attitudes with *questionnaires* and *interviews*; or (2) organize your ideas for a *group presentation* to the class; or (3) prepare for an oral *debate* on a topic related to the reading you have done.

To prepare for a debate, consider both sides of the issue, not just your own. Write down the main arguments you want to make and consider what the response of the opposing side is likely to be. Then think of how you could respond most effectively to the opposing point of view. Oral presentations, too, benefit from advance planning and writing. Guidelines for writing questionnaires and conducting interviews are on page 238.

Timed Writing   To answer a timed writing question, you need to schedule enough time to analyze the question carefully, decide on a thesis statement, make a brief outline to be sure your answer will stay focused on the thesis, write the answer, and have a few minutes left for proofreading at the end. Following are suggested schedules for a thirty-minute answer and a sixty-minute answer:

Schedule	*30 Minutes*	*60 Minutes*
Analyze question, write thesis	5 minutes	5 minutes
Outline answer	5 minutes	15 minutes
Write answer	15 minutes	35 minutes
Proofread	5 minutes	5 minutes

Notice that when you have a longer time period, it's better to spend comparatively more time planning and organizing your answer than writing it. If your thesis statement is logical and your outline is detailed and organized, you should be able to write quickly. (*Never* take the time to rewrite your answer; instead, neatly cross out parts you want to delete and write above the line to insert new sentences.)

In timed writing, it is important that you take part of your writing time to *conclude* your answer so that it doesn't seem to stop in mid-thought. Read the following sections of this chapter to prepare for timed writing:

Focused Essay Topics   The *Focused Essay Topics* ask you to respond to a reading in greater depth than either the *Reading Journal* or *Reading for Meaning* questions. To answer these questions fully, you will need to analyze the reading itself and then think carefully about the topic. Read *Analyzing a Reading,* page 237; *Overview of the Writing Process,* page 243; and *Writing an Essay,* page 255 for a variety of useful strategies for writing essays.

EXTENDING THE CONTEXT

Extending the Context assignments at the end of each unit ask you to write essays based on the connections you have drawn among several of the reading selections. For example, you might be asked to compare and contrast two authors' viewpoints on a given subject. (See page 264 on *Comparison and Contrast.*) No matter what the particular assignment asks you to do, remember that you probably already have class notes, freewritings, journal entries, and reading notes from the chapter. Review all your notes before deciding on a thesis or a direction for the development of your essay. The section called *Drafting* on page 247 outlines questions to ask yourself while writing, and the *Revision Checklist* on page 251 may be helpful as you move toward a final draft.

PART TWO
SUGGESTIONS FOR WRITING FROM READING AND INFORMAL RESEARCH

Most of the essay assignments in this book will ask you to read about your topic and incorporate ideas from your reading into an essay. As you read and write, remember that no essay should be a patchwork of other people's ideas. Your own ideas are the most important; use other people's ideas to support and develop them. Since your first step in responding to others' ideas is understanding them, begin by analyzing the reading text in writing.

ANALYZING OTHERS' IDEAS

Answer the questions outlined below to understand an author's ideas completely and to begin to generate material for your own essay.

- In one sentence, what is the author's main point?
- What three reasons or examples best support this point? List them.
- Are there any other reasons or examples that the author doesn't mention, to support this point?
- What reasons, examples, or facts can you think of that make the author's point of view seem wrong, misguided, or unclear?
- Which of the author's points do you disagree with, and why?

CONDUCTING INTERVIEWS AND WRITING QUESTIONNAIRES

Sometimes your own ideas will provide sufficient details for writing an essay. Other times, it may be helpful to ask others what they think or how they feel about a topic to prepare for writing. If your instructor has asked you to conduct an interview or use a questionnaire to survey others' attitudes or opinions about a topic, be systematic in your approach to gain the most useful information.

☐ **Getting the Information** Use these brief guidelines to help you design questions that will give you the information you need.

- *Organize your thoughts* about exactly what you are trying to find out. Write down the two or three most important pieces of information you are interested in gathering from each person.

- *Decide how to form your questions* to elicit the response you want. For example, if you want to find out the reasons someone holds an opinion, you will need to ask "Why?" after he or she has stated the opinion. If you want to discover someone's preference for one choice over another choice, ask your question in an either/or format. If in using a questionnaire you will gather and count only "true" or "false" answers, then design the questionnaire as a series of statements that can be responded to with simple agreement or disagreement.

- *Write down your respondents' answers carefully*, particularly if you have asked for an opinion or attitude. It is wise to read your notes back to the person to verify that you have stated his or her response accurately.

☐ **Analyzing Results** Be careful to keep your analysis accurate when reporting the results of a survey. For example, suppose you survey ten Americans to find out what they consider the most important qualities of a happy life, and you give them the following choices: a well-paying job, a busy social life, close friends, close family ties, and a sense of independence. Of the ten respondents, two mention a busy social life, two mention close friends, and two mention close family ties as being important to happiness. In your report, you could say that "the majority of the respondents mentioned having other people in their lives as a source of happiness," but you could not say that "nearly all" or "the vast majority" mentioned other people as being important. These phrases imply more agreement on the question than you have actually received. The most precise way to report this result would be to say that "60% of the respondents found interactions with other people to be an important component of happiness."

LIBRARY RESEARCH

In this book you will not be asked to write formal research papers. However, your college library can still be an invaluable resource for finding out what published authors have to say about a given topic. Become familiar with the library as soon as possible, and always ask a librarian for assistance if you cannot find the information you need.

USING SOURCE MATERIAL

Once you have analyzed a reading and conducted any necessary research, you may be asked to summarize an author's or respondent's main ideas or to write an essay using the ideas you have gathered. Summary, paraphrase, and quotation are three techniques for restating someone else's ideas in your essay. (See *Signal Verbs*, page 242, for a list of verbs that may be used to introduce a summary, paraphrase, or quotation.)

PLAGIARISM

Plagiarism occurs when you use someone else's ideas or words without crediting that person as the author—in other words, when you pretend that someone else's ideas or words are your own. Plagiarism is considered a very serious offense in colleges and universities; a student caught plagiarizing may fail the course or be expelled from the university. However, not all plagiarism is deliberate. To avoid inadvertent plagiarism, take the following steps whenever you summarize, paraphrase, or quote someone else:

- *Copy carefully.* Do not make careless mistakes when copying someone's words.

- *Double-check your notes against your source.* In summary and paraphrase, you should *not* use the author's words or sentence structure. In quotation, you *must* use a set of quotation marks around the author's exact words.

- *Always put publication information on your note cards.* In your notes, always include the author's name and the book (or article) title from which you took your information. This information allows you to indicate your sources in your essay, and it helps you locate your source again if you need additional information later.

FORMAL RESEARCH PAPERS

If your instructor assigns a documented research paper—that is, a research paper that includes full publication information for each source you have used—ask him or her which citation style you should use. The Modern Language Association (MLA) citation style is typically used in English, history, and other humanities courses. Other citation styles include the APA style, used in psychology, sociology, and anthropology, and the CBE style, used in the sciences. A good college handbook usually includes guidelines for using citation styles.

GUIDELINES FOR WRITING SUMMARIES

A summary is a *very brief* restatement of an author's major points rewritten in your own words. You may be asked to summarize a work of literature, a film, or an article to show your instructor that you have understood its main ideas. To write a summary, first identify the writer's thesis statement if it is stated. Rewrite it using your own words and phrasing. If the thesis is not stated, write a sentence that summarizes the main idea that the whole piece of writing implies. (Or, if you are asked to summarize only a paragraph or two, find the main idea of that part of the essay or article and do the same.)

Next, write a sentence to begin the summary that states the author's full name, the name of the article or essay, and the thesis statement written in your own words.

For example, Matthew Schifrin states in his article "Horatio Alger Kim" that Korean small business owners in the U.S. succeed because they work long hours, support one another, adapt themselves to new circumstances, and retain control over all aspects of their businesses. (A sentence of explanation for each point follows this introductory sentence.)

Three additional points when writing summaries are:

• *Keep your summary brief.* Make sure that you don't include minor details in your sentences. Focus on the author's most important ideas.

• *Do not use the author's own language.* Restate the author's ideas in your own words. If you must use a few words of the author's, refer to the *Guidelines for Writing Quotations* below, to make sure you credit the author.

• *Do not mix your own ideas with the author's.* Your own ideas should not appear in the summary. If your instructor asks you to comment on a summary, make it very clear to the reader which ideas are the author's and which are your own:

"I agree with Schifrin that…"

"Although Schifrin argues that…, I believe…"

GUIDELINES FOR WRITING PARAPHRASES

"Paraphrasing" means restating someone else's ideas in your own words. Unlike a summary, which is brief, a paraphrase gives all the details of the original source, but in different language and sentence structure. Use paraphrase when you need to reproduce the exact details of a few sentences or paragraphs of a source. Identify the source of the material in your paraphrase for your readers. Use the guidelines below to write accurate paraphrases:

- *Your paraphrase typically will be as long as or even longer than the source.*

- *Don't distort the source's meaning.* Use the same order of ideas and emphasize the same points that the author did.

- *Use all your own words and sentence structure.* Find synonyms for the author's key words. Check your paraphrase against the original passage to make sure you haven't used its words or sentence structure.

GUIDELINES FOR WRITING QUOTATIONS

When you quote someone's exact words, be sure to copy their words precisely, and put the words inside a pair of quotation marks:

> Discussing American values, L. Robert Kohls notes that Americans connect change with "development, improvement, progress, and growth."

Notice in the example that the quotation is integrated into the student writer's own sentence structure. Never quote an entire sentence from a source without introducing it and then explaining its significance to your own thesis.

Quotations should be used sparingly in your essays. To decide if someone's words are worth quoting directly, ask yourself the following questions. (Use quotations only if you answer "yes" to all three questions.)

- Is the language or style of the quotation so appropriate that it would be difficult to achieve the same impact using your own words?

- Is the authority of the person you are quoting particularly impressive?

- Do you need the quotation to emphasize one of your own ideas?

SIGNAL VERBS

Summaries, paraphrases, and quotations can be introduced by a number of verbs, each with a different meaning. Use the verb that most accurately conveys the author's meaning. The first group of signal verbs on the chart below can be used to indicate that an author is merely stating an opinion, belief, or fact. Use a verb from the second group when the author is making a claim, refuting someone else's argument, or conceding that a different point of view has some merit.

THE AUTHOR'S PURPOSE	SIGNAL VERB
TO STATE A FACT OR BELIEF	acknowledges adds believes comments declares indicates notes observes points out reports states suggests thinks writes
TO MAKE AN ARGUMENT (stronger than a statement) To Confirm or Conclude:	argues (that) agrees that asserts claims concludes confirms contends emphasizes insists
To Refute:	denies disputes objects refutes
To Concede:	admits concedes

PART THREE
OVERVIEW OF THE WRITING PROCESS

Writing effective essays is a process of finding ideas, figuring out the best way to explain your ideas to your readers, and making sure that your writing conforms to accepted standards of structure, grammar and punctuation. The diagram illustrates the stages you should go through in order to produce an organized, well-developed essay.

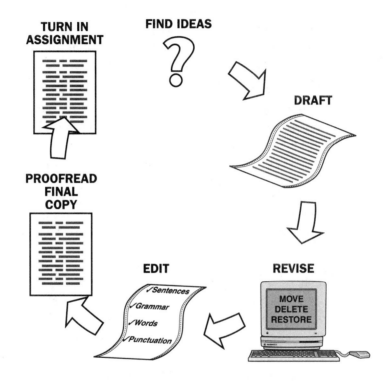

What follows is an in-depth explanation of the various startegies you may use in writing your essay. You needn't use all these strategies each time you write. Feel free to try them all to see which best suit your own individual writing style.

FINDING IDEAS

As you write to discover possible ideas for essays, let the words flow freely. In this first stage of writing, write your ideas as they come to you without censoring or criticizing them. Often, an idea that seems unimportant will spark another idea that is worth exploring. The most important assets you have at this stage of writing are all your ideas, written down so they can be examined and explored later.

If your instructor has assigned a topic, write it down. If you can choose your essay topic, pick any general subject or problem you want to consider. For example, the subject might be "culture shock" or "how people can preserve their own culture while living in another."

Freewriting   Freewriting is a useful technique when your instructor has assigned a general subject and you need to decide which aspect of the subject you would like to write about. In freewriting, follow these guidelines:

- Decide to write for a certain period of time, say ten minutes. Keep writing until the time is up.

- Write down all ideas you have about the subject, in any order. Don't be concerned about writing in complete sentences, spelling correctly, or using proper grammar.

- When the time is up, read your freewriting and underline any ideas that seem worth exploring further. Explore those ideas by freewriting again or using one of the other invention techniques given below.

Here is a student's freewriting on the subject of culture shock:

> In China it is rude to act like you "know it all," but it seems to be an American value . . . even when people don't know what they are talking about they act like they know everything. In my classes American students argue with the professor. I thought they were being very offensive. I thought the professors had *lost face*. But the professors argued with them, so I thought that I should learn to question their teaching too. But I have not argued. The other problem I have in the US is that *people seem very bold*. They say "no" anytime they want to, even to their guests. In China we would not say "no" to guests. It is very impolite. My main idea about culture shock is that in America *people are very direct*. It is difficult to be so direct for me.

Brainstorming   Brainstorming is a strategy for finding ideas that is often used when a group of people are working together to find solutions to a problem. To brainstorm with a group, do the following:

- Write down the problem or general topic.

- Have group members call out as many ideas as they can about the topic. No one criticizes any ideas, no matter how silly they may seem.

- Have a member of the group write down all the ideas.

- Have each group member write down the ideas he or she wants to focus on in the next stage of writing.

Below is an example of brainstorming on the subject of "How to preserve your own culture while living in another":

> have friends from your country
> talk in your own language with them
> tell Americans about your culture
> cook your own food or teach an American friend how to cook a dish
> if you are in a big city, find a neighborhood where people from your country live
> tell stories of your culture to Americans
> make decisions based on your understanding and values, not just on what American friends think is right

Clustering Like brainstorming, clustering is a method of generating ideas quickly. It differs from brainstorming in that it offers a picture of the relations among your ideas. To cluster, follow these steps:

• Write down a general topic in the middle of the page and circle it.

• Jot down ideas about the topic as they occur to you. Circle them, and draw arrows or lines back to the circle that inspired them. Keep creating new circles and connecting them back to earlier ideas.

• After you have finished, decide which clusters of ideas seem most interesting or important. Star these clusters.

• Try to summarize your most important ideas in a sentence or two.

An example of clustering on the subject of "happiness" follows.

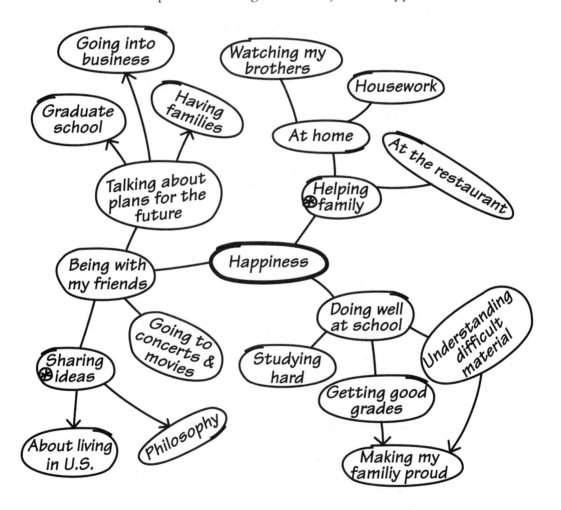

For me, happiness is being with the people I love: my family and friends. I have always enjoyed helping my parents and playing with my brothers. Now that I'm in college, I really like being able to talk with my best friends about life in general and our plans for the future.

Informal Outlining Jotting down notes in an informal outline is a more structured method of generating ideas about a topic than freewriting, brainstorming, or clustering. Before you attempt to arrange your ideas in outline form, take the following steps:

- Make a list of all the ideas you have had about the topic. This list can be composed of words, disconnected phrases, or sentences—whatever best expresses your thoughts. (This list may have come from freewriting, brainstorming, or clustering.)

- Examine your list for similar types of items. To do this, think about generalizations you can create from your specific ideas. For example, suppose your topic is "How people can preserve their own culture while living in another," and your list includes the following items: *speaking your first language, speaking up when stereotypes of your culture are discussed, wearing clothing from your culture, addressing older people respectfully, and observing cultural holidays and celebrations.* Generalizations derived from these specific items might be based on where each action could be carried out, why each action is important, or who is involved in each action.

- Now group the items from your list under the appropriate generalization. Here is an example based on where each action to preserve one's culture can be carried out:

Actions you can take at home:

Speak your first language
Address older people respectfully
Observe cultural holidays and celebrations

Actions you can take at school:

Speak up when people discuss stereotypes of your culture
Wear clothing from your culture of origin
Address older people respectfully

- If some of your listed items don't seem to fit into the categories you have developed, you have several choices:

You can discard the item if it isn't important.
You can think of other, similar items and group them all together under a new heading.
You can change your generalizations so that the other listed items will fit under them.

Outlining your ideas can help you decide where you will need to generate more details for your essay. For example, you may have a generalization that you think is important to include, but you have only a single specific detail listed under it in your outline. You can do further listing, brainstorming, or clustering to develop new details to support this generalization.

Purpose   After thinking about which aspects of a subject you would like to cover in your essay, consider why and to whom you are writing.

- *What might be your purpose in writing about this issue?* Figuring out a purpose for writing will help you make decisions about how best to convey your ideas to your readers. Do you want your readers to understand your personal experience? Do you want to inform your readers about an important issue? Do you want your readers to think or act in a new way once they have read your essay? Write a few sentences about what you want your readers to feel, understand, or do after they read your writing.

Audience

- *Who are you writing for?* What will your readers need to know for you to achieve your purpose? How much do they already know about your topic? For example, if you are explaining a technical process to an audience with no technical training, you will probably have to explain unfamiliar terms; give very specific, concrete examples that illustrate how the process works; and perhaps compare and contrast the process with everyday events that your readers are already familiar with. If your audience is a group of engineers, however, you can assume they have already done some sophisticated thinking about your topic. You can use technical terms without explanation, provide detailed statistical data, and so on. Write a few sentences describing your audience. Keep this group of readers in mind as you draft the essay.

DRAFTING

Once you have developed some ideas and thought about your purpose and audience, draft a tentative *thesis statement*. A thesis statement tells your readers two things they will need to know as they read your essay: (1) the main idea you are discussing, and (2) your attitude, stance, or approach toward the main idea. A thesis statement is not simply an announcement of an idea, such as "In this essay I will describe my first experience in the United States." It is a statement of your attitude, stance, or approach to the main idea, for example, "My first experience in the United States was both frightening and exciting." The words *frightening* and *exciting* tell the reader how you will focus your ideas about your first experience. The purpose of an essay with this thesis statement might be to share your reactions to being in a new country with American classmates, many of whom have probably never traveled outside the United States.

By writing a tentative thesis statement, you commit yourself to focusing on a single idea in your draft. This focus on one main idea is an important characteristic of English essays. After you finish the draft, you can check the details and explanations against the thesis statement to make sure these supporting points are clearly relevant to the thesis. As you continue to draft, however, either your main idea or your attitude toward the main idea may change, and thus you may need to continue to refine your thesis statement to ensure its accuracy. (See *Thesis Statements* on page 258.)

☐ Questions to consider as you draft your essay

- What kinds of details do I need to prove or support my thesis (my main idea and my attitude toward it)?

- How many details or how extensive an explanation do I need to give to achieve my purpose for writing to these particular readers?

- How specific do I need to make these details to explain my view thoroughly?

- How can I best organize support for my thesis—details and explanations—in separate paragraphs to achieve my purpose with these readers?

Take some time to revise with the organization of the draft. Pretend to be a reader and decide whether the overall organization of the essay is logical. (See *Writing Essays* for a discussion of the format of English essays.) Switch the paragraphs around to discover the most effective order for your ideas. Examine each paragraph to make sure it clearly relates to and gives new information about the main idea. Cross out any paragraphs or sentences that would not help a reader understand your attitude toward your main idea or that do not add new information.

REVISING

To make your essay as effective as possible, plan to revise your draft at least once. An effective essay focuses on the writer's exploration of a single idea. The essay contains a sufficient number of relevant, specific details to explore that single idea in depth. These details are organized logically, one point leading into the next in a smooth and orderly transition of ideas. Finally, each sentence in an effective essay is as error-free as the writer can make it.

Guidelines for an Effective Essay

- Unified by a single main idea

- Focused by the writer's attitude toward the main idea

- Developed by an adequate number of relevant examples, reasons, details, facts, and other supporting evidence

- Coherent through the use of transitions and the repetition of key words

- Correct because of the writer's careful attention to editing and proofreading.

Improving Unity by Focusing on a Single Main Idea The thesis statement controls the content of the rest of the essay. To improve the unity and focus of your essay, make sure the thesis is stated precisely and that the rest of the essay—every paragraph and every sentence—develops the idea and attitude stated in the thesis. Make sure that every paragraph offers a new idea that directly supports the thesis statement. Cross out any paragraphs and sentences that digress from the main idea of the essay, and decide what other information would more clearly explain and develop your attitude toward the main idea.

Checking Development by Giving Enough Supporting Details A well-developed essay (and each paragraph within it) offers the reader enough information to create a clear and complete picture of the writer's approach to the main idea. How much information your reader will need depends on the scope of your thesis statement, your purpose for writing, and your readers' existing knowledge of the topic you are developing. (See *Strategies for Developing Essays and Paragraphs* on page 263.)

Increasing Coherence by Using Transitions and Repeating Key Words "Coherence" means that all the sentences in your essay are logically related to each other. You can help the audience follow your logic by using transitions that specify exact relationships between ideas and repeating key words and phrases throughout the essay.

☐ **Using Transitions** Transitions are words, phrases, and sometimes whole sentences or paragraphs that help readers understand the logical connections among your ideas. When considering which transition to use, be sure to select one that expresses your exact meaning. On the following page is a chart of some transitions and the logical relationships they signal.

RELATIONSHIPS	TRANSITIONAL EXPRESSIONS		
Addition	again also and and then	besides equally important further furthermore	in addition likewise moreover too
Comparison	in a like manner in the same way	likewise on the same hand	similarly
Concession	after all although true and yet	at the same time granted naturally	of course perhaps
Contrast	after all although true at any rate but despite	even so for all that however in contrast in spite of	nevertheless on the other hand on the contrary still yet
Example	consider for example for instance incidentally	indeed in fact in other words in particular	namely particularly specifically that is
Result	accordingly as a result consequently	hence then thereby	therefore thus
Sequence	finally first eventually	gradually last next	second third ultimately
Summary	actually, apparently, certainly, conversely, fortunately,	in brief in conclusion in short obviously, on the whole	to conclude to summarize undoubtedly, unfortunately,
Time	after a short time after a while afterward at last	at length hereupon (formal) lately presently	recently shortly since then then

☐ **Repeating Key Words and Phrases** Key words and phrases are those that carry the most important messages to your readers. In the thesis statement "My first experience in the United States was both frightening and exciting," the most important words are *frightening* and *exciting*. Using variations of these words, such as *scary, fear, afraid, excitement,* and *stimulating* throughout the essay will help your readers remember your purpose for writing: to share your conflicting emotions. You can signal the relations among your sentences by using variations of key words whenever you think readers may lose sight of your main point.

Revision Checklist Answering the following questions about your draft will help you decide which revisions you need to make. If you want to get feedback from a classmate to help you revise, switch drafts and ask your peer reviewer to answer the questions about your essay.

Thesis Statement

☐ Is the main idea and your attitude, stance, or approach to the main idea stated early in the draft?

☐ Does the thesis statement adequately express the main idea?

☐ If not, how could the thesis be improved?

Unity and Focus

☐ Do all the supporting ideas—details, facts, examples, and explanations—illustrate the writer's attitude toward that one main idea?

☐ Are there any digressions from the main idea? If so, where do they occur?

Development

☐ Which of the paragraphs or sentences most effectively develops or proves the point the writer is making? What make these parts effective?

☐ Has the writer supported the main idea with sufficient evidence? Are the examples, quoted authorities, statistics, and other supporting details convincing? Where does the writer need to add more supporting details?

Coherence

☐ Is the organization of ideas between paragraphs logical and fluent? Do all the paragraphs seem to be connected to each other in terms of meaning?

☐ Does each sentence flow logically from the one before?

☐ Does the writer need to add transitions to make these connections clear to the reader?

Purpose and Audience

☐ Was the writer's purpose clear? What did the writer want the reader to know, do, or feel after reading the essay?

☐ What group of readers does the writer seem to be addressing? What makes you think so?

Just as questioning your own drafts helps you decide which parts to keep, change, or omit from your essay, questioning the feedback you receive from a peer reviewer is important. Read your classmate's comments and then reread your essay to decide which suggestions seem valid and which do not. Make sure that your thesis, purpose, and intended audience stay in the forefront as you make decisions about your draft.

EDITING

Once you feel satisfied that your essay is complete and logically organized, put your draft aside for a few hours or days. It will be easier to find errors once you return to your essay. When you are ready to edit your draft, examine one sentence at a time. Mark any sentences that don't seem complete or correct, and then use the editing checklist below to make sure that each of your sentences is clear and grammatically accurate. If you can't figure out how to correct an error, consult a grammar handbook or a college dictionary.

Editing Checklist Notice the correction symbols listed on the left. When your instructor reviews your draft, he or she may use these symbols to point to problem areas.

Sentences and Paragraphs

frag	Is each sentence a complete thought or is it a *fragment*? Does it have a subject and a complete verb?
r/o	Is each sentence only one sentence? Have you incorrectly joined two or more sentences together in a *run-on* sentence?
choppy	Can you join any simple sentences into longer, more complex ones which are related in meaning?
?, awk	Have you phrased your ideas in standard English, or have you translated ideas from your native language instead making them seem *awkward?*
trans	Are your ideas connected logically and clearly so that readers will understand the flow of your ideas? If not, add *transitions.*
pron ref	Are *pronoun references* clear?
pron agr	Do *pronouns agree* with their antecedents in person and number?

s-v agr	Do *subjects and verbs agree* in person and number?
//	Have you used *parallel* grammatical form for words, phrases, or clauses that are paired or grouped in a series?
¶	Have you broken ideas into paragraphs appropriately? Does each *paragraph* focus on only one idea or set of *closely* related ideas?

Words and Punctuation

ww	Have you used the wrong *word*? Consult a dictionary or thesaurus to find a better word.
wd form	Have you used the correct *word forms*, such as forms of adjectives and adverbs? Do the verb endings indicate the appropriate tense? (Check *-s* endings and *-ed* endings especially.) Have you correctly used present and past participles, such as *bored* and *boring*?
om,∧	Check for *omitted words*, such as *a, an,* and *the.*
∿	Check *word order.*
pron	Are all *pronouns* in the appropriate case?
P	Are there *punctuation* problems? Does every sentence end with a period, a question mark, or (rarely) an exclamation point? Are commas used correctly? Check the use of apostrophes, semi-colons, and colons.
" "	Do pairs of *quotation marks* properly enclose direct quotations, as in dialogues or in quotations from research sources?
sp	Are any words *spelled* incorrectly? Check the dictionary if you are not sure about the spelling of a word. (Keep a list of words that you commonly misspell and check your drafts against this list.)
cap/lc	Is every proper noun and proper adjective *capitalized*? Does the first word in each sentence begin with a capital letter? Check all capitalized letters: should they be changed to *lower case*?

Checking your essay for matters of style, usage, and correctness is a very important stage in the writing process. Attending to these final details shows respect for your readers and allows them to respond to the content rather than the form of your essay.

Essay Format Guidelines for essay format are as follows:

- Written work should be typed, double-spaced, on 8 1/2" x 11" white bond paper (avoid "corracable" bond paper because it smears).
- Print should be dark and easy to read.
- Include your name, page number and draft #.
- Use staples (not paper-clips) to hold your paper together.
- It is a good idea to photocopy your paper before submitting it. (Just in case your work is misplaced or lost)

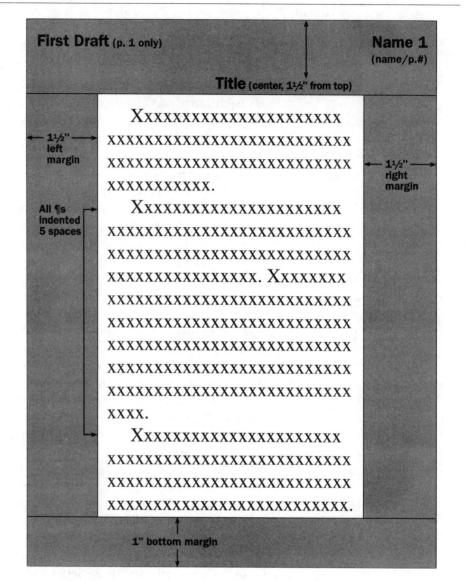

Proofreading

Before you begin the final draft of your essay, check your format against the format diagram above, or use the guidelines your own instructor has given you. When you have copied, typed, or printed out a final version of the essay, check each sentence and word one more time for careless mistakes. Look especially for words you may have omitted, spelling errors, and mistakes in capitalization and punctuation. Make any final corrections neatly in handwriting, as in the following example:

James M. Barrie noted that **the** "secret of happiness is not in doing what on**e** likes but in liking what one has to do."

PART FOUR
WRITING AN ESSAY

An essay is a focused exploration and elaboration of a writer's ideas about a given subject. The word "essay" comes from the French *essayer* meaning "to try," or "to attempt." Thus an essay is a trying out of ideas, an attempt to test ideas on an audience of readers. Even when it includes research, an essay focuses on the ideas of the writer, not on the ideas of the writer's sources.

An essay can be classified by the most important purpose it serves. A *personal* or *experiential* essay relates a writer's experience in narrative form and suggests why this experience is memorable. An *informative* essay explains or clarifies a topic so that readers will understand it better or realize its importance. An *argumentative* essay tries to persuade readers to adopt the writer's point of view on a topic. Essays you will be asked to write for your college courses typically will range in length from five to twenty-five pages.

No matter what type or length of essay you write, however, the English essay follows a pattern based on English thinking patterns. The characteristic English thought pattern is a straight line of development; that is, to get from Point A to Point B, the writer does not digress from the most direct route. Often, an English essay begins with a statement of its central idea (*thesis statement*) and then subdivides the main supporting ideas into separate paragraphs, as in the illustration below.

ESSAY FORM

Introduction

One or two paragraphs that present and focus the controlling idea (the "thesis statement") of the essay.

Body Paragraphs

The body is the longest section of the essay. Each body paragraph clearly relates to and supports the thesis; each paragraph adds a new and distinct idea to the essay.

Body Paragraph A	Develops the thesis by focusing on a single point or a set of closely related points.
Body Paragraph B	Further explores the thesis by offering a second point or set of related points.
Body Paragraph C	Further develops and explores the thesis with another point or set of related points.

Conclusion

In one or two paragraphs, the conclusion sums up, restates, or otherwise provides closure for the essay.

THE INTRODUCTION

The main purpose of the introduction is to whet your readers' appetite, to make them want to read the entire essay by sparking their interest. Above all, your introduction should attempt to answer the question, "So what?" about your thesis. In other words, why should readers care about your thesis? Why is it important? What do readers have to gain from considering your ideas? Here is a list of strategies that can help you draft an interesting and effective introduction.

☐ **Start with a brief anecdote** An anecdote is a short narrative (story or chain of events). Anecdotes make abstract concepts more concrete for readers. In an introduction, an anecdote should be clearly related to the thesis.

> One taste of kimch'i, *the fiery pickled cabbage with a mind-bending aroma that is Korea's national dish, made* Today *show host Jane Pauley lose her composure and drove her off the NBC set after she sampled it for viewers just before the Seoul Olympics. Few other Westerners take to* kimch'i, *either, which helps explain why most Americans have never set foot inside a Korean restaurant in the U.S. Too bad, because if they did, they might get a lesson in economics even more stimulating than a mouthful of* kimch'i.
>
> **"Horatio Alger Kim"**
> Matthew Schifrin

☐ **Offer a strong opinion** Stating a controversial opinion with great force can grab readers' attention by suggesting an idea they may not have considered before. Even if readers disagree with your opinion, you entice them to read further to find out how you could possibly justify it.

> *I don't know what's happening to our standards. I fear that we in the mass media are creating such a market for mediocrity that we've diminished the incentive for excellence. We celebrate notoriety as though it were an achievement. Fame has come to mean being recognized by more people who don't know anything about you. In politics, we have encouraged the displacement of thoughtfulness by the artful cliché.*
>
> **"Media Courtesans"**
> Ted Koppel

☐ **Start with a quotation** A quotation can lend your thesis strength, especially when the person being quoted is an authority on the topic you will be discussing in your essay. Quotations should be chosen for interesting content and fresh use of language, and they should have a direct relation to your main idea.

> *Philosopher's still debate the definition of happiness, but scientists, who've dubbed it life satisfaction, generally agree on a definition: A state of well-being, filled with positive feelings toward oneself and the world. Philosophers and researchers alike agree on the importance of their subject. "For most people, happiness is the major goal in life," says Jonathan*

Freedman, who surveyed one hundred thousand people for his book
Happy People. *"Almost every decision we make is based on what we think*
will bring us the most happiness. Everything important to us—love, faith,
success, friendship, sex—is actually a means to the end of achieving hap-
piness."

"What Is Happiness"
Catherine Houck

☐ **Open with a question** When you start your essay with a provocative
question, the thesis and the rest of the essay attempt to answer that
question. Be careful not to ask a question that is so vague or general
it cannot be answered.

If someone asks, "Why do people marry?" he meets indignation or aston-
ishment. The questions seems absurd if not immoral: the desirability of
marriage is regarded as unquestionable. Divorce, on the other hand,
strikes us as a problem worthy of serious and therapeutic attention. What
explains marriage?

"The Invention That Isn't Working"
Ernest van den Haag

☐ **Begin with a statement of facts** If your essay is serious in tone and
content, as many academic essays are, you won't want your introduction to sound "gimmicky." Presenting your topic with appropriate
detail (for example, using statistics or data), and then stating your thesis is an appropriate introduction to a college essay.

Surveys show what everyone already knows: People are more likely to
report themselves as very happy when they're happily married. (Who
would deny the delights of loving and being loved?) However, the unat-
tached can take some comfort in evidence indicating that singles—now
one out of every three American adults—are not only happier but health-
ier than the unhappily *wed.*

"What Is Happiness"
Catherine Houck

Avoid These Ineffective Introductions

- *Repetition of the assignment.* Don't merely restate the assignment in the introduction. Move directly to the position you will take about the assignment.

- *Complaint or apology for your inability to write on the topic.* Don't detract from your credibility by apologizing. Do your best to develop an interesting and informative introduction.

- *Vague announcement of your plan for the essay.* Statements such as "In this paper I will attempt to show" . . . distract readers' attention from the thesis by emphasizing the writer instead.

- *Dictionary definition of a term used in the essay.* If you need to define a term, use your own words.

THE THESIS STATEMENT

The introduction to an essay typically includes a thesis statement, one or two sentences that tell the reader what to expect from the essay: the main idea and your attitude, stance, or approach to that idea.

A thesis statement . . .
- *is* a complete thought about a subject.
- *has* a subject that identifies the main idea and a predicate that states the writer's approach or attitude to the main idea.

A thesis statement *is not* . . .
- a broad, general topic ("values," "culture shock")
- a statement of fact ("Americans eat more beef than any other nationality.")
- an announcement ("I plan to discuss American individualism . . .")

Here are two examples of well-written thesis statements.

          main idea   attitude toward main idea

1. | *Learning about American values* | is | *difficult but rewarding.* |

Each paragraph of this essay will focus on a new idea about how learning American values is *difficult* and *rewarding*. The key words that the writer has to explain are *difficult* and *rewarding*.

2. *My understanding of the phrase "culture shock" was incomplete until the day I registered for my college courses.*

The writer of this thesis promises to explain several ideas to readers: what she used to think about culture shock, what she thinks about it now, and what happened during registration that caused her understanding to become complete.

Often the thesis is placed toward the end of the introduction, although its placement will vary depending on the writer's purpose and audience. You may develop a tentative or "working" thesis statement at any stage in the writing process to help you focus and shape your ideas. As you rethink and revise the ideas in your body paragraphs, make sure that your thesis continues to reflect their content accurately.

THE BODY PARAGRAPHS

The thesis is further developed and explored in the body paragraphs of the essay, each of which focuses on a distinct idea or set of closely related ideas. The *topic sentence* of each body paragraph clearly supports, develops, or explains some aspect of the thesis statement. The other sentences in the paragraph support the topic sentence, just as all the topic sentences together support the thesis statement.

The writer's purpose, audience, and thesis will determine the best way to develop each body paragraph. See *Strategies for Developing Essays and Paragraphs*, pages 263.

THE CONCLUSION

A strong conclusion reinforces the major ideas discussed in the essay. It is a logical extension of the rest of the essay in both content and tone. The conclusion fulfills the reader's need for closure and completeness; and for the writer, it is a way to make sure that readers have understood the main thrust of the essay. Some effective strategies for conclusions are listed below.

☐ **Create a vivid image** that will leave readers with a lasting impression of your idea.

> *America's Declaration of Independence guarantees every one of us the right to the pursuit of happiness. But because the Declaration is a political document, it does not warn us of the frustration of trying to exercise that right, because the pursuit of happiness is the wrong goal. You don't become happy by pursuing happiness. You become happy by living a life that means something. The happiest people you know are probably not the richest or most famous, probably not the ones who work hardest at being happy by reading the articles and buying the books and latching on to the latest fads. I suspect that the happiest people you know are the ones who work at being kind, helpful, and reliable, and happiness sneaks into their lives while they are busy doing those things. You don't become happy by pursuing happiness. It is always a by-product, never a primary goal. Happiness is a butterfly—the more you chase it, the more it flies away from you and hides. But stop chasing it, put away your net and busy yourself with other, more productive things than the pursuit of personal happiness, and it will sneak up on you from behind and perch on your shoulder.*

"When All You've Ever Wanted Wasn't Enough"
Harold Kushner

☐ **Warn readers** of what might happen based on the facts you have presented.

> *A society which assumes its members are honest is humane, comfortable, habitable. A society which treats everyone like a criminal becomes harsh, unfeeling, punitive, paranoid. The human connection is severed; fear of detection and punishment becomes the only deterrent to crime, and it's a very ineffective one. Somehow, sometime—I don't know when, but it was within my lifetime—we changed from the first type of society to the second. Maybe it's too late to go back again, but the road we are now on is a dark and descending one.*

"Severing The Human Connection"
H. Bruce Miller

☐ **Stir readers to or make a plea for action** based on their new understanding of the consequences of inaction.

> *My son, Wind-Wolf, is not an empty glass coming into your class to be filled. He is a full basket coming into a different environment and society with something special to share. Please let him share his knowledge, heritage, and culture with you and his peers.*

"An Indian Father's Plea"
Robert Lake

☐ **Quote an impressive authority or statistic** that sums up or further reinforces the facts you have detailed.

The NIMH's biological-psychiatry branch is now investigating the relationship between mental states and brain chemicals. Eventually, scientists hope to learn the most effective ways of dealing with brain-chemical imbalances that lead to addiction and other problems. For the moment, they're experimenting largely with the uses of synthetic drugs, but few researchers believe synthetic chemicals will be the final answer. "Drugs, which assault the whole brain at once, will never be as subtle as our own natural neurochemicals, which can be released just in one spot and not another," says neurochemist Candace Pert, a leading NIMH researcher on endorphins.

"What Is Happiness?"
Catherine Houck

☐ **Tell a final anecdote** that shows the main idea in action.

A few weeks ago, I cleared my throat and asked the children, now mostly grown and fearsomely smart, whether they felt any stirrings of ethnic or religious identity, etc., which might have been, ahem, insufficiently nourished at home. "None," they said, adding firmly, "and the world would be a better place if nobody else did, either." My chest swelled with pride, as would my mother's, to know that the race of "none" marches on.

"Cultural Baggage"
Barbara Ehrenreich

☐ **Estimate the significance of your conclusion** for the group most affected by the problem you have described.

The outlines of a possible great and truly democratic commonwealth become discernible. Its form would be that of the federal republic; its substance a democracy of nationalities, cooperating voluntarily and autonomously through common institutions in the enterprise of self-realization through the perfection of men according to their kind. The common language of the commonwealth, the language of its great tradition, would be English, but each nationality would have for its emotional and involuntary life its own peculiar dialect or speech, its own individual and inevitable esthetic and intellectual forms. The political and economic life of the commonwealth is a single unit and serves as the foundation and background for the realization of the distinctive individuality of each nation that composes it and of the pooling of these in a harmony above them all. Thus "American civilization" may come to mean the perfection of the cooperative harmonies of "European civilization"—the waste, the squalor and the distress of Europe being eliminated—a multiplicity in a unity, an orchestration of mankind.

**"Assimilation in America:
Theory and Reality"**
Milton Gordon

☐ **Ask a concluding question** to reinforce the thesis.

But those days of trial and uncertainty are over, and the open-admission policy has been eliminated. Anybody who enters the City University's senior colleges must now have an 80 percent high school average. And I am one of those fortunate individuals who in a unique period of

American education was given a chance to attend college. But I wonder what will happen to those people who can learn but whose potential doesn't show in their high school average; who might get into street crime if not given a chance to do something constructive? I wonder, because if it weren't for open admissions, the likelihood is I would still be swinging baseball bats on the streets on Friday nights.

"Open Admission & The Inward I"
Peter Rondinone

Avoid These Weak Conclusions

A poor conclusion can water down the effects of even a carefully developed essay. Here are some types of conclusions you should avoid:

- Repetition of the thesis. In a short essay, don't insult your readers' intelligence and attention span by simply repeating your thesis statement.

- Apology for the argument. If you have taken enough time to think and write about your topic, you have no reason to apologize for your efforts.

- Introduction of a new topic or a new line of reasoning. Don't lead readers to believe that you will now begin a new discussion. The object of the conclusion is to end an essay, not begin a new one.

PART FIVE
WRITING A PARAGRAPH

A paragraph is a group of sentences that together express one central idea in some detail. The topic sentence of a paragraph focuses the reader's attention on this central idea. The topic sentence is often the first sentence in a paragraph. All the other sentences develop the topic sentence by explaining it, giving examples or details of it, describing it, telling a story about it, or supporting it in some other way. In an essay, each paragraph introduces and develops a new idea that supports the thesis statement.

Each paragraph has an indented first line, as shown in the accompanying diagram. This indented line lets readers know that now you will shift to a new idea, one that is distinct from the idea in the paragraph that precedes it. If you are handwriting, indent from the left margin about one inch. If you are typing or using a word processor, indent five spaces.

**First Line
Indented**

**All Other
Lines Go
to Margin**

James M. Barrie noted that the "secret of happiness is not in doing what one likes, but in liking what one has to do." I have found this attitude to be very helpful as I learn about the North American way of life. . ...

THE TOPIC SENTENCE

The topic sentence of a paragraph has three qualities:

- It is a complete sentence.
- It includes the paragraph's main idea.
- It gives the writer's attitude or stance toward the main idea.

Just as the thesis statement controls the content of the body paragraphs of an essay, the topic sentence controls the content of the other sentences in a paragraph. The rest of the paragraph then explains, describes, or discusses the topic sentence. In many paragraphs, there is also a concluding sentence, just as there is a concluding paragraph in an essay.

THE BODY OF THE PARAGRAPH

What kind of information a paragraph will include depends on the topic sentence, the writer's overall purpose, and the intended readers. See *Strategies for Developing Essays and Paragraphs* on page 263 for a variety of strategies you can use to develop your paragraphs. Just as important as the strategies you choose are the way you present your material to the reader. Following are some of the choices you have as a writer.

☐ **Use Chronological (Time) Order** If your paragraph details a series of events for your reader, for example, if it tells a story or shows how to do something, time order is an effective organization. You can talk about the events in the order they occurred (past-present-future order) or you can show how past events led to later ones by beginning in the present with the result and then telling the story of how the situation came into being. *Transitions* useful in time order are given on page 249.

☐ **Use Spatial Order** In describing a scene, an object, or a person, spatial order is useful. You can move from foreground to background, from left to right, from top to bottom, or in any other logical order. Only include the features that are important for your readers to understand in order to grasp the main point you are making.

☐ **Use Emphatic Order** Emphatic order allows you to emphasize the most important of several details, reasons, or examples. An effective order is to begin with the least important detail and end with the most important detail. Journalists often switch this order (using most important to least important order) because people often read only the first few paragraphs of a news story. In academic essays, however, it is more effective to begin with the least important and end with the most important example or reason.

☐ **Use General-to-Specific Order** Many academic paragraphs in English begin with a general statement and then move to specific details about the general statement. This order is effective when you have a series of brief examples that together are evidence for an assertion made in the topic sentence. The topic sentence is the first sentence in a paragraph organized in general-to-specific order.

☐ **Use a Group of Paragraphs** In longer papers you might sometimes need several paragraphs to explain a complex aspect of your subject. In this case, you can develop a topic sentence that encompasses the next several paragraphs of the essay. To develop these paragraphs effectively, you will probably need to use a variety of strategies (See pages 263-265).

THE CONCLUDING SENTENCE

The concluding sentence in some paragraphs fills the same function as the concluding paragraph in an essay: it gives readers the sense that the topic has been fully examined, that the discussion is complete. What kind of concluding sentence to write depends on the content and tone of the paragraph as well as your purpose for writing. Just be sure that you don't leave your readers dangling in the middle of an explanation of your paragraph's topic. Read your paragraph out loud. Does it sound complete and finished? If not, consider adding a concluding sentence.

PART SIX
STRATEGIES FOR DEVELOPING ESSAYS AND PARAGRAPHS

Each of the following strategies can be used to develop a single paragraph or an entire essay. Likewise, a single paragraph can be composed of one or several of the strategies. Whatever strategies you use to develop the points in support of your thesis statement or topic sentence, make sure that the effect of these strategies is to make your topic clear to your readers.

NARRATION

Narration shows readers what is happening or what has happened. You can narrate (tell) a brief story or anecdote that explains your attitude about your main idea. For example, narration would probably be used to develop the thesis statement, "My first experience in the United States was both frightening and exciting."

- *Organize the narrative around the most important point you want to make.* For example, if you want readers to vicariously experience your conflicting feelings of fright and excitement, emphasize the events that provoked the strongest feelings.

- *Keep the time frame clear.* Whether you move from the present to the past or from the past to the present, make sure the chain of events is clear to your readers. See page 250 for a list of transitions that help keep narratives coherent with time order.

- *Use dialogue to show a person's character in action or to make the relationship between people come alive for your readers.* Remember to use quotation marks when reporting someone's exact words.

DESCRIPTION

Description appeals to your readers' senses. Recounting the sights, sounds, smells, textures and even tastes of an experience can help your readers gain insight into your perception of events.

- *Focus your descriptive details* around a single important impression. Don't describe any details that are unimportant in creating this impression.

- *Avoid generic words* such as *good, bad, great,* and *interesting,* and clichés such as *fresh as the morning dew* in your descriptions. Use fresh, vivid language that invites readers to see the world through your eyes and ears.

- *Use spatial order* to help keep a descriptive paragraph organized (see page 262).

EXAMPLES

Examples are often the clearest way to explain a general statement. Many essays and paragraphs you will write in college will follow the standard English pattern, starting with a general statement (thesis statement or topic sentence) and then giving an example or series of examples that explains or proves the statement. You can organize examples from least to most important (emphatic order), or from most to least important. You can also organize examples as they occur in time (chronologically). See page 262 for more information on emphatic and chronological order.

DEFINITION

Definition can help readers grasp concepts that have more than a single meaning. Abstract terms such as "justice," "values," and "responsibility" have different definitions for different people. If an exact understanding of *any* term—abstract or concrete—is important to the information you are presenting, you should define the term precisely. You can define a term by showing how it is like or unlike other things and by giving examples of what it is and is not.

COMPARISON AND CONTRAST

Comparison and contrast shows readers how an unfamiliar person, place, object, or idea is similar to or different from something they already know or understand. One of the most important ways people learn is by relating the unfamiliar to the familiar. In a paragraph or essay, you can examine a point under discussion by showing how it is similar to something else (comparison), how it is different (contrast), or both. For simple comparisons or contrasts, you can first discuss all the attributes of one item and then all the attributes of the second item in the same order. In more complex comparisons it is better to compare the two items in alternating fashion, attribute by attribute. Consider what your readers already know about your topic to decide whether comparison and contrast would be an effective explanatory strategy. (See page 249 for *transitions* that signal comparison and contrast.)

CLASSIFICATION AND DIVISION

Classification and division are particularly useful when you are explaining a complex event, object, or process. *Classification* is grouping separate items into categories according to qualities they share. The categories you set up should be mutually exclusive—that is, one item cannot fit into more than one category. *Division* is taking an item and breaking it into its parts to explain it. As in classification, the parts must be mutually exclusive.

For example, suppose you want readers who have never used a computer to understand the parts of a computer. You could divide the computer parts by functions: the keyboard allows the computer operator to access and input information, the monitor allows the operator to retrieve information and see current work, and so on. If you wanted to explain the American system of government to someone completely unfamiliar with it, you might classify the responsibilities of the three main branches of government (the executive, legislative, and judicial branches).

General-to-specific order can help organize these types of paragraphs and essays (see page 262).

CAUSE-AND-EFFECT

Cause-and-effect reasoning shows readers why an event occurred (cause) or what happens because of an event (effect). Be certain in using cause-and-effect that one event did, in fact, cause another. Remember that most effects have at least several causes: do not assume that because one event occurred before another event, it necessarily caused it.

PROCESS ANALYSIS

Process analysis helps you explain to readers how to do something step by step. A process is an orderly progression of events that leads to a certain result. One event follows another: first you do one thing, then another, and then something else. In process analysis, it is important that you keep the sequence of events clear for the reader by using time order. Also, try to anticipate which steps of the process will be difficult for readers to understand or do, and be especially careful in explaining these parts.

Chronological order and spatial order can be effective organizing strategies for process analysis paragraphs (see page 262).